Earl Shinn

The art treasures of America being the choicest works of art in the

public and private collections of North America

Vol. III.

Earl Shinn

The art treasures of America being the choicest works of art in the public and private collections of North America
Vol. III.

ISBN/EAN: 9783743304482

Manufactured in Europe, USA, Canada, Australia, Japa

Cover: Foto ©Thomas Meinert / pixelio.de

Manufactured and distributed by brebook publishing software
(www.brebook.com)

Earl Shinn

The art treasures of America being the choicest works of art in the

public and private collections of North America

ÉDITION DE LUXE

THE

ART TREASURES OF AMERICA

VOL. III.

ONLY ONE THOUSAND COPIES OF THIS EDITION PRINTED FOR SALE.

THIS COPY IS No. **780**

SPANISH CAFÉ

ARTIST

JOSÉ JIMENEZ Y ARANDA

BORN AT SEVILLA.   PUPIL OF THE ACADEMY AT SEVILLA.

●

EDITION DE LUXE

THE

ART TREASURES

OF

AMERICA

BEING THE

CHOICEST WORKS OF ART IN THE PUBLIC AND PRIVATE COLLECTIONS
OF NORTH AMERICA

EDITED BY

EDWARD STRAHAN

THE

ART TREASURES

AMERICA

AN ARABIAN TRIBUNAL

ARTIST
T. MORAGAS

BORN AT BARCELONA, SPAIN.   PUPIL OF ACADEMY OF BARCELONA.

COLLECTION OF
MR. J. PIERPONT MORGAN, NEW YORK

THE FLIGHT OF CHARLES II.

FAC-SIMILE OF AN ETCHING BY NEUMANN FROM THE ORIGINAL PAINTING BY CARL HOFF.

COLLECTIONS OF EX-GOVERNOR E. D. MORGAN AND OF MR. J. PIERPONT MORGAN.

CRYSTAL FROM A DESIGN BY M. LELOIR.

Bagage de Croquemitaine," in Governor Morgan's collection, in New York, a canvas of 3 by 4½ feet, by Lobrichon of Paris, is a terrible warning to infant depravity. These bad children have evidently broken the whole decalogue of the nursery. Mademoiselle Lili has eviscerated her doll, and incidentally met her first disillusion. Mademoiselle Lulu has kicked off the covers; and now shivers by the cellar-window, an outcast. Masters Toto and Fanfan and Pipi have broken windows, stolen jam and liberated canaries until the measure of their

sins is complete. There is nothing for it but to deliver them up to Croquemitaine, the Bogie of Fear, who will carry them off to a doom all the more terrible for being entirely indefinite. The painter, with a rare knowledge of childish character, has discriminated his various personages like a dramatist; it is easy to distinguish the child who roars frankly at every rebuff, the child who seeks solitude when in disgrace, the sly child who hides peeping till the danger is over, the child who sulks in self-justified rebellion, and the child who is carried outside of his own interests by pure delight in another's woe, and unselfishly exults in mere joy that the other child is catching it. These various natures and dispositions are piled into a porter's hotte or basket, and leaned up against a wall provisionally. Such is the limbo of criminals as a French child understands it. No actual punishment is shown in the scene, but instead, a mighty brooding sense of ill, a foreboding of the reckoning to come, well calculated to depress the stoutest rebel of the nursery. The dangers of Croquemitaine, indeed, are imaginary. He is the spectrum of terror, the *alter ego* of fear; when fear is absent, he cannot exist. Confronted by a valiant heart, he and his frowning castle sink into the earth, as has been wittily developed in L'Epine's fanciful *Légende de Croquemitaine*, written in 1863. Timoléon Lobrichon, the painter of this whimsical and not inartistic group, was born at Corned in the Jura, and received his education at Paris, in the atelier of Picot, obtaining a medal in 1868; his best pictures represent children.

"Breton Washerwomen," or "Lavandières Bretonnes" (8 × 5 feet,) by Jules Breton, is a fine example of the authoritative power with which this master can impress a plain country eclogue on the mind. The personages here are rustic folk, engaged in the humblest of occupations. The Breton race, a tribe originally from the greater Britain across the channel, and still preserved singularly pure from French intermarriages, often shows a serious, grave beauty, based upon simplicity of character and fine physical health. These people, dressed like the English of the Tudor dynasty, move about their avocations with a quiet directness and an absence of coquetry that often yield to the artist some attitude of statuesque grace or a motion free and large as that of an animal. In the present picture we have a washing-scene. The mature woman at the right assumes the white coif, in shape like that of any of the queens of Henry VIII.; but the younger troop beside her have rejected the external winged cap, and only wear the close inner bonnet, which protects them from the shame that would ensue if a single lock of their golden hair should become obvious to the male spectator. A dozen of these simple, proud beings are gathered at their task beside a little rill that flows into the sea. A noble looking girl stands and turns up the sleeve from her large brown arm, the serious purpose of salutary labor shining in her clear, tranquil, dark eyes; on one side of her a maiden, shaking out the cleansed linen to be dried upon the rocks, looks as if she were showing a graceful signal to some vessel out at sea; and on her other side, a damsel, whose washing is done, occupies herself with spinning flax, her absorbed look ocean-ward giving her an air of contemplative grace. The other women wield the heavy bat, apply the soap, or let the wide cloths float in the living pool. The unapparent skill and ease with which the painter collects these figures into a beautiful and well-balanced group, without affectation or conscious attitudes, forms the *sculptural* part of his merit; but the sculptural side is only a beginning of his art; besides this felicity and grace of design, the glowing tenderness of color which envelopes and unites all the personages, the unity of the light which plays on the figures with that which bathes the late afternoon sky and shining sea, make this picture an orchestral composition, vibrating throughout with harmonies subtle as lofty.

"The Flight of Charles II" is a painting of small dimensions, by the picturesque costumer, Carl Hoff, in which the most is made of the elegant dresses of the cavaliers. Charles lies in bed, without undressing, watched by Major Carlis, who can scarce keep from slumber as he sits, and by a maiden and the Giffard household. The furniture is that of a well-to-do farmhouse, but, in its treatment and that of the figure of the

damsel, our painter has not been able to divest himself of his familiar surroundings, both being entirely German in character. The scene of weariness and watching is, however, impressive and touching enough to make us forget any slight inconsistency with the manor of White-Ladies. Carl Hoff, born at Mannheim in 1838, pursued his art studies at Düsseldorf under Vautier, and remains one of the most elegant, light-handed and graceful exemplars of the Düsseldorf school.

Defregger's "Prize Horse" (4 × 3 feet) is a lively study of German manners. The hero of the incident is a stout black cob, who arrives from the village fair, decked with ribbons and followed by a flag of triumph. The old men, sitting on the ale-house bench, blink at his points critically, while the children stare, the blacksmith looks at his shoes, and the debauchees of the neighborhood propose unlimited orgies in his honor. Dickens has somewhere pointed out the awfully corrupting influence of this specious animal as a comrade. Those who pass the most time with him are the most fatally smitten with the degradation which emanates from his contact; they become idlers, drinkers, betters and bankrupts, just in proportion as they addict themselves to the society of this chartered profligate. The four-footed blackleg of the picture is about to work his destined evil, and lead off a crowd of these simple rustics to a night of soaking and gambling.

Dieffenbach, a young artist who treads with all his skill in the footsteps of Knaus, came out in 1862 with "The Eve of the Wedding," in plain emulation with "The Golden Wedding" of the older painter. "The Eve of the Wedding" (6 × 4 feet) is a composition which knits together a whole universe of country interests and joys; it shows the artist's determined effort to squeeze out the uttermost drop of dramatic capability in rural life, to prove that its narrow comparisons are as entertaining, as well contrasted, as brilliant, as animating, as any historical, intellectual or ideal subject that might solicit the painter's brush. Knaus, for his part, perfectly succeeds in beguiling the spectator to the momentary belief that nothing on earth can be more interesting than his laughing peasants and frugal homes. This he does by his miraculous eye for character. His imitator, furnished with a more conventional budget, with faces that have been painted before, with actions that are calculated rather than invented, determines to make a success by dint of multitude, by numerically piling up the interests of his scene. Anybody can see that the young painter is possessed by the importance of doing a great representative work, by an uneasy rivalry with a recognized renown, and by the conviction that the world must needs listen if he engages pieces enough for his orchestra. In effect, he has been successful, according to almost any criterion, and it is unnecessary to deny that the engraving after Dieffenbach's "Eve of the Wedding" has sold as many copies as the "Golden Wedding," after Knaus. The difference between the works is immense, however, and the laborious accumulation of laughter and festivity in the present picture is but a mechanism emulating the spontaneity and fling of Knaus's country revels. The ambitious painter, like a man conscious of doing his first grand work, seems to ask us if we are not in conscience satisfied with the abundance he

The Baggage of Croquemitaine

ARTIST

TIMOLÉON LOBRICHON

Born at Cornod, France, 1831.

Pupil of Picot

COLLECTION OF

EX-GOVERNOR E. D. MORGAN, NEW YORK

has provided for us. Here is a fat priest—adept in the sly joke permitted for the occasion—grasping with both hands the plump fingers of an intended bride, as he makes his congratulatory visit the afternoon before the wedding; the would-be groom, also on a visit, stiff as a post, duly overcome with bashful pride, and twirling his hat in the usual stage-loutishness; a peddler, spreading his wares on the table before some aunts or cousins, and making an inventory of the bride's charms to be retailed with his pack of gossip as he traverses the country; maidens in front stringing garlands, which lads

and Hals and Van der Helst treated similar scenes of assembly,—Night-watches, Syndics of the Trade Guilds, or Ratifications of Peace,—how clearly they felt their artistic responsibility, and how dimly they felt their historic or narrative responsibility, and accordingly what masterpieces they made of such subjects, we are constrained to own that art among their successors has made a sad decline, and taken the direction of a fatal literary and explanatory tendency. Push this direction to its extreme, and it would arrive at picture-writing or hieroglyphics, like the Egyptian. A paint-

THE PRIZE HORSE.
FACSIMILE OF AN ENGRAVING BY HIM AFTER THE ORIGINAL PAINTING BY P. DEFREGGER.

in the background are looking at the eaves. An oven with a baker drawing out loaves, a butcher cutting up the ox, beer and musical instruments unloading higgledy-piggledy from a wagon; children bringing flowers, dames plucking geese, neighbors drinking healths—the whole shop-window of country joys in a conspicuous, well-set-forth, almost boastful expression of themselves,—such are the concomitants of this picture so well-known as almost to be famous, so ingenious that genius itself almost seems present.

Wilhelm Lindenschmitt, one of the most distinguished professors of Munich, is the painter of "A Meeting of the Reformers at Marburg, in 1529" (8 × 5 feet), a picture executed in 1867. This is historical painting in the strictest but not the broadest and best sense; the more purely artistic problems of the composition are kept subordinate to the emphasis of the history narrated. When we remember how Rembrandt

ing like this of Lindenschmitt's is evidently composed after much cogitation of Van der Helst's "Arquebusiers" and Hals' "Trustees of the Clothweavers;" but where are the magic lights and shades, the respirable air of the room, the frank and unarranged look of life in the figures? Instead, we have a balanced, formal arrangement of scholars, in their black sixteenth-century gowns, and duly contrasted with them, the captains and politicians of the protestant Philip of Hesse, who are committed to reconcile the Reformers. Luther, reading a manuscript at a great table, faces the lean and subtle Zuingli; Melanchthon affectionately leans on Luther's shoulder, and Bucer and other intellectual rebels are near. Books and authorities are collected in heaps, especially by the side of Zuingli the learned. The friction of a great moral engine, the clash of Zurich with Wittenberg on the eucharist, is explained, to the intellectual sense, with a keenness and lucidity that eliminate all mystery; the artistic eye requires something quite different, and, in presence of this clear, historical statement, asks for certain art-beauties which statement-painting never can convey.

The lively Paris painter, Firmin Girard, contributes to this collection a scene of "Fishing," painted in 1874. A Paris husband and wife, with their little girl, all three stamped from head to foot with the inexperience belonging to city people, are astray in a country scene, and engaged in fishing in a showy and play-acting way. The husband, perched on a wall by one of the little French rivers, casts his line for minnows as gravely as if they were salmon, his wife gives

bars with his mighty form the castle-path from the interloper, is a pleasant touch of humor. M. Girard is also seen in the collection in a picture called "Reverie," a life-size lady with a book of hours, painted in 1874.

Luis Alvarez shines with all the colors of a dying dolphin in his "Spanish Birthday Festival" (4 × 2 feet,) a quaint *olla podrida* flung together in 1875, at Rome. The scene gives the manners of the Spanish capital under Godoy, the Prince of the Peace. On the wall of a glittering saloon is hung one of Murillo's Conceptions, flanked on one side by Goya's Charles IV, on the other by his portrait of the queen and infanta. Music is going on in the foreground, a young

FIGURES FROM "THE EVE OF THE WEDDING."
FROM THE PICTURE BY A. DARPENTRACH.

half her thoughts to his success and half to her beautiful summer toilet, and the young infant, feeling for the moment as professional as a Billingsgate fishwife, collects the scanty prey in a tub. Firmin Girard is also represented here by "The Betrothal," a color-study in small of the picture he selected to represent him at the International Exposition of 1878. A party, in the costumes of Louis XIII, are passing through the woods of a château, from a family chapel or oratory, seen in the distance; at this private temple a solemn promise or vow has been ratified, one of those formal agreements which in old time were only less sacred than marriage. The gallant young chevalier, walking in front with his affianced, makes with her a winning and graceful pair. To see the formal courtesy with which he leads her by the hand is a pretty thing, because this ceremonious style is associated in our experience only with very old-fashioned people, and here it is practised in conjunction with full-flushed hope and youth. The gallant resistance made by the young lady's poodle, who

beau sitting in the midst and delicately picking a guitar, while a graceful girl in white stands by him singing from *La Tirana.* An old abbé sits by a bull-fighter on a sofa, in that charitable reconciliation of secular and ecclesiastical interests which made so picturesque the lazy and degraded Bourbon reign which Napoleon temporarily disturbed. The picture is fresh, amusing, delicate and superficial, in its pretty frivolity and airy fan-painting manner.

Scipione Vannutelli shows a "Venetian Masquerade" (4 × 2 feet,) painted in 1875. The massive and determined revelry of the old Republic—"balls and masks begun at midnight, burning ever till midday"—has in this case invaded the whole Piazza of St. Mark's, and the portico of the Ducal Palace is filled with stately and noble-looking maskers. Conspicuous in front is a jealous husband, casting burning glances of suspicion towards his beautiful wife, one of the gayest and most careless maskers there. The picture is a good example of the vivid decorative style of modern Italian genre.

WASHERWOMEN OF BRITTANY

ARTIST
JULES A. A. L. BRETON

BORN AT COURRIÈRES, FRANCE, 1827   PUPIL OF DAGNAN

COLLECTION OF
EX-GOVERNOR E. D. MORGAN, NEW YORK

Baugniet's pair, "The Toilette of the Bride" and "Departure of the Bride," (each 30 x 18 inches,) represent, first, a

FISHING.
FAC-SIMILE OF A SKETCH FROM THE ORIGINAL PICTURE BY FIRMIN GIRARD.

handsome girl in white—the image of Marie Röze, the singer, at the time of her Parisian début. The Breton *bonne* arranges her lace flounces, a sister spreads her veil, another takes the white kids from a sumptuous glove-box, while, in the background, the regretful mother, in widow's weeds, is consoled by a charming little school-girl sister. In the companion picture the bride is in hat and cashmere shawl, ready for the wedding-journey; sympathetic sisters are kissing, watching, weeping over the dismantled orange-wreath,—the scene taking place in the maiden chamber, where so many sisterly despairs are originated and consoled. The *bonne* carries a handbag to the door, the horses must be pawing underneath; with these kisses and tears breaks the last tie of the old family life.

Bouguereau's "Bohemian Girl" (2 x 4 feet,) a painting of 1867, shows a damsel of twenty, standing and leaning against a hand-organ, on which she rests her tambourine. A fillet of wide gold braid is tied around her hair, and she looks upward with a homesick and mournful expression—a sort of Mignon of the Tuileries Garden. The same artist's small canvas of "The Elder Sister" shows a plain barefoot girl of ten, with no beauty but that of health and good temper, smiling at the spectator as she nurses a sturdy boy laid across her lap.

Kaulbach's ample and highly-finished crayon drawing for the painting called "Mother-Love" (3 x 4 feet) is a conspicuous item in Gov. Morgan's collection. This last survivor of the

great doctrinal art-school of Cornelius and Schadow is interesting for all he does, but there is something a little freakish in his addiction to laboriously-finished paper-pictures, prepared elaborately for the paintings he executes, as if the scheme of his compositions occurred to his mind rather as a dingy shadow than as a harmony of natural colors. The even and monotonous shading of this prodigious exercise is rather puzzling than enjoyable. Why should a colorist work out his conception in a preliminary experiment of gray and white—an experiment necessarily false to his intended harmony—and carry that experiment onward so remorselessly? Schoolboys, in the preliminary stage, are allowed to show their neatness of hand, and try what large spaces they can cover with faultless expanses of cross-hatching and line-work; but in the history of art it has been rare indeed that a fresco-painter of acknowledged position has sought to commend himself with elaborate feats of crayon-drawing, such as this cartoon of "Mother-Love," or the similar one in Mr. Pierpont Morgan's collection, or the "Reformation," belonging to Mr. Durfee, of Fall River. The "Mutterliebe," a group of four children and a dignified imposing-looking woman, has been already noticed as occurring in the form of a small painting in Mr. Gibson's gallery at Philadelphia, while the large and finished picture is to be found in Mr Probasco's collection in the city of Cincinnati.

Gustav Richter, of Berlin, contributes "Queen Louise of Prussia," a picture of cabinet size. It is a young girl of serious and even grief-stricken mien, descending some garden-steps towards the spectator. The tranquil, foreboding beauty of the face is made more interesting by the fact that it is an idealized and spiritualized likeness of the mother of the present venerable Emperor of Germany, represented in the dress and environment of her youth, and studied for modern times as a specimen of noble or regal demeanor in the beginning of the century. Louise, deceased in 1810 at the

THE BETROTHAL.
FAC-SIMILE OF A SKETCH FROM THE ORIGINAL PICTURE BY FIRMIN GIRARD.

early age of thirty-four, was daughter of the Grand-Duke Charles of Mecklenburg-Strelitz, and became the wife of the present Kaiser's father (Frederick-William III). She was celebrated for the enmity of Napoleon. Richter's larger picture of this subject is at Cologne. Gustav Richter died on the first of September, 1881, having just attained his fifty-eighth year. From his birthplace, Berlin, he went in youth to Paris, to study in the atelier of Léon Cogniet. He was a member of the Academies of Munich, Vienna, and Berlin, in which latter city he was a professor in the governmental art-school. He received a grand medal at Berlin in 1864, and a second medal at the Paris Exposition of 1855, other medals at Brussels, Vienna, and Philadelphia, to the exposition in which last-named city he sent a portrait of the historian Bancroft. It is agreeable to come upon the work of Gustav Richter, not at all abundant in this country. Alone among the painters of Germany he has arrived at theories of sumptuous color which place him on a line with Makart and the Vienna tone-painters, as well as with a class of experimenters in brilliant effect now coming forward in every national school of art. It is curious that this man of the past, born in 1822, should have arrived, by paths of his own, at the same resuscitation of Venetian splendor which we find, so differently achieved, in the works of Makart, of Semiradsky, of Pradilla and Agrasot and Valés, of Henri Regnault, of Pinchart, of Simonetti and Maccari.

Cesare Maccari, himself, an Italian representative of this modern resuscitation of Veronese and the Venetians, is represented by "The Zither-Player" (4 × 5 feet,) a sitting figure of a girl in an enormous garden-hat, occupied with the tinkling instrument, which gives astonishing play to a set of flexible and taper fingers. The picture is radiant with color and self-conscious with modish grace. Maccari, born at Siena in 1840, enjoyed high consideration under the last king of Italy, being employed to decorate the Quirinal Palace for the new royal occupation of Rome; in that regal residence his fresco represented the "Triumph of the Graces."

Among the sculpture to be found at Governor Morgan's residence, the work of highest consideration is "Hiawatha,"

A MEETING OF THE REFORMERS AT MARBURG, IN 1529
FAC-SIMILE OF A SKETCH FROM THE ORIGINAL PICTURE BY W. LINDENSCHMIT.

a sitting figure of remarkable ideal beauty and anatomical accuracy. It is an early work of Augustus Saint-Gaudens, of

New York, and clearly predicts the celebrity since become so conspicuous.

SKETCH FROM A DESIGN BY C. VANNUTELLI

F the small but precious collection got together by Mr. J. PIERPONT MORGAN, of New York, perhaps "The Cardinal's Fête" (4 × 3 feet,) by the Cavaliere Scipione Vannutelli, of Rome, is the greatest rarity. The picture was painted in 1875. The dashes of glitter, the mixture of pomp and piety, the indulgent and complaisant clergy, the palace decked with tapestry and with the sacred banners, afford an opportunity to the painter for the resources of a glittering palette. The ceremony represents the festival held on some anniversary of the Cardinal's election. On this ferial day the prelate sits in state in the sala di ricevimento, the ceremonial chamber in the palace of the cardinalate, receiving the visits of priests and laity, who earn a five years' exemption from purgatory by a single kiss of his hand or his red robe. Cardinals' nieces have a prescriptive right to be charming, and their sweetness and affection form a bouquet of loveliness that takes the place of filial tenderness in the old man's childless lot. Young boys of chosen beauty, selected from the most honored branches of his family, bring flowers or hold aloft the emblazoned banner of his race. A group of youths and maidens, in the rich costumes painted by Masaccio and Lippi, carry on a concert of voices and mandolins. The aged Cardinal, dumb and motionless as an idol, sits in his burly scarlet by the estrade which divides the saloon, whose rich decorations are all of a religious character, and give to his palace the aspect of a church. His secretary, an aged Benedictine monk, who may have served his superior through many years and under several popes, stands at his right to regulate the ceremony of hand-kissing, while priests of divers orders occupy seats along the wall, and look down upon the bevy of richly-dressed girls, whose white veils form a bower around the aged prince of the church. This picture, a reflective historical study of manners during the brightest lustre of the papal power, marks the highest level of contemporary Roman art, and exceeds in interest the "Venetian Masquerade," painted by the artist the same year, and just considered in the collection of Gov. Morgan.

By Luis Alvarez, a modern Spanish painter, whose brush is a pointed weapon of wit and brilliancy, the collection has two pictures. "The Ladies' Pet," or "Coqueluche des Dames," represents the familiar abbé of eighteenth-century society. Introduced as a household plaything among the frivolous beauties of the Rousseau epoch, he was expected to advise during the visit of the hairdresser, to bring news, to run errands, to carry the latest gossip of the greenroom and the latest scandal of the frail world. A picture by the modish contemporary artist, Lavreince, represents this holy ecclesiastic actually assisting at the morning array of a beauty in her bedroom, and choosing her silks or ribbons, with the legend "Qu'en dit l'Abbé?" He was permitted to hand the powder-puff, to put on the slippers. Scribe represents such

mirror, or ask his opinion of their costumes, he sits among them supremely at his ease, enjoying all the pleasures of the ball except actual participation. To tread a minuet in public would probably be forbidden by his cloth, but short of positive dancing he gets all the flavor of the orgie. The artist has comprehended and revealed a character perfectly accepted among the southern races, but unknown to the Anglo-Saxons—the boy who is not in the least afraid of ladies. This precious personage, at a boarding-school age when we were so dreadfully afraid of our sisters' friends, is completely acceptable and harmonized among the girls. Neither embarrassed, nor pompous, nor affected, nor cere-

THE CARDINAL'S FÊTE.
FACSIMILE OF A SKETCH FROM THE ORIGINAL PICTURE BY GIOVANNI B. TIEPOLO

an abbé, in the well-known play of *Adrienne Lecouvreur*, seasoning with gossip and gallantry the toilet of a princess: "It is your duty to know all the news," she says, "and it is for that reason the ladies receive you in the morning while dressing themselves. Give me the patch-box. Would you stick this patch on the cheek, or at the corner of the left eye? What, not approve of patches? You are precipitating the revolution! With your bashful and Sunday manners, who would suspect you of being such an insurrectionist among the Levites?" Such was the tone in which the tame pet of the boudoir was addressed, and with such hints did he learn the duties that were expected of him. Alvarez depicts a very youthful specimen of this privileged class. With the clerical cravat sticking out from his chin, and a crown of roses on his head, he permits some masquerading beauties to dress him off out of the toilets provided for the carnival. As they array themselves, try on their masks, adjust their dominoes at the

monious, acting no part and evoking no distrust, he has learned the gentleness that reassures them, with the order of ideas that entertain, and sprawls among the petticoats, completely accepted as being of their own species.

By Alvarez, likewise, is the "Gondola Flirtation." On the placid water of the Grand Canal, where it broadens towards the Lido, passes a gondola, with an embroidered canopy in place of the black cab which was exacted by the sumptuary laws of the Republic's greater days. The liveried gondolier skillfully urges the boat, his long oar fixed in the curious notched rowlocks of Venice. The family in the boat are people of quality, not of the grand old times, but of the licensed age of Rousseau and Casanova. The *cicisbeo* forms an admitted article of the family group. While the stupid old husband nods, the gallant is permitted to clasp the hand of a ripe beauty in powder, who shelters the transaction with her fan. The daughter is engaged with a flirting chevalier, and the little girl, learning her life's mission by metaphor, is herself angling,—beguiling fish while attending the capture of hearts. The artist's copy of this picture, owned by Mr. Cutting, has been already catalogued among the possessions of that collector.

"The Slipper Shop" (30 × 24 inches,) by Villegas, not illustrated in these pages, is a further demonstration of the rich, iridescent, tile-painting style of the enameled art of Spain. It is extraordinarily sumptuous in its flash of Oriental color and costume.

By T. Moragas is "The Court of Justice in the East," a canvas of 1873. This scene takes us to the lands where the

Fortuny is represented in the collection by a water-color study of a "Contadino." In this little picture, rejecting his usual fancy for glittering dresses and iridescent colors, he represents an ordinary laborer of the Campagna in the plain and heavy costume of his labor,—the ugliest dress, Hawthorne declares, in the world.

In each of the collections described in this article is to be seen one of Kaulbach's large cartoons or crayon drawings— a more ample fragment of paper than can usually be found, however covered with ornament, in a modern house. As the gallery of Governor Morgan included that artist's "Mother-Love," so this collection exhibits his "Vogelsang," or "The

FLIRTATION IN A GONDOLA.
FAC-SIMILE OF A SKETCH FROM THE ORIGINAL PICTURE BY S. ALVAREZ.
COLLECTION J. P. MORGAN.

judge still sits in the gate, administering the law as in the day of Boaz. The naked prisoner, his wrists fastened in wooden handcuffs, lies on his back in a court-yard of splendid architecture. A rich carpet is spread on the pavement, and the ancient cadi sits cross-legged and barefooted, in a semicircle of seven assistant judges and primitive lawyers. A couple of mounted guards, armed to the teeth, boldly bring their horses into this simple court-room; while, further back, another officer on horseback deals blows right and left with his sword, to keep back the thronging crowd of spectators, not permitted to approach within a dozen feet of the scene of judgment. A bloody garment, presented as the chief piece of evidence, is spread before the cadi, in witness of some ruffianly deed of violence, the witness pointing to it and making it the prime article of conviction. The bare soles of the criminal, helplessly stretched towards the judge, invite the bastinado. This animated and lifelike scene is painted in a thorough-going though somewhat heavy method, in a style of photographic minuteness recalling the earlier manner of Fortuny.

Bird-Song," illustrative of Schiller's poem. A shepherdess, seemingly fresh from a bath in the pool which spreads at her feet, lies on the grass in a simple drapery of white; her crook and flower-crowned hat lie beside her, her sheep are pasturing on the hillsides in the distance, and she half repels and half yields to the embrace of a wandering minstrel who has discovered her retreat. The intruder, in the garb of the ancient minnesingers, his guitar strapped to his back, his cap crowned with dancing feathers, with his face so near that he can perceive the odor from her rose-wreath, pours into her ears the spirit and allurement of his songs. The embrace takes place "unter den linden"—a title sometimes given to the picture, which is very popular in various styles of reproduction. The original, here seen, with its life-size reality of presentation, conveys a certain hardness, not to say coarseness of management, which would be almost painful in a full sun of oil-colors, but which the gray effect of the crayon and the flatness of a monumental style of drawing carry safely off into the remoteness of ideality and symbolism.

"La Blanchisseuse des Amours," or "The Laundress of Cupids," is one of the most audacious and original of the fancies of that poet of the palette, Hamon. The picture is

THE PORTER OF HORACE.
FAC-SIMILE OF A SKETCH FROM THE ORIGINAL PICTURE BY H. LEROUX.

like a song, and conveys a delicate impression of music and perfume, rather than of form or color. In a pearly scene of dawn, a maiden cleanses her conscience of its loves, at a fountain which ought to be filled with holy-water. This frankest of painters, who can make poetry out of the commonest incidents of commonest life, is not afraid to represent the washing-bat and the soap, the clothes-pins and stretching line, in a scene outwardly clothed in classic guise. Such a confusion of epochs really adds to the grace and piquancy of his ballad-like art. Nothing can tell a clearer story than the dejection of the freshly-drowned Cupid pinned to one end of the line, with hanging head and straightened curls; and the recovery of natural instincts goes on successively through the ranks, until the dryest of the Loves, though caught still by the wings, lifts his sunny head and begins to play with the butterflies which circle around him.

Hector Leroux, so well known for his Vestal and other Roman groups, shows in Mr. J. P. Morgan's collection "The

Servant of Horace," delightedly studying out the primitive circus-poster, and forgetting in his interest the errand on which the poet has sent him. On the wall are sketched the two styles of gladiator, the myrmillo, or Gaulish swordsman, and the net-thrower with his trident. Contemplating the announcement of the coming contest, the lazy knave quite forgets to carry home the wine,—a beverage which the painter imagines as enclosed in wicker-covered flasks, not different from the modern.

There is a truly magnificent specimen of Corot in the collection of Mr. J. P. Morgan. It is called "Le Gallais," and contains in the fullest degree his charm of mystery and pearly tenderness.

By Diaz, painted in 1870, is a capital example, "The Promenade." It is one of his purposeless groups of figures, aimless except for the juxtaposition of their lusciously colored dresses. A gallant and lady are represented, with dogs on either side. Out of vague romantic forms like these, telling no story and illustrating no drama, the colorist contrives a melody of hues that strikes the eye as one of Schubert's symphonies affects the ear. This important specimen of Diaz, of great purity amid its opulence, is called the "Promenade à la Robe Bleue."

THE BIRD-NEST (VOGELBAD).
FAC-SIMILE OF A SKETCH FROM THE SKETCH BY W. VON KAULBACH.

Heinrich Schaeffels shows a complicated and ingenious scene of "Queen Elizabeth Returning from Knighting Admiral Drake." This artist, who paints in a style that seems to emulate Baron Leys, but only attains to Piloty, is here redeemed in his commonplace by the background of sails, rigging, and old-fashioned galleons, which involuntarily, as it were, spread for him a decorative groundwork of quaintest originality for his queen and court and their burly dresses. Useless to complain that the "imperial votaress" and her gallant knights look like pen-wipers at a fair! Behind them stretch the tackle, the looped sails, the carved poops of the caravels, cutting the heavens with strange lines and patches; the stage in this instance almost makes the drama—and worthily, for it is set with the very properties of Shakespeare, the scenery of the *Tempest*, of the choruses in *Henry V*.

Elihu Vedder, an American "mystical" painter, is shown in a quaint and certainly interesting composition of "Nausicaa and her Maidens." The figures illustrate that fresh, breezy, primitive and most beautiful passage in the *Odyssey*, where the princess, after washing out the clothes of her royal family, engages in a game of ball with her maidens prior to discovering the shipwrecked Ulysses. The spirit of sweetest idyl, fit to be set to music by a young god in the morning of the

world, here intrudes into the stern and warlike story of Homer; and it is not surprising that painters of all ages have been inspired by the figure of Nausicaa—so pure, so useful, so joyous and so princely. Mr. Vedder has made of this Homeric group a decorative panel. He extends the line of playful maidens in a long sequence, varying as much as possible their graceful attitudes and the daring flutter of their draperies. His style is partly inspired by the frieze of Greek marbles, partly by the more opulent variety afforded by renaissance painters. This troubadour variation, played on the plain Greek air, is a very popular thing just now, particularly in England; and Mr. Vedder's Greek draperies, just beginning to lose their holy simplicity in the torments of Bawdinelli and Bernini, have an air of vexed innocence that would appeal to Mr. Burne Jones, to Mr. Albert Moore, or to Mr. Rossetti.

While mentioning the specimens by Luis Alvarez, it may be observed that Mr. J. P. Morgan owns that artist's sketch of his "Selling Tickets for a Charity Bull-Fight," of which the painter's finished work has been noticed in the collection of Mr. Stebbins.

CATALOGUE OF EX-GOVERNOR E. D. MORGAN'S COLLECTION.

CATALOGUE OF MR. J. P. MORGAN'S COLLECTION.

La Soubrette

ARTIST

D. RAIMUNDO DE MADRAZO

BORN AT ROME, ITALY, 1841.　　　　　　　　　　　　　　　　PUPIL OF HIS FATHER

COLLECTION OF

MR. A. J. DREXEL, PHILADELPHIA

COLLECTIONS OF MESSRS. A. J. DREXEL AND J.W. DREXEL.

CONSIDERABLE proportion of decorative pictures of the modern Spanish school characterizes the collection in Mr. A. J. Drexel's West-Philadelphia home—a delicious *rus in urbe*, whose groves and parks are spread in the midst of city squares. We remark the names of Madrazo, of Rico, of Luis Jiminez. The frank, sensuous enjoyment of bright color for its own sake, the fearless contrast of positive hues, is at once characteristic of the canvases which scintillate over the walls inside, and of the flower-petals and butterflies dancing in the garden-beds without. The artists of the pictures within might seem to have taken their lesson from the delicate works of Nature under the windows. These painters of the South indeed have the courage to go straight to the lessons of creation; the flowers and birds of the tropics teach them a series of audacious contrasts, of risky harmonies that tremble on the verge of discords, and they possess the bravery of spirit that incites them to take these hints directly from the external world, without trying to teach the parrot or the cactus to be gray. Their united productions tend to give a tone of enchantment to the premises where they are preserved. None of the asceticism of a timid taste, reducing the color-melodies of the world to still uniformity, or extolling the beauty of faded tints, can remain in a home thus brightened with daring coruscations, and sparkling with the gaieties of the solar spectrum from every wall.

One of the notable decorations of Mr. A. J. Drexel's mansion is the life-size picture by Ramon de Madrazo, a subject known by the *nom de théâtre* of "Dindon Tendre." Here we have a life-size standing figure, without any Rembrandt contrasts or Caravaggio shades, relieved against a light background, and itself seeming made of crushed roses and swansdown. The theme is a creature of the footlights, or a dancer at opera balls, careless and audacious yet veiled with the weariness of sleepless midnights, and armed with a hundred piquant graces which are supposed, like a metropolitan dialect, to be comprehended and interpreted and uttered only at Paris. Her mask, her opera-cloak, a foot made muscular with much waltzing and swelling out of a low dancing-shoe and a silk stocking, the toleration and fearlessness of the expression, the bouquet and the letter at her feet for trophies of conquest, compose the expressive traits of the type. Here is epicurean life, an existence reduced to the exploration of sensations; no surprise could greatly shock

SENTINEL OF THE REPUBLICAN ARMY OF THE VAR.
FAC-SIMILE OF A SKETCH FROM THE ORIGINAL WATER-COLOR BY J. L. E. MEISSONIER.

this being enervated with novelties, and no alarm could deepen the expression of the face, habituated to receive pleasure and pain alike with one unalterable fatigue. The style in which this truly nineteenth-century symbol is painted is that singular and sensitive manner frequently chosen by Madrazo, in which he seems to demand of oil-color the delicacy, the tenderness, of pastel. To prove that there is nothing in the robust wooden palette coarse, nothing stolid, nothing unsusceptible of all caprice, seems to be a mission of Madrazo's; and he is constantly surprising us with modish, powdery effects fixed in oil—with a bloom that seems fallen from a plum, or from one of the pastels of La Tour, yet which is made unalterable with the most permanent method known to the colorist. We must not forget that for the artist this slightness of effect is a thoroughness, not a negligence; it is a tremendous effort, this of grinding down the obstinacy, the resistance, of oil-color painting, until something is produced as volatile, as aggressive, as piquant, as the dust of the diamond. To have attained this daring outlook from the finer summits of art, to have wrung the triumphs from different methods and fixed them as a plume upon his own originality, it is evident that Madrazo must have been a personage with a history. He is in fact, though so decidedly an inventor and an innovator, a man saturated from infancy with the traditional teachings of art. The Madrazo family—one of the honorable pedigrees of old Spain—can be traced back at least to the middle of the eighteenth century. At this period the great-grandparents of the painter lived at Santander. They were in modest circumstances, and wrought industriously from the rise of the sun till the going down of the same, but they had the good fortune to propagate a genius. The grandfather of our artist, the first known to have pursued the profession in his family, was this prodigy; he became Don Jose Madrazo of Santander, having been a designer, and even a painter, from his most

tender years. It is a home tradition that the initiator of his genius was the curate of the parish, who introduced him into the sacristy of his little church and allowed him to copy to his heart's content the paintings there preserved. The progress of Jose was rapid. He soon obtained an appropriation from the *Deputacion provincial* enabling him to live in Madrid and study in the Art Academy of the capital. The gallant grandsire became a personage of consequence, came to Paris and studied under David, traveled to Rome, was named painter in ordinary to the king, Charles IV, then professor at the Academy, and finally director of the Prado Museum. He died full of honors and of years in 1854. Two of the sons of Jose—Federico and Luis—walked in the footprints and received the advantages of their father. Federico, in his turn, became the director of the Academy of Madrid, where, at least until lately, he still continued his functions. He had two sons, Ramon and Ricardo, who are both painters: of these Ramon, the painter of "Dindon Tendre," was born in Rome in 1841. He came to Paris during the Exposition of 1855, but remained for only a short visit. Six years later, he returned to the French capital to reside, and became a pupil at the Beaux-Arts School; he also entered, of all places, that rule-and-line atelier of Léon Cogniet, where the master, though almost perpetually absent, contrived to rule according to the most rigid lines of the old traditions—to be an intermittent influence of permanence. It was thus that, from his professor, from his father, and from his grandfather, Ramon received an almost irresistible bent towards the false classic of the David or Overbeck school, became one of the most erudite of critics in the discussion of the old masters, and

PORTRAIT.
ENGRAVED BY FALES FROM THE ORIGINAL PICTURE BY RAMON DE MADRAZO.

seemed like to make the Dryasdust of some new eclectic laboratory of painting, comparable to that of the Carracci in their day. From this fate he was preserved by the force of his individuality. Exhaustive student of the early painters as he was, and equipped like none other with the erudition of art-history, a tireless traveler and a profound expert, he shut himself in a Paris studio and endeavored to paint directly from models and arrangements of still-life, deriving no more from the example of the ancients than would cling like an aroma around his style. It was thus, with his eyes clouded with visions of Titian, Raphael, Velasquez and Murillo, that he became an original by a prodigy of will. What he formed, was not a unity of personal style, but a flexibility: in none of his various manners, however, is he really stronger than in his development of the experiments of Goya in giving a blonde bloom of pastel-dust to the effects of oil. This painter, who applied himself to one of the few things left for art to do, and succeeded, prepared his soul for the combat in the privacy of a strangely secluded studio. He never exhibited in the annual Salon of Paris, resembling in this his future brother-in-law, Fortuny. The two young men worked side-by-side—in a companionship that was to be perfected later by a close family tie—in adjacent chambers of the palace of Queen Christine, in the Champs-Élysées. It can hardly be said that Madrazo was truly appreciated before the Exposition of 1878. During the lifetime of Fortuny he had kept himself carefully in subordination to that brilliant relative. At the exhibition in question, Fortuny having already reached his apotheosis, the brother-in-law came forward with a surprising manifestation of himself. His numerous canvases, in so great a variety of effects, had the result of initiating the public into an unsuspected creed. Madrazo is original because he does not issue from any of the preceding painters, although he knows how to assimilate what is suitable to himself in the method of each. He knows the schools and masters, with an intimacy possible to few. The problem of being a versatile modern painter, of original style, when living in the midst of Paris life, is quite as difficult an one as that of being conversant with old masters without becoming imitative in that direction. But Madrazo has avoided taking color from the moderns also. Spite of his sojourn among the most skillful of contemporary realists, with their logical

VENICE.
THE SHADOW OF A VENICE FROM THE ORIGINAL PAINTING AT A. J. DREX.

and convincing styles, spite of his intimacy with Fortuny, Domingo, Rico and Zamacois, Madrazo has never been hustled from the ground which he conquered for himself. The hidalgo in him resists all attempts at absorption, and he

is no more a pseudo-Meissonier than he is a pseudo-Raphael; the sangre azul of the grandee flows through his veins and rejects all mixture. His nationality seems to give a personal quality, comparable with that of a Velasquez or a Franz Hals,

BUVETTE ESPAGNOLE.
ENGRAVED BY SAENЗ FROM THE ORIGINAL PICTURE BY LUIS JIMINEZ.

to all his portraits,—to portraits of celebrities, like that of Coquelin senior in the Annibal of l'Aventurière, or to those of anonymas, like the unheralded dancing-girl Dindon Tendre, born to flutter in the gas-light awhile and then fade into a canvas like the present.

Still as portraitist, but with the addition of subject-interest this time, is Ramon de Madrazo to be viewed in the canvas of "Master Drexel." The entirety with which the articulated human form is hung and jointed, its pliancy and flexible strength, are infallibly comprehended by the painter; the animated machine depends together with an admirable expression of tension, the little weary legs seem ready to pull the vertebræ apart, and the hands are half-braced and half pendent, as becomes a child wearied to the last degree with hanging in mid-air, at a painter's pleasure, in an adult conversation-chair. Family legends tell the amount of specie which the little fellow drew from a convenient banker as a premium for each sitting. The artist casts his human body in the seat with the secure rightness only possible to the anatomist and the draughtsman. The careful drawing of the extremities, the dexterous modeling of the round infantine head in its umbra of dark hair, the relief of the picturesque velvet which forms the scabbard to this highly-tempered little body, all are expressed with masterly ease and enviable vigor.

Luis Jiminez, whose birthplace and age were just given in the article on the Lankenau collection,—a son of Seville and pupil of her art-Academy,—contributes a "Scene at a Lemonade Shop," or "Buvette Espagnole," which smacks of the soil as the work of such a child of Spain should do. The pretext is one of those booths scooped in the walls, for the sale of summer drinks, which abound in Seville, each kept by a gipsy girl with a rose in her hair; one can hardly find a street in Seville without such a *limonadière*, or without the *buñoleras*, in striped costume, who employ so many provocations and blandishments to attract passers-by under the awnings where they fry their fritters in olive oil. Before the booth and before the gipsy girl and before the crystal arsenal of bottles and glasses, stands a bull-fighter, tumbler in hand, conversing with a barefoot Carmelite monk. The humor of the picture is in the excellent understanding which subsists between the man of blood and the man dedicated to heaven. Evidently the superb bull-slayer has often gratified the palm of the begging monk when on his quests, and the church has no grudge against the gladiator for his sanguinary occupation. This group, made savory with a full Spanish flavor as obvious as the pervasive garlick of a Seville salad, is one of those which the young artist sent in the beginning of his career from Italy, and the style of which surprised the spectators to a singular degree. What artist, before, ever sent Spanish genre-subjects from Rome? The history of Luis Jiminez shows strong individuality, and pictures like this form a part of it. Placed by his father in the Art-Academy of Seville, as soon as he manifested a sparkle of the graphic talent, young Luis labored like a galley-slave, under the guidance of masters committed to the falsely classical and to *ennui*. All the while, beneath a mask of docility, the youth was goaded by the ambitions of his age, which spurred him towards the land of imagination, of eternal memories, of golden sunshine. He dreamed of Rome, of Italy—he dreamed, we might suppose, of the immortal relics attesting a workmanship now inimitable, of grandeurs which the step of time has not been able to extinguish. Rome was the goal of the dark Spanish boy's thoughts, copying frigid casts in the Seville Academy; but between the dream and its realization existed an obstacle, the lack of money. The father refused further subsidies, and the disappointed youth was about to pack up his hopes in the budget of human disappointments, when a person of means in his vicinity took the rôle of a Mæcenas, and gave the ambitious young artist the means to run about the world with a free foot. His first Mecca was the city of the popes; but here, instead of interesting himself in the works of Michael Angelo or the relics of Latium, our painter took a very different course. Using the sky of Italy and the inspiration of the throng merely as a stimulus, Luis Jiminez sat upon the ruins of the Cæsars and sketched, with renewed ardor, the very scenes of Spain which he had just left, and which now hummed in his head with far greater persistency than ever before. During a ten year's residence in Rome, the Seville painter incessantly sent back incidents of the home life of his youth, of which the present picture of a "Buvette Espagnole," painted in Rome in 1873, is a specimen. It was not until 1875 that he betook himself to Paris, whither he was drawn by the warm reception accorded to his works by Goupil, and where he continues to pour out the dramas of life around Seville with unmitigated vigor. Only a Spaniard, perhaps, has this

nostalgia of home themes; only a roving artist brought up in the gipsy crowds of Seville would have the street-throngs so photographed on the gray matter of the brain, that whenever he goes into his closet, or is left alone, the beloved scene develops before him in all the spangles of its sunshine and all the vivacity of its life.

Simon Durand, who shares with Benjamin Vautier the distinction of being in the foremost rank of the genre-painters produced by Switzerland, is represented by "The Wedding at the Church" (4 × 3 feet.) This forms a companion to Durand's equally celebrated picture at the exposition of 1878, "The Wedding at the Mayor's Office." The lumbering dignity of an old-fashioned Geneva family is represented in this good-natured picture. The ponderous carriages deliver their loads at the portal of the church. The bride is entering the sacred edifice, on the arm of an elderly citizen, her father, who looks honest and sentimental, as Rousseau describes his parent, but who is glad enough to "caser," or get rid of, the stylish girl and her milliner's bills. The groom, in garments never designed by Dusautoy, and in large white gloves, helps a bridesmaid out of the ancient carriage, on whose tail-board a bare-legged street Arab has been stealing a ride. The usual throng of loiterers hangs around the church-door and tastes the spectacle like a gourmand's dish. The painter works with a fat, loaded, unctuous brush, which expresses architecture with peculiar breadth and solidity, as where the irregular walls and gables of the narrow street-perspective are buttered by the reeking Southern sunshine.

Beside the Durand might be placed the "Reception of the New Mayor" (2½ × 3 feet,) another bourgeois ceremony in Southern Europe, by Chierici. The great man of the village, in his smart official coat, enters a little mountain hamlet in Italy, of which he is the newly-appointed syndic or mayor, and whose real estate he possibly owns almost in its entirety. Great awe, approaching to consternation, is shown by the estimable population of smugglers and poachers whom he has come to rule. The men, standing in their wooden shoes, almost efface themselves against the long wall at the right. The women, on the contrary, have nothing to fear from a gentleman of taste and gallantry; and their representative, a handsome contadina in gala costume, who is seen in a back view, as she stands prominently forth at the left, evidently intends to get the *lionne's* share of the great man's attention.

Henri Dupray, "the dreamy painter of melancholy sublieutenants," an artist whose sentimental treatment of war-themes is so entirely national that few of his pictures have been chosen for American purchase, is represented by "The Versaillists Entering Paris after the Commune" (6 × 4 feet). In this canvas, painted in 1876, we see the bald heads of the hills around the capital covered with snow, and just lightly bearded with the sparse trees which push through the white integument. The army of law and order trudges gallantly into occupation, cold and cheerful, over the snowy road. The squad of tramping privates, with much French character in the bulge of their baggy red breeches stuffed into well-worn gaiters, is very good, and there is less of lachrymose affectation in the picture than is usual with this troubadour of the armies.

Charity

ARTIST

WILLIAM A. BOUGUEREAU

BORN AT LA ROCHELLE, FRANCE, 1825.　　　　　　　　　　　PUPIL OF PICOT.

COLLECTION OF

MR. JOSEPH DREXEL, NEW YORK

Meissonier signs the "Republican Sentinel of the Army of the Var," a by no means small water-color in the A. J. Drexel collection. It is very high in tone, and the light facings and gaiters seen against the sky give the figure the air of a little marble statuette. The rigid perfection of the modeling, in this small scale and high key of values, reminds us of those few patient Dutchmen who are able to carve intaglios in diamonds. Diamond carvers and Meissoniers are about equally rare.

"Venice" in Rico's canvas (4 x 3 feet) is seen from all across the Giudecca, whose full width occupies the front of the calm pale picture; the campanile, the Palace, the domes of the cathedral, form a band of glittering stones, like an opened girdle, across the middle of the view, between sea and sky, while a covey of fishing-boats make for the Quay of the Slaves. Rico's "Seine" is a smaller painting, measuring 3½ by 1½ feet. Moya has a "Reception of Victor Emmanuel at Venice" (10 x 5 feet,) showing the first occupation by an Italian king of the sea-city, in 1867, after the Austrian usurpation—a change attended by fairy-like fêtes never to be forgotten by those who happened to be present. "Com' è bella Venezia!" exclaimed the stolid king on this exceptional occasion.

Biard has a "Crossing the Channel" (5 x 3½ feet,) showing people on deck, reading or sick, dressed in the fashions of 1860; this painting has formed the theme for one of the large engravings in mixed mezzotint and stipple so popular in England. The American Knight's pair of pictures, each 6 x 4 feet, of "Harvest Rest" and "Market Scene at Poissy" have great perfection and refinement of drawing, and a tinted reserve of color, altogether characteristic of the teachings of Knight's instructor, Meissonier. The crowded groups are photographically faithful, evidently studied directly from living models. What Anthony Trollope's novels are in literature, such in art are these accurate nineteenth-century records, set down to teach the ages of the future.

A COLLECTION impregnated with geniality, generosity to artists, and a sort of catholic embrace for every kind of good painting, is that of Mr. J. W. Drexel, in New York. Mr. Drexel's largest object is Bouguereau's serene, tranquil, gracious picture of "Charity" (5 x 9 feet) painted in 1878, and one of the most highly finished pieces of sculpture with the brush ever achieved even by this magister emeritus of elegance and grace. The replica of this canvas, in Mr. Hawk's collection, having been already mentioned, it may be well to specify the slight difference in the accessories; the group in the two pictures being similar, that of Mr. Hawk's is the one with landscape background, and that in an architectural setting belongs to Mr. J. W. Drexel.

"The Muezzin," by Gérôme, shows the pomegranate-shaped dome of a minaret, up to which the blind muezzin has climbed to cry in the moonlight, "Prayer is better than sleep." The stars, too bright to be extinguished by the moon's rays, sprinkle the clear heavens, under which the roofs of Cairo are basking. Night-hawks perch over the copper dome, and the moon lays on the platform a sharp mosaic of the shadows of the muezzin and his assistant. These last are both blind. Moslem law forbidding any male to climb the minarets capable of seeing the women who may be reposing on the city roofs. The picture of the "Muezzin" is one of the very few in which the artist has undertaken to represent a night effect. It belongs to his enormous collection of Eastern scenes betraying the accuracy of the photograph, and allowing the untraveled western world to appreciate bible lands with an exactness never before attainable. Less romantic and less gorgeous than the oriental pictures of his predecessors, Marilhat, Decamps, Belly, and Delacroix, the Turkish themes of Gérôme are marked by a clarity of demonstration that convinces and satisfies. They are composed by the artist with indefatigable care; the pencil-sketches of his albums, and the color-patterns and indications hastily jotted with the brush upon a multitude of fugitive sheets of canvas, form the foundation of these tourist's reports; with such memoranda, and with an exhaustive acquaintance with all the Turcos and Arab vagabonds who may be hired in Paris as models, the artist contrives to arrange his Eastern scenes with a fullness and sufficiency leaving nothing to desire. With these genuine models, arranged amid an enormous stock of real costumes and accessories, the learned painter can at any moment construct a veritable Orient in a corner of his studio, the arrangement being always brought to the test of a most categorical memory. Gérôme has written in his notes various hints of his methods of work. The camping grounds at sunset were his harvest-seasons during the journeys, in which he hastily put together the recollections of the day or the actualities of the spot. Of his first march in the desert, camping at El Ariseh, he writes: "Nothing is more pleasant and poetical than these encampments in the solitude. There is also the added charm of the unexpected, the unknown, and of novelty. Although tired with such long marches in the hot sun, I set myself to work ardently as soon as the halting-place was reached. But alas! how many things one leaves behind, that can not be carried away except in recollection—and I love better three touches of paint on a canvas than the most vivid of recollections! But one must mount and on again, carrying one's regrets on the horse's crupper!" The lament over the insufficiency of remembrance is only what Gérôme must share with every artist who undertakes traveler's themes. But few can accuse their recollections with less justice than he, and it is the reconstructing power of an almost infallible memory that enables him to build up again such themes as "The Muezzin," a subject he could never have been permitted to paint after nature, and whose night-effect must have been largely contrived from imagination.

Some of Mr. J. W. Drexel's canvases represent historical painting, as Tack's "Breaking out of the Thirty Years' War"

(4 × 3 feet) and E. L. Henry's "Declaration of Independence." Some are able restorations of antiquity, as Savini's picture of 1873, "Pompeian Interior" (3 × 2 feet). Schreyer's "Alarm" and H. Robbe's "Sheep" are fine specimens of animal painting. Diaz's "Fontainebleau Forest," Corot's "Landscape" and Andreas Achenbach's "Sunrise on the Rhine" are, in very different ways, able specimens of nature's color-impressions and form-impressions, while Oswald Achenbach's "Naples" (24 × 12 inches) gives in his rich scenic way the turmoil of vetturini and beggars in the modern Parthenope, with the threatening extinguisher of Vesuvius elevated over all. The specimen of Angelica Kauffmann,—that romantic nymph celebrated for an unusually mistaken matrimonial venture,—is a canvas presented by Marie Antoinette to the American Consul, and by him to De Witt Clinton.

Meyer von Bremen, whose pictures are never slighted and never marked with fatigue, polishes and repolishes a little scene of "The Rustic Toilet." A fair peasant-girl, beautiful with the brief morning bloom of the lymphatic temperament at twenty years of age, puts on her armor of conquest in the solitude of a snug châlet. The table with the lamp, the oval mirror on the wall, the chair and narrow maiden bed, together with the items of a humble provincial costume, make up the poor child's battery of fascination. As she puts up her tresses, she might quote Pope's line, that "beauty draws us with a single hair." Will she capture the wandering prince in disguise, or only bluff Hodge by the church-door—will this anxious toilet command a future of opulence, or merely the ordinary fate of connubiality in Germany, toil between the cart-shafts, and a husband's perpetual tobacco-smoke?

The life-size standing marble figure of Psyche is by Carl Steinhäuser, a sculptor with a studio in Rome and a professorship in Carlsruhe. This sculptor, having sold in Philadelphia his "Hero and Leander," a quarter of a century ago, became a great favorite with the artistic circles of that city and was commissioned to construct the monument for the tomb of the Burd family, to carve a couple of figures for Mr. Henry C. Carey, and about the same time, doubtless, to place this "Psyche" in the collection of a connoisseur well acquainted with Philadelphia galleries. The art-resorts of that city form, in fact, a little propaganda for the fame of Steinhäuser, otherwise scarcely known out of Europe. Carl Steinhäuser is a sculptor of high rank in the German school of the art. His "Herman and Dorothea," in the palace garden at Carlsruhe, is one of the finest conceptions with which the genius of Goethe has inspired a sculptor's chisel.

CATALOGUE OF MR. A. J. DREXEL'S COLLECTION.

CATALOGUE OF MR. JOSEPH W. DREXEL'S COLLECTION.

GARDEN OF THE DARIO PALACE, VENICE.
FAC-SIMILE OF A DRAWING BY G. MARTIN RICO.

THE COLLECTION OF MR. J. C. RUNKLE.

O N this page is given in fac-simile a pen-and-ink
drawing by Rico, in the possession of Mr. J. C.
Runkle, of New York. The copy is of the same size
as the original, and affords an accurate impression of
the powers of one of the most accomplished manipu-
lators of line now living. Señor Rico has deeply
studied the expressive capacity of white paper and
black scratches, and can now decide with infallible
acumen how much of his effect can be safely represented by the blank white of the sheet. This is to

be considered as a color, inlaid upon which are the "vigors" made by dark objects and crisp shadows. The tone of the

THE ARRIVAL
FAC-SIMILE OF A SKETCH FROM THE ORIGINAL PAINTING BY R. RICO.

sheet thus becomes not a passive recipient, but an active element. Rico *paints* with his white mat of cotton-pulp, as distinctly as if it were a mass of limewash loaded into a brush. A more vigorous study can nowhere be found than this robust impression of a garden in Venice—that of the Dario Palace. It is surprising that no etchings by Rico are published, since in pen-and-inks, of which this work has now given two (see Cutting article), he shows evidence of a power with the point which would rival dangerously such aquafortists as Whistler, Haden, and Méryon. Another of Rico's fine drawings, "The Seine," is in the collection.

The painting by Roybet, "The Death of Roxana" (29 × 25 inches) illustrates Racine's tragedy of *Bajazet*. Many readers may have seen Rachel in this part, or have watched Bernhardt personate the great actress Adrienne Lecouvreur playing the same rôle. Roxana, in the play, is a sultana who allows herself to love the sultan's brother, and is put to death by the monarch for her treasonous passion. The tragedy is one of the most animated of all Racine's. Amurat, the fourth sultan of the Turkish empire, ascended the throne in 1623. From among the royal consorts he selected Roxana to bear the style and title of sultana. Her destiny ordered that she should be smitten with an irresistible tenderness for Bajazet, the brother of her husband. Bajazet, preserved by his pure affection for Attalida, resisted temptation, and his

assassination was ordered by Roxana, who herself soon met her death by the executioner sent from the camp by Amurat, who had been privately made aware of his unhappy queen's intrigues. We are in the present picture again reminded of the addiction to hazardous splendors of coloring, recognized by Théophile Gautier in another of Roybet's paintings. "The red of the dress is magnificent in tone," said Gautier once in describing a Roybet, "solid and strong, with ruby transparencies and reflections of purple; we no longer find these reds, which the French school seems to be afraid of, except in the pictures of Bonifazio and Giorgione. This splendid red note bursts out like the peal of a trumpet." A critic as eloquent as Gautier might detect in the artist's "Roxana" a whole keyboard of hues equally splendid on which to wreak his descriptive powers. There is, in the hardy foreshortening, the confused adjustment, and the dashing rather than accurate drawing of Roxana, an evident challenge to Delacroix. Ferdinand Victor Léon Roybet was born April 12, 1840, in the little town of Uzès (Gard department), France. His father and mother were keepers of a small wine-shop on the Boulevard du Petit-Cours. The prudent wine-seller and his dame felt a timorous repugnance to allowing their son the freedom of a career so precarious and irregularly profitable as that of painting, but the inclinations of the lad were fixed, and at seventeen, in the year 1857, he entered the beaux-arts school at Lyons. He faithfully pursued the course of a local professor, one Vibert, and tried his hand at engraving, at lithography, and drawing. After two years of preparation he essayed painting, and made his début with a recognized masterpiece. Inspired with the study of the most eloquent of the old painters, those who are picturesque and impassioned, he struck out a style of painting based upon the inventions of the Venetian colorists, Tintoretto, Titian and Veronese, and sent to the salon of 1866, for his first specimen, a "Jester of Henri III," which received a medal, and was immediately

LANDSCAPE.
FAC-SIMILE OF A SKETCH FROM THE ORIGINAL PAINTING BY PH. ROUSSEAU.

bought by the Princess Mathilde. By this time Roybet, arrived in Paris, had formed a friendship with Ribot, the painter of the miraculous "Sebastian" of the Luxembourg, and with Vollon, the still-life painter, and to the subtle counsels of these two he partly owed a success which was absolutely forced upon the public rather than solicited. From the day when he was crowned and baptized by Gautier and by the reigning family, the temporal success of the young artist was assured, far above the predictions of evil heard occasionally in the form of croakings from the liquor-bar where his mother sold brandy in the town of Uzès. His pictures have passed

enormous white lappels and in top-boots, his hair cropped *à la Brutus* and his hand grasping the knotted stick or *pouvoir exécutif*. He listens to a friend who reads *Le Père Duchesne*, a satirical journal of the day. These figures, like the "conspirators" in a familiar opéra-bouffe, tend to set the fancy working over the pregnant period when Napoleon's power was taking form.

Goubie's "Return to the Château" is a picture executed in 1876, and shows, in a clear, bright, able style of painting, a

ROXANA.
FAC-SIMILE OF A SKETCH FROM THE ORIGINAL PAINTING, BY F. ROYBET.

into all countries; Russia possesses his "Page with Dogs," Cologne retains in its Museum his "Gathering of Hunters," and America has some of his finest works, but *L'Art* and the *Gazette* and the *Deux Mondes* are silent concerning Roybet, because he is not placarded with the throng of annual exhibitors. His studio is thus a hermitage for the powerful young painter. His fame, co-extensive with the civilized world, is imperfectly known to the Paris lounger of the Salon.

Something of a rarity is an early picture by Detaille, painted before he felt the mission to illustrate the woes of the French army. "Les Profonds Politiques" is a little picture in Mr. Runkle's collection, painted in 1869. A perfect emblem of the dandyism of the French Directory is the hero in

couple of fine horses conducted up to a park gate, which the dismounted rider of one of them unfastens. The delightful look of animation in the eye and the bearing of a gallant steed returning home is all concentrated in the principal animal figure, sketched with much sober knowledge and solid sympathy for horse-flesh. Jean-Richard Goubie, a pupil of Gérôme, born at Paris, received his unique medal in 1874—it was one of the third class—for his clever painting of a "Riding-School in the Eighteenth Century."

Among the landscapes, which are truly remarkable for high quality in Mr. Runkle's collection, is an exquisite little Théodore Rousseau, which may be called "The Château," as a pignon of some dignity is seen lifting its gable between the principal trees in the centre. No landscape ever painted, since Hobbima's masterpieces of restrained intensity, has excelled this small panel for the glorious impression of heat and sunshine, which seem to feed every spear of grass with nourishment and delight.

J. F. Millet, the wonderful interpreter of French peasant-life, is represented by three small paintings; one of them depicts a partly nude girl, "The Laundress." It is characteristic of the early period of Millet's career, just before the great change which made him the poet he became. At this epoch, his biographer, Sensier, says: "Standing before Deforges' window one evening, Millet saw two young men examining one of his pictures, 'Women Bathing.' 'Do you know who painted that?' said one. 'Yes,' replied the other, 'a fellow called Millet, who paints nothing but naked women.' These words cut him to the quick; his dignity was touched; coming home, he told his wife the story. 'If you consent,' said he, 'I will do no more of that sort of pictures; living will be harder than ever, and you will suffer, but I shall be free to do what I have long been thinking of.' Madame Millet answered, 'I am ready, do as you will;' and, from that time on, Millet, relieved in a sense from servitude, entered resolutely into the rustic art which became his specialty." Of the rural scenes by Millet, in his more familiar manner, one is a fine farmyard episode, and the other that graceful figure of a young girl bearing on her shoulder a copper milk-jar shaded with leaves, which the artist, charmed with his success, repeated several times—once in the specimen to be found in the Borie gallery, already considered, once in the Newcomb gallery at Louisville, and finally in this delicious example.

"Falling Leaves" is the title of an unusually pathetic picture by Gustave Jacquet. The figure is life-size, and repre-

THE MILK-JAR
FAC-SIMILE OF ORIGINAL SKETCH, BY J. F. MILLET.

sents a thoughtful girl in garden costume, in an autumnal park where the brown leaves are floating down around her. The picture refers to a celebrated elegy by Millevoie, a poet whose book the lovely creature holds in her hand. The old brown binding of pine-tree leather, and the small, thick duodecimo size, have all the character of a work published in 1812. "Companions of my sad life-journey, now dispersed abroad, O my friends! O you who were so dear to me! gather up my faulty songs as your legacy,—save from oblivion a few of my verses. And you for whom I die! Women! You whom I forgive, your outlines still present themselves before my troubled vision, like a sunbeam in autumn or a dream at daybreak. Gentle visions, approach! My shade implores of you one final memento of regret and love. Strew at the foot of my cypress the leaves of the roses which live but for a day." This is an extract from the most celebrated elegy of the invalid author, the one which obtained a prize at the "Floral Games." In the 1812 edition of Millevoie's "Elégies, followed by Emma and Eginard," there is a frontispiece showing the poet sitting, bare-headed, under trees which are shedding their foliage; the engraving bears the title of the poem it illustrates. A happier inspiration is seldom met with by a painter in his desultory readings of half-forgotten authors; nothing finer than this canvas has yet been supplied by way of corollary to Millevoie's favorite and proverbial lines, which ring in every French ear but heretofore have found no adequate representation,—

Deux fantômes, venez! mon ombre vous demande
Un dernier souvenir de douleur et d'amour.
Au pied de mon cyprès effeuillez pour offrande
Les roses qui vivent un jour!

CATALOGUE OF MR. J. C. RUNKLE'S COLLECTION.

PENETRANTES IN INTERIORA MORTIS.
FACSIMILE OF A SKETCH FROM THE ORIGINAL PAINTING BY JAMES TISSOT.

ADDITIONAL ART TREASURES OF PHILADELPHIA.

HERE we gather together, in a more arbitrary fashion than hitherto, the private galleries and isolated works of art which particularly challenge notice in the city of Philadelphia. The same plan will be followed in other centres. Not to swell the present work beyond a compassable form, yet at the same time not to neglect any work of eminence, it becomes necessary to exercise a somewhat rigorous test, and to measure simply by a few selected standards many a collection on which it would be a pleasure to dwell.

INITIAL FROM A DESIGN BY B. ABBOT.

Mr. T. A. DOLAN's pictures include an eminent example of James Tissot, of unusual size; it was painted in 1860, and bears for title the Latin sentence: "PENETRANTES IN INTERIORA MORTIS." It reveals the time when this painter was most strongly under the influence of Baron Leys, and like him was addicted to much study of the German Little Masters. To them he has gone for his costumes and manners, and to Holbein and other ancient designers for the subject—that "Dance of Death" of which the early Northern painters were never weary, and in which they displayed the grisly skeleton interfering with human projects in a thousand ways. In this picture Tissot seems to fancy himself painting on some church wall of Flanders or the Palatinate the familiar lesson derived from the warning sermons of St. Macarius, and called after him the *Danse Macabre*. A jester and two other musicians go piping in the van, and leading after them a motley procession of which Death brings up the rear. First come a pair of infatuated lovers, a Faust and Marguerite, or Aucassin and Nicolette. Then comes a fierce and mighty soldier between a maid and a matron; then an aged husband, whose blooming wife allows a gallant to kiss her hand, while she neglects her little lonely toddling infant; then four drunken knights, trampling over a corpse as they advance roystering, like the hardy companions of Pantagruel entering Paris; then a bloated seigneur purchasing with a bag of gold an unwilling damsel from her duenna; then the motley crowd of age and infirmity, madly suing to a buxom beauty, the last of whom turns with horror as he finds himself in the skeleton grip of Death, who darts after the crowd bearing a coffin. No mediævalist ever told the importunate story with more consummate emphasis. Another Tissot in the collection, "The Return from the Promenade," represents a lovely girl warming her foot at the fireside. Tissot, a native of Nantes, pursued his labors at Paris until the time of the Prussian war, exhibiting in the Salons up to 1870 inclusive, and gaining a medal in 1866; then he was suddenly missed, and has lived since in great artistic honor at London, illustrating antique English life in a style of originality and quaintness derived from his study of old illuminations and frescoes, and of the reconstructive works of Leys; since the execution of this early *Danse Macabre* he has gained in drawing and accuracy, but has never invented a more impressive legend.

Mr. Dolan's collection also includes "The Ladies' Luncheon" (36 × 24 inches,) by C. D. Hue, representing a crowded well-known fashionable cake-shop on the Place Castiglione, Paris, and recalling Taine's remark on English heroines, "What a quantity of little tarts they contain!" the same artist's "Morning Chocolate;" J. Worms' "Spanish Estaminet" (12 × 14 inches,) with a bull-fighter and gipsy-girl; Escosura's "Painting from the Model," a picture of 1871, showing a contadina and baby posing in a modern atelier, while Escosura paints, and a number of more or less celebrated artists gossip; Troyon's "Milking," with cows, calf and several human figures; Rothermel's "Macbeth and Wife;" Schreyer's "Drinking Horse," associated with a crouching Arab; and G. Petti's "Page and Court-Jester," a picture of 1871.

analytically through eye-glasses, glaring in rabbit-like fright, discussing together "with hands of wild rejection," or mopping a broad face and listening to the ear-whisper of chicanery. The workingmen are skillfully discriminated; behind the burly and guileless leader is the lean workman crazed with wrongs; then old age in penury, reflecting on the futility of effort; then a philosopher of the cabarets, and lastly, whispering behind his hand, the police spy intruding into their counsels to betray them. Outside a demagogue addresses the mob. The art of telling a story well, as distinguished from the art of painting well, could hardly be carried further, whether by Hogarth or Hasenclever.

Atilio Simonetti, a Roman painter, was the only pupil of Fortuny. He contributes to Mr. E. B. Warren's collection a

COAST SCENE WITH FIGURES.
FAC-SIMILE OF A SKETCH FROM THE ORIGINAL PAINTING BY J. C. NIBBY.

Mr. Ferdinand J. Dreer, best known as a collector of fine portrait engravings, can boast the most important work of the Düsseldorf artist, Hasenclever, (1810–1853) in any country. It represents an episode of 1848, when, as Heinrich Heine says, the troubles that unseated Louis Philippe "made the red curtains of a German throne or two catch fire." "A Deputation of Workingmen" shows a session of a city council in convention at a great table in a splendid civic hall. Half-a-dozen workingmen enter with a petition for more generous legislation in their behalf. The leader,—a simple, noble fellow,—halts abashed as he finds himself in an atmosphere of concentrated contempt, and is ready to drop the paper. The member to whom he offers the document rejects it utterly —his hands are too much occupied with a fine snuff-box. Opposite at the table, bearing the mace or sword of office, is a magnate whose look of amazement, as of a warrior before an unexpected enemy, is of worse augury than any refusal; the various forms of Jack-in-office surround the board—pushing it away as in comprehensive rejection, peering at the visitors

large and elaborate subject, though one kept strictly in the triviality of genre art,—"A Proclamation in front of the Pantheon." This scene of Roman manners shows the heralds, or messengers, of the *sindico* going their rounds, proclaiming a fast-day or a decree, followed by a pair of military drummers, and attended by choice specimens of the lazzaroni of that central and popular quarter which stretches around the Pantheon. The scene is like a chapter from Story's *Roba di Roma*. The crowd of urchins, mostly barefoot, run on ahead of the heralds, treating with painful disrespect their beadle-like cocked hats and cloaks and gilded staves; two gymnastic rascals turn cart-wheels on their hands; others beat an impromptu drum, or drag along a short-stepped little brother in a shirt. One makes *la nache*, as the French call it, for the benefit of the pompous officers; that is to say he plays an imaginary flageolet on his nose; this, however, is not characteristically Roman; a child of the papal city wishing to express contempt, scrapes one forefinger briskly with the other in the face of the insulted party; Simonetti must have introduced his reminiscences of French or English customs when he depicted *la niche* in front of the Pantheon. Around the drummers is also seen a tributary crowd, inspired by the rat-tat-too with more military feelings, and exercising imaginary muskets as they march behind the reveille. For background are seen the mighty columns of the Pantheon portico, filled in with the palisades which a modern Pope has added to their hoary antiquity. Mr. WARREN, besides his large Simonetti, has a pleasant little picture by Erdmann, of which a sketch is here presented, showing "Lisette," bearing the pousse-café on a salver, and saluted by an eighteenth century gallant who parts the portière; V. Palmaroli's "Convalescent," revealing a languid girl in Empire costume, on a silken sofa of the style of 1800, reclining on the shoulder of an older lady, who reads to her the second volume of Amadis de Gaul, while a pretty

finished, in Vibert's manner, and filled with half-sarcastic study of character—while the marine sketching is a vertigo, a mad struggle of paint with nature, resulting simply in a vast corrugated plaster; in this paste are stuck the highly-finished figures,—like a leaf of Anthony Trollope accidentally bound in a volume of Walt Whitman. By Chaplin, Mr. Antelo has a pretty decoration (similar to Mr. John Wolfe's), and such as Marie Antoinette might have admired. The "Girl with Doves" sits in dazzling nudity, made all the more emphatic by circumjacent draperies; some doves fly into her bosom, from one of whom she unties the long fluttering neck-ribbon, resembling a modern telegraphic despatch—and indeed doubtless conveying some message from Cyprus. A pretty, trivial allegory by Hamon represents "Hope," bearing her anchor and crowned with her star, occupied in drawing

A DEPUTATION OF WORKINGMEN AT FRANKFORT, IN 1848.
FACSIMILE OF A SKETCH FROM THE ORIGINAL PAINTING BY J. P. HASENCLEVER.

sister weaves garlands at a side table; Bouguereau's "Little Marauders" (22 × 40 inches,) with a girl helping her younger sister to steal "les pommes du voisin;" Schreyer's "Arab Chieftains" (4 × 3 feet) and his small pictures of "Kabylian Soldiers" and "Russian Sledge-Traveling in a Storm;" Robbe's "Sheep in Stable" (20 × 25 inches); Vibert's "Two Sous a Slice," where a portly street-vendor sits by his melons in gayest Spanish costume, holding up two fat fingers to designate his tariff; and Dagnan-Bouveret's "Lovers' Quarrel," a picture of 1880, where a modern pair are seen holding off from each other in a temporary tiff, silent and moody among the luxuries of a sumptuous drawing-room.

Some choice pictures are brought together by Mr. A. J. ANTELO. For instance, from the earlier experiments of Vibert an unusual specimen is produced. It is a "Coast-Scene with Figures," a picture perhaps three feet across. A great splashing breaker comes shattering and booming against a cliff, filling the air with exploding foam; on one of the rocks a party of tourists of twenty years ago—ladies, dandies, and an accidental priest in his black frock—is printed against the white ruin of breaking waters; the human part is highly

the tiny boat of human life; the boat is a walnut-shell; and the *Ilias in nuce* is neither more nor less than the human embryo and his struggles and destinies, floating down the stream of time, convoyed by Hope, who moves with graceful treachery in the air above. Edouard Richter, a Paris pupil of Hébert, contributes an odd and clever study, representing the "Aquarium at Brussels;" ladies in modern costumes cling like limpets against the enormous artificial rock-work, upon whose surfaces the cross-lights, shot through the glass tanks, play and splash like rainbows. The forced picturesqueness of factitious rock-work is faithfully given, and the fashionable visitors have a pantomime air, as if ladies from an audience were to be caught up and fixed in the spangled caves and colored illuminations of a theatrical transformation-scene. A "Greek Soldier," by Eugène Delacroix, looks as if he might have run away from the salon of a Rothschild. The picture is small, pointless, perhaps out of drawing—and it is a masterpiece. It represents a foot-soldier, who might have been of the band of Bozzaris, standing in a simple attitude, his many-folded white petticoat falling to his knees, a damasked mantle over his shoulder, and his right hand resting on one of the large silver pistols, which, with a long sword, are thrust into his girdle. There are spurts of color and breaking lights here and there in this little picture which only Delacroix could have commanded, and which Giorgione would be tempted to come out of his immortality to see. By Troyon there is a beauty—a landscape with a fine storm-effect: against the darkest cloud, from among a herd of cattle, stands forth a symmetrical white heifer, her skin, creamy as the bosom of Io, shining like silver tissue on the sky. Lecomte-Dunouy contributes a sitting figure of a Pompeian market-woman. By E. de Beaumont there is a "Shipwreck" (3 x 2 feet,) a coast-scene, with figures discovering a corpse. G. Brillouin shows "The Artist,"—three figures in a studio. Corot is seen most richly in "The Village,"—a town, a river, a peasant and his wife on the *sentier* at the left. Munkácsy gives a spirited sketch, "The Dying

Mr. JOSEPH W. BATES' collection reveals here and there a broad play of healthy humor, and we find, hung up in a place of honor, the amusing picture of Erskine Nicol, entitled "The Duet." Two Irish flute-players, in burly frieze coats, having exhausted the beer and pipes on the table before them, are soaring into the realms of fancy on the breath of their tuneful tubes. The anxious effort of the amateur virtuoso is caught quite irresistibly, and one of the lusty poets looks heavenward, as if, like Wilson's famous mocking-bird, to "recall his very soul, which expired in the last elevated strain." German humor is present, too, especially in a study by Hasenclever for his celebrated picture of "The Wine-Tasters," where every variety of German gourmand, fat or thin, critical or voluptuous, finds a place and a drop of comfort. A pleasant childish scene is delineated by Gavin, "A Juvenile Game,"

A PROCLAMATION IN FRONT OF THE PANTHEON.
FAC-SIMILE OF A SKETCH FROM THE ORIGINAL PAINTING BY A. RINOVETTI.

Brigand." Michetti has an exquisite and fragrant pastoral, "Two Children," wading in a sea of herbage, carrying flowers. Fortuny affords a valuable lesson in water-color art, with "The Dead Donkey," where an Arab with a water-jar stands by his lifeless favorite. Meissonier is found in a prosaic mood with the study of a "Paris Commissionaire." Alvarez has a canvas of 1872, "The Spinners," modeled on a celebrated Velasquez. Vallez is seen in a modish conversation-piece, "The Gallant." P. de Coninck is shown in a life-size figure, well-known from the photographs, "The Violin-Girl." Compte-Calix displays an ambitious mountain-scene, of six figures, with lady tourists kissing a beggar's baby. L. Jiminez contributes a little picture of 1872, a standing "Bull-Fighter." Madrazo is represented by a head, his usual "Gipsy-Girl." Fromentin has a fine composition, "The Cavalcade." Jules Worms shows a romantic fancy, "Consulting the Sorcerer." R. L. Legrand contributes a realistic "Ambulance," with three wounded soldiers. H. Schaep shows a marine, "The Wreck" (5 x 4 feet), and Robbe a "Cattle-piece" (4 x 3 feet).

where a number of little ones are linked hand-in-hand in a long chain, and jump through their own entanglement in the rosy joy of a rustic game; contemplating this picture we recall what modern London reviewers have claimed for their national painters, that they are unapproached in entering into the feelings and sympathies of childhood. There is in this well-seasoned collection a view of an "Italian Seaport," by Clarkson Stanfield, seeing whose surface-style and distemper tone, combined with very spirited drawing, we recall with mixed feelings how the "Oxford graduate" styled this painter "the leader of the English realists," and placidly remarked that "one work of Stanfield alone presents us with as much concentrated knowledge of sea and sky as, diluted, would have lasted any one of the old masters his life."

In the collection of Mrs. J. GILLINGHAM FELL, "La Folle," by the late Hugues Merle, painted at Etretat in 1871, cost fifty thousand francs, and is one of the best specimens of his art left by the painter. The subject is direct, rustic, unaffected, and dark with a homely horror worthy of the ballads of

Wordsworth or Crabbe or Cowper. A village bride, on the loss of her baby, has gone distracted; she wanders to and

LISETTE.
FAC-SIMILE OF A SKETCH FOR THE ORIGINAL PAINTING BY G. GERMAIN.

fro, long after the mourning garment assumed for the lost innocent is in tatters, and is seen by the pitying townsfolk, who come on sunny afternoons to draw water at the well, sitting on the curb, nursing against her soft mother's-breast a senseless bit of wood, which she wraps in the cradle-blanket. The artist shows her thus, her rich black hair shaken out so as to shade her thin face and dark, spectral-looking eyes,—the splendid dower of her former beauty hanging its latest shreds and graces about her, while all her little world looks on. Two lovely village maids stand beside her—one a sweet blonde, whose dewy eyes look out of her face seen in shadow, the other a more proud and self-sustained character. On the other side, two children are placed by the maniac—the younger a fine sturdy boy, such as *hers* might have grown to be, who has run away from bed in his shirt, and will push forward and lay his wandering face on the madwoman's knee; a girl of twelve restrains him, with an instinctive action of her hand on his shoulder, while she turns her large liquid eyes with a world of meaning on those of the unconscious invalid. This simple head of a fair French child, painted with a perfect fidelity to nature, unspoiled by any improbable degree of

prettiness, and thrilled with expression, is one of the finest things ever done by Merle; in painting quality it perhaps equals his "Good Sister," in Mr. Belmont's gallery, while as a type it is better selected: its arrested look—where the natural animal selfishness of childhood is crossed for the first time by the full maturity of womanly abnegation and divine pity—is thoroughly understood and eloquently expressed. This large picture is a statement of all that Merle could do, the resumption and compilation of his art. The tone is unusually atmospheric for the painter, and the drawing skillful. The piteous nature of the subject—a legend as sad as that of Paquerette in Hugo's *Notre Dame*—does not prevent this group from multiplying upon the spectator, as often as he sees it, its mysterious chainlets of fascination. Another large composition forms a pendant to the Merle, in Mrs. FELL's collection; it is the "Imogen carried by Arviragus," from *Cymbeline*, painted by Edward H. May, one of the veterans of the American colony in Paris. The young disguised prince, bending his noble head over the trailing body of his sister, steps with rapid and sure foot up the rocks that lead to the cavern; Imogen lies in his arms like a bruised lily, her white neck shining in the gloom, and one long arm depending. Among Mrs. FELL's pictures there is an excellent strain of the bucolic melody of J. F. Millet, before which we may pause and pour out all the loyalty and admiration we have learned from other inspections of his work. Here is a scene of sober-colored cheer; in the background a husband spading his garden among the shadows of the apple-blossoms, in front the humble Baucis scattering grain from her apron into a group of eight or nine hens that focus their heads under the descending shower. Truth of color, truth of sentiment, truth of values and relief, are all here perfectly developed under a guise of rustical severity. Bright immortals might descend and sit, with appetite and benediction, between a couple so pure, so simple, so true and accessory, in their cheery industry, to the happy impulse of fecund nature. Take, for another example full of simplicity but full of style, the Corot

THE WINE TASTERS.
FAC-SIMILE OF A SKETCH FROM THE ORIGINAL PAINTING BY J. F. HASENCLEVER.

in this collection, the "Nymphs of Dawn." Has a man the right to call himself a landscape-painter who has never shown that he commands the ability to draw a single leaf, who seems profoundly ignorant of the difference of the various

THE DUET.
FAC-SIMILE OF A SKETCH FROM THE ORIGINAL PAINTING BY KNAUS FEYEN.

tree-growths, who would fall flat before the most lenient examination of the Ruskinists about cumulus and cirrhus and cirrho-stratus? Let the accomplished Sapience of meteorology learn that there are other eyes for such things than his. Was the cloud-student or the reader by the midnight lamp ever sleepless, and constrained to wander forth among the wooded hills an hour before the day? At such a time the beech-grove, with its leafy depths, its domes, its dreaming nests, is a sanctuary of pillared clouds; it upholds against the colorless sky its mere presence, a hesitating outline. In the fern amid which its stems are buried, two of nature's jewelers—blind partners, the spider and the dew—are spreading those parures of diamonds which shall presently flash in the festival of sunrise—now, dim webs of watery nothingness. But a glint from here and there, whether of May-dew or of star-shaped flower, bursts out, penetrates the vapors, and makes the ground about it seem darker. Obscurity weaves itself around, and hangs and catches from trunk to trunk: there seem to be mysterious movements and stirrings. Toward the east the bewildered sky is losing star after star. What are those that move so stealthily from behind the trees? Are the fauns and dryads still alive, in this age of the wisdom-tooth of good *père* Corot, or are these mere vines that gad and trail behind the wind, or stealthy creatures of the wood? But the impulse awakens and increases, even among the eastern mountains, that have been folded together, sacred and dusk; veil after veil seems to fall away; the whole orient, with its everlasting hills for petals and the crepuscular incense for perfume, is one expanding violet, in whose heart there will directly be a seed of intolerable gold. And now, in the last watch of the night, in the confiding moment of a dynasty that is fated, the trailing shapes and dryads, for one instant, reveal themselves; brown in the hollows, pale against the light, we catch the movement of a dancing limb or a beckoning hand; and one, see! one fair grace, who is wrapped with gauzes unwound from the steaming rivulets, dips her head, crowned

only with the honors of her twilight hair, visibly into the expected sunrise, to be crowned with its rays and then to die. This is the description, perhaps, of a visionary poet's morning dream; but it is also the description of the great landscape, Corot's "Nymphs of Dawn," in this collection.—It is far from detrimental to an epigrammatic painter of crowds, like Oswald Achenbach, to miss in him the suddenness and visionary revelation, as of a brush from the wing of one of the hours, which distinguishes Corot. Instead of the unity, as of a seal stamped at a blow, we expect to find in his large balanced schemes the evidence of composition, arrangement, and theatric effect. O. Achenbach's noble "Ball-Players Before the Villa Torlonia, Rome," a picture that has focussed admiring crowds at many a public exhibition, belongs to the GILLINGHAM FELL collection. The villa gardens form the relief and setting, in front of which, relieved against the bronze of the cypresses, ilexes, and stone-pines, a mixed crowd of priests, poultry-sellers, teamsters and children watch the game of ball. Action and character are given to each of the players, the adjustment of the light is most artful and striking, and the artist's personal liking for a rich irregular spot of black somewhere about the centre of a composition is fulfilled by

TOO MUCH CRIMSON.
FAC-SIMILE OF A SKETCH FROM THE ORIGINAL PAINTING BY A ZAMACOIS.

the scenic group of strong dark trees, rusted like mountains of iron in the sunset. Decamps himself might have been

THE LAST DAY OF A MALEFACTOR

ARTIST
MICHAEL MUNKACSY

BORN AT MUNKACS, HUNGARY, 1844.   PUPIL OF THE ACADEMIES OF VIENNA AND MUNICH.

COLLECTION OF
MRS ANNA H. WILSTACH, PHILADELPHIA

tempted to admire Düsseldorf as personified in this canvas.— Emile Breton, in a "Village Street" of remarkable vigor,

AT THE WINDOW.
FAC-SIMILE OF A SKETCH FROM THE ORIGINAL PAINTING OF F. BRAUN.

shows moonlight after rain, the sky iced with white-edged clouds, and the deep ruts in the unmacadamized cartway filled with pools that are mirrors.—Rousseau contributes to this collection "The Plain," modeled with rare skill to the utmost horizon, shaded in the foreground and bathed in intense rays at distance, and supporting three or four bour-geoning trees.—Dupré has a "Meadow," with white clouds dappling a faint blue sky.—Daubigny shows a "Heath," an endless plateau teased by the wind, which stirs the yellow broom-flowers, bends the ash-trees, and wrings the clouds into coils.—Diaz, in that pursuit of forest intricacy wherein no man could easily show himself his master, has shown a broad extensive scene of ferns and forest oaks, the dry gray trunks wrought here and there into frosted silver by the burnisher of the sun, and the thick rich leafage paying away all its moisture to the greedy sultriness of the air. These examples of four French landscapists recently dead are indeed choice and instructive specimens of the national art, showing its contempt of flippancy, its voluntary restriction of subjects, and its direct aim at the simple impression of nature in each study.—A fine bit of character and philosophy by Gustave Doré is in the FELL collection, and shows a group of four life-size "Spanish Beggars" (4×8 feet); by methods of his own, unfamiliar to life-size figure art, the rapid sketcher contrives to limn for us a knot of varlets worthy of Gil Blas. By Eugène Isabey there is "The Letter," a precious bit of dash and energy; a young lady at a postern gate receives a

billet from a page just dismounted from a white horse; her duenna, starting with wrath or apprehension, leans out of a low window at the side; each figure is filled with animation, and the color is strong, of the first jet, and vivid; overhead, the old slated walls and dark peaked towers of the château are built high into the clear dark blue.—By Troyon there is a "Milking-Lass" in *chapeau de paille*, caressing her piebald cow, a group studied for some larger landscape, and needing landscape accessories to give it the true value.—By the present head of the Munich school, Carl Piloty, the FELL collection shows a specimen unusual for quietude, self-control, conscientiousness, tender gradation, finish; in "The Sick Mother," a peasant girl, a watcher by the sick bed, has been overcome by her healthy animal craving for sleep, and drops her great bible, which she has been reading by the aid of a candle and reflector; dawn comes at the close of the vigil, and the invalid mother awakening clasps prayerful hands, blessing the dereliction with a true mother's love that condones even faults, when the faults are the rebellion of her own flesh and blood. The subject gives scope for treatment of broad dying suffusions of light, and the painter distinguishes himself in his opportunity by delicate manipulation and skilful gradua-tions.—Hübner contributes a specimen of his earlier and better manner, before a too faithful attachment to stencils and repetitions gave to Düsseldorf its present peculiar odor of satiety in the world's nostril; in "The Diligence Station,"

PERSIAN CAVALCADE.
FAC-SIMILE OF A SKETCH FROM THE ORIGINAL PAINTING BY A. PASINI.

a family of peasants, keeping the postal inn, and praying with much introversion over their dinner while the five travelers stare as they wait for their relay of horses, has character, individuality, and study of humors; the types of the devout, half-grown, loutish Suabian post-boys, and that of the wiry little white-headed father who insinuates a grace with all the consciousness of taking a liberty with heaven, show every talent that need have been wanted to equip a valuable career; Hübner greatly declined in later life; but should not a man be judged by his prime?—In a "Council of War" by Stroebel, showing a white-headed steward giving testimony before some Cavaliers who surround a table, the attraction is the curious brilliancy of a square casement's refraction thrown on the wall, giving a relief to the broad chapeaux of the inquisitors like that of Van der Meer's famous "Conversation."—Of American work, besides the "Imogen" of Mr. May, there are

marked individuality of the WILSTACH cabinet is that on a large proportion of the pictures the same date is signed. Many industrious brushes were tapping together, in cities far from these shores, to construct the magnificent result we see. The fact creates an illusion of preciousness and precariousness; it is strange to find pictures accepted only in the moment of their achievement, as if a Zamacois or a Vollon of five years' earlier date would have been as useless as a bottle of champagne popped a se'nnight ago. It is enough to point out in few words this peculiarity, which sprung naturally from the conditions under which the works accumulated. A connoisseur, an expert in the qualities of a good picture, feels a combative ambition when he enters one of the great spring Salons of the Champs Elysées. These yearly openings, so

MID-OCEAN

FAC-SIMILE OF A SKETCH FROM THE ORIGINAL PAINTING BY W. T. RICHARDS

in the FELL collection a good specimen of Boughton, the "Puritan Soldier"—a staunch old Pilgrim standing guard in the bitter New England mist, keeping watch for the Indians with the particular eye that is not bandaged from a former encounter;—and a pair of portraits by Gilbert Stuart, of which that of Mrs. Greenleaf, née Allen, a Revolutionary belle, is of true distinction, both by aristocracy of carriage and Stuart's occasional almost matchless pearliness of tint.

The WILSTACH collection, now the property of Mrs. W. P. Wilstach, was amassed under unusual circumstances, and under such as seldom lead, as happened in this case, to great critical selectness. The canvases were mostly purchased in a two or three years' artistic trip to Europe. The cream of the French Salons of 1868, 1869, and 1870 was drained into the gallery. Mr. Wilstach, a gentleman peculiarly and almost technically interested in art, made the purchases,—generally in the company of the now deceased artist Robert Wylie, whose professional taste doubtless confirmed many a doubtful choice, and made the gallery what it is, a true artist's selection. The

different from the swept-up exhibitions of America, are, in one respect, great picture-fairs. What with the dealers, and the art-illuminati, the strong works are found out, estimated, and bought, before the varnishing-day, or at most before the private view, is over. An American whose head is furnished with critical knowledge, entering upon one of these novel "first representations," where gray Hebrews in spectacles and lofty exquisites with jumelles are intriguing and doing battle among the pictorial gems, feels the spark kindle within him, and is soberly triumphant if he can disappoint the native competitors—still gladder if the jury attaches the Médaille to any work of which he has become the proprietor. On some such terms were called these glowing neighbors, many of which hung together, about as closely as they do now, in the Champs Elysées in the years from 1868 to 1870. The canvas which was secured under the most interesting circumstances is "The Last Day of a Condemned Man," by the Hungarian painter Munkácsy. This work was executed amid all the obstacles of struggling genius, and illustrates one of the

Pauvre Folle!

ARTIST

HUGUES MERLE

BORN AT SAINT-MARCELLIN, FRANCE, 1823. DIED, 1881.   PUPIL OF COGNIET.

COLLECTION OF

MRS. J. GILLINGHAM FELL, PHILADELPHIA

many romances of obscurity of which only the happily-issuing cases come to our ears. The "Condemned Man" was

THE COMMUNE.
FAC-SIMILE OF A SKETCH FROM THE ORIGINAL PAINTING BY LEON GLAIZE.

Munkácsy's first Salon picture. Fate in hostile array, with its most crushing weapons—poverty fighting like an armed man against the acquisition of every ounce of paint laid on the palette—the artist's very freshness and youth turning enemies, and holding him away from serviceable publicity—a fine idea long kept in abeyance, and restrained in the utterance, by lack of the commonest means—a creation finally brought to pass by one of application's miracles, acting without the needful, without the indispensable—finally, success, a brilliant uncurtaining in Paris, the frank surrender of the great critics, and their quick freemasonry of unreserved approval, a concentration of regard and blushing renown on the young head—such were the steps by which this admirable composition emerged to the light. An American collector—in whose dealings with distressed Art passionate thanks such as those poured out by the Hungarian were nothing new—bore off from disappointed princes and maddened dealers the work of which he had been the material creator. Stand awhile before this rare acquisition of an art-student's first success, saved with the freshness of its history still upon it, saved with the sap of his earliest strength, the dew perhaps of his tears. Munkácsy's picture shows a Hungarian prison, partly obscure, partly pierced with shafts of light. According to local custom, the condemned prisoner for murder receives on the day before execution visits from his townsmen, who bring offerings of money destined to pay for a mass for his victim's soul. Two principal characters make up the dramatic antithesis in the painter's scheme; the murderer, known, exposed, and shamed, and the accomplice, looking at him from his place of safety in the crowd. The culprit sees to-day the long privacy of his confinement interrupted by a sudden and glaring publicity. Here he sits before the throng, moody and distraught, his head sunk on his breast, his hard workman's hand clinched on the white cloth of the sordid board. Sad hero of a miserable pageant, he faces the firmament of eyes and takes no heed. Strong, young and savage, he merely endures the ever-circulating throng of villagers, who enter, look, linger,

drop their obolus and go their way. His poor wife buries her head in the corner nearest her husband, standing up against a wall to cry, as children and rude people do, turning her back to everybody, and forgetting their baby, who wanders off neglected. There is endless individuality in the crowd of visitors, who stand apart, and among whom is found one whose attitude is studiously quiet, and who sinks his head as he stands to glance obliquely at the prisoner—the confederate of his crime, the guilty soul dismissing him to his doom as a scapegoat. The rest of the village crowd, their eyes shining in the dark, are kept at a strange, conscious distance from their old comrade by the moral bar separating innocence from guilt, or impunity from detection. The women curse him, or they contemplate him with pity made ineffectual by foolishness and stolidity. At the lost man's feet is the bowl containing the coins which every one has thrown in for the murdered one's mass—a terrible memento for the eyes of the assassin, who has risked another man's soul besides his own. A copper is rolling away; an unkempt child, a wary young bird-snarer, glides towards it into the foreground of the picture, his foxy figure strung high with the conflict between avarice and fear of detection; if he can once cover it unobserved with his grimy foot, the infamous treasure will be his own. Facing his fellow-villagers, the condemned keeps up his privacy of shame; he is no longer of them, no longer of to-day. Alone with his terrible morrow, he neither knows that his confederate is spying, nor that the women, his old

ROUSSEAU AND MME. DE WARENS.
FAC-SIMILE OF A SKETCH FROM THE ORIGINAL PAINTING BY CH. HUE

sweethearts, are pitying. These many figures, about half the natural size, Munkácsy paints in the truly personal manner found out by himself;—a touch massy and positive, the illuminated faces kept as broad as possible, the shadows inky

A SPANISH CAFÉ
FAC-SIMILE OF A SKETCH FROM THE ORIGINAL PAINTING BY F. PERALTA.

and almost incisive. It is victorious, male painting, every tone broadly yet not harshly uttered, with no trace of the prentice hand, though the artist's first composition. This work gives us what so very seldom reaches us—an anecdotic subject painted with distinction of style. While reaping an uncommonly full and early harvest of popular honors, Munkácsy does not forget that his fame pertains, in its beginnings, to America; that his portrait, in its outlandish Hungarian boots and cloak, is made at home in the Philadelphia album, just as it was conferred with all the fervor of the young carpenter's gratitude; and that, however his laurel may broaden by the Danube or the Seine, its first branch is kept green beside the Delaware.

Willems's very graphic invention, "J'y Etais!"—well known by photographs and other reproductions—shows one of Van Tromp's admirals, a glorious old moustache, uttering the exclamation, as he looks at a picture on the wall to which his daughter points with her fan—a representation of large-hatted Dutch troops disembarking from a fleet to take some town. Like Æneas seeing the sack of Troy painted in a Carthaginian temple, the old sea-wolf is touched at the scene of which, originally, magnum pars fuit. This painter shows also in the collection a porcelain girl, in alabaster satin, "Sealing the Letter." A formal little page waits for the missive, and from the mutual expression of lady and confidant the seal must read, "J'aime qui m'aime comme j'aime quand j'aime!"

Of three capital subjects by Zamacoïs in the WILSTACH collection, the largest, "Too much Crimson!" gives the remark of a politic priest to his fellow, as the self-satisfied painter daubs-in the streaming life-blood of a hideous crucifixion on a chapel wall; while his smaller studies, racily representing "The Cavalry Boot"—ruefully regarded by a wooden-legged trooper who will never need it more—and "A Cavalryman Buckling on his Spurs," show that peculiar union of farcical or anecdotic subject and high technical quality which is always surprising in modern Spanish work.

Cabanel is represented in the WILSTACH collection by one of his most serious, studious canvases, a picture without illustrative subject, and the better for the fact, as is inevitable. This is painted almost as well as the "Saint Louis" in the Luxembourg collection. It represents an "Italian Maiden," lowly sitting, clothed on with humility, her pure dark face swept by the shadow of her rayless hair, whose abundant honors crown her again and again with their hovering chaplets. Lovely, large-eyed, contemplative, and never glad, this incarnation of Shadows eludes the definition of words, yet holds for him who can interpret her mute lips the most sympathetic of individualities.—Jarring as it may seem to pass at once from an image like this to subjects of still-life or nature morte, yet we had better yield to the spirit of such a place—what is a picture-gallery but articulated dislocation?—and willingly admire, while yet our sense of admiration is fresh and unjaded, a picture or two which it required courage to buy and convey so far, and which give the collection its strongest cachet of originality, connoisseurship and sapience. About 1870 a very odd young painter took a couple of fish into his studio, worked like a maniac for just thirty minutes, and achieved a picture of them all inimitable for sliminess, scaliness, and wetness, which he exhibited and which got him a medal. This was in Paris, and all the world knows the significance of a Paris medal. The rabid youth became a rage, and Vollon's masterpiece in America, "The Accessories of the Ball," is in this gallery, painted in his peculiar way in a series of fits or possessions—partly enameled over with minute detail, where every thread of a gold fringe is marked, but generally thrown together as if the man had discharged his brushes at it from across the room. At the proper distance it composes into a picture, and one of seldom-equaled power. The effect sought is a peculiar one; if we were to put a gold ewer just behind a pencil of sunlight and against some dark relief, it would seem to throw off little

FIGURES FROM "GRANDFATHER'S PET."
FAC-SIMILE OF A SKETCH FROM THE ORIGINAL PAINTING BY LOUIS LELOIR.

coruscations like gold-dust: bright objects, in certain confused illuminations, often thus puzzle the eye as to their outlines;

CONVALESCENT

ARTIST
V. PALMAROLI

BORN AT MADRID, SPAIN, 1837.   PUPIL OF

and this richly-cut flagon, on its broad patera, in front of its velvet curtain, seems to charge the dark around it with magnificent sallies of its own rich substance. Close by lie a lady's mask and domino, her bouquet and fan, her scented Eastern beads and jewels; among the latter, some ornaments in Genoa filigree work, seeming like glossy things made of spider-web. The very lace-paper around the flowers,—and what can be less amenable to the grand manner than stamped paper?—is treated with distinction, and rolls from light to shadow like sea-foam. We can pass from this tumbling, flickering apotheosis of ball-room baubles to another composition of still-life, so admirable that before it anything else

quantity of angular facets, like shattered bits of mirror on a table, only inclined enough to take different reflections of the canopied grays above. The liquidity of it all, the placid calm, like even heart-beats, the unctuous lap of water in a clouded moon, is truly there, and even an impatient spectator would agree that this liquid bit of subtle, crystal quality overmatches the most energetic marines of kicking waves and courtesying ships.—By Otto Weber this collection has a scene of "Gathering Firewood," a quiet story of the dappled Fontainebleau forest, as restful to the thought as a leaf-scented walk in the country; our very hearts go out in an odd affection for these cheerful, easy-going laborers who pile

A SNOW-STORM IN RUSSIA.
ENGRAVED BY W. HOLLENGE FROM THE ORIGINAL PAINTING BY L. SCHREYER.

seems unreal and evaporating: a heap of "Peaches," by Philippe Rousseau,—pure lusciousness bagged in dry and dinted velvet—laid in a dish, upon a napkin which pulsates precisely the grateful coolness of fresh linen on a sultry day; and has that sense of body without the aid of gum or starch which is in its way the aristocracy of table-napery. As these gourmand's refinements flatter our senses, around them we perceive grouped the rich berries of the mountain-ash, and a great brass vessel and a tall and singular vase, all real to the eye with a sort of self-possession that does not insist upon and demonstrate its own likeness to nature, as does a certain much-praised class of Dutch and other still-life.—Dutch, say we? The word shall be the talisman to carry us to this matchless "Dutch Marine," by P. J. Clays of Brussels, whose command of silver grays seems to prolong for modern eyes the old triumphs of Van Goyen and Ruysdael. Under a sky marbled with mixed clouds lies a fleet of Dutch schooners, fixed upon an endless flat of water that just breaks into a

the firewood from the lopped branches into decorous little stacks, confined by stakes and withes into cubical form, unloading for the purpose a lumbering two-horse cart; it is because the air is sweet and the leaves are green and the trunks are gray, that the picture makes us happy. But rural toil has sterner and less easy-going phases, and here is Jules Breton with a "Brushwood Fire," that shows energetic peasants, who hurry through smoke and flame, and pass away into gray perspectives of twilight air, as they burn and heap together, and fling up on forks in trailing tresses of fire, the weeds of the field and the black snapping stumps of buckwheat-harvest. It is so mysterious, and the sultry dusk so enlaces and blots the figures, that one is fain to give allegorical significance to the whole, and think of human lives made pure for fruitfulness "athwart the smoke of burning weeds." In another specimen, Breton, with the plainest and most rustical accent, quite clear of moral or afterthought, gives us the luxury of childish repose in a "Tired Gleaner," who has cast off her wooden shoes and lies upon the harvest straw, pillowed by a bag of grain.

But how particularize, how dwell upon, this WILSTACH collection, which contains no resting-places of poor or unnoteworthy works—no pieces that one can pass with charity and relief? This, we are to remember, is a gallery that knows absolutely no inferior pictures: it is such a collection as a well-trained artist gathers when fame and success have given him the means. I therefore must be allowed to name only, with pleasant souvenirs, the rich Terburg-like interior by Leys, with sleepy guards who play at dice on a drum-head, or listen to the reading of the order for the night; the "Arnaut Soldier"—no one but Gérôme can give this finish, this ivory-carved relief and saliency, to the statuesque oriental, standing with native pride in front of his tent, between his saddle and his dog; the lady in superb Persian shawl, "Going to the Promenade," by Alfred Stevens, and turning with such perfect arrested motion to leave directions for the government of the household in her absence with the supernally wise dog at the door; the Diaz, "Love's Persuasions," where, in loveliest carnations, Cupid teases a rosy girl, tampering with her drapery as she leans against a rock; the other Diaz, in his landscape-mood, "In the Fontainebleau Woods," with dry ferny ground, stems of lichened beech trees, and profound azure heavens over-fretted with their twigs; the simple, dreamy Corot, "The Batteau," with low banks, flat stream, square houses, square boat, and forms everywhere horizontal, a hazy scene, lying in Nature's storehouse until wanted, until a breeze shall ruffle them and a general burst of sap tickle them into detail; or yonder most refined, deftly touched, palpitant scene, in Corot's manner, the "Landscape" by César de Cock, where the air seems all tremulous with the twirling leaves of the ash-trees, and their graceful, swan-neck stems bend over to admire themselves in a pond so limpid as to seem immaterial; or the Fromentin, "Arab Horsemen Nearing a City;" or Schreyer, with his large and important example of "Russian Horses." To have found these pictures, to have worried them out among the afflicting masses of trash that are poured upon the buyer in Paris, seems to argue the possession of a sixth sense, a touchstone of the artistic.

And then the fine, pompous pictures showered upon the WILSTACH gallery by the German dealers! Carl Becker's "Grandfather's Birthday," for instance, with the elegant old grandfather receiving the bouquets and birthday addresses of the little children, who march in, conscious, gala-robed and happy, in the convoy of their elders, who help them on in their rôles with the most shameless prompting and coaching, a sort of velvety, high-lived lesson of family sentiment, in a composition of nine figures; and the sad, stony "Martyrdom of St. Ludmilla," by Gabriel Max, showing the fair votaress strangled with a black drapery as she kneels against her bed; and the Gustave Brion, so much more variegated and glowing than his wont, "Reading the Bible in Alsace," where a grand old burgher from the neighborhood of Strasburg reads the daily bible lesson to a crowd gay with red petticoats and figured head-kerchiefs; and the Riefstahl, "The Return from the Christening," one of his admirable scenes of mountains

and Styrian blue with a procession of most vivacious, most expressive little bonshommes; and the crayon drawing by Vautier of Düsseldorf, intensely finished for engraving purposes, showing the first or aristocratic pew in a German church, with collection-taking; and the canvas, by Vautier too, representing "The Hopeless Scholar," some modern Quentin Metsys, a blacksmith's son, who does nothing with his slate but scratch and scribble caricatures, and is brought to the forge by the distracted schoolmaster that the father himself may hear of the matter; and C. F. Lessing's covey of "Monks Reposing," a tired band who rest their dusty frocks and aching bones in the dry, powdery road, over which the green trees wave; and Oswald Achenbach, with his staircase street in an "Italian Town," excellent in its way; and Andreas Achenbach—the storm is past, the illuminated poplars show bending bright against the dark sky, the washed red roof and latticed windows of the mill glitter in the sunshine, and the overcharged sluice pours its little Staubbach down the valley. Such, with a veritable menagerie of the bronzes of Barye—the sole professor whose lessons were enjoyed by Mr. Wylie, the adviser of many of these acquisitions,—in the style of selection observed in the only gallery yet encountered whose fine works were contemporaneously achieved.

To the collection of MRS. J. GILLINGHAM FELL should have been added in this account the skillful and conscientiously-finished "Washerwomen" by D. R. Knight, the American artist. It faithfully represents the types of modern French peasants as found in the neighborhood of Poissy, where Mr. Knight has taken up his residence near the studio of Meissonier. This genre-painting of a high and intelligent order, not quite French in quality, perhaps, because it is somewhat more attentive to depicting minute shades of character and expression than to securing breadth, unity of composition, impasto and fullness of savor; it may rather be compared with the work of such a painter as the Swiss Durand, whose "Marriage at the Church," in Mr. A. J. DREXEL's collection, is a scene of genre-painting similarly full of character and of graphic delineation, here applied however not to peasant life, but to the pursy and self-satisfied middle class burghers of a provincial town, fussy over their family alliances and filled with a pleasant full-dress importance.

In the collection of T. DONALDSON is seen the diverting picture of "Rousseau and Madame de Warens," by Charles Hue (2½ x 3 feet). It is an episode described in the "Confessions," when the young adventurer finds a refuge at the age of sixteen with the pretty pensioner of the King of Sardinia, in her cottage at Annecy, not far from Geneva; in return for her royal annuity, this lady was understood to bind herself to make as many converts as possible from among the Swiss protestants, and the means of attraction used in the case of her candid young secretary were the vials and retorts in her little laboratory of drugs. "I fancy I might have arrived at the love for medical science," declares Rousseau, "if my disgust for it had not produced so many playful scenes by which we were perpetually kept in a state of gaiety; it was perhaps the first time that the craft ever produced such an effect. I pretended that

ADJOURNMENT OF THE GRAND COUNCIL, VENICE

ARTIST
LOUIS MOUCHOT

PUPIL OF DROLLING AND DE BELLON

BORN AT PARIS.

COLLECTION OF
MR. WM. B. BEMENT, PHILADELPHIA

I could tell a medicine-book by the smell, and what is divesting is that I hardly ever made a false guess. She made me taste the most nauseous drugs. I might run away or defend myself as much as I choose; spite of my resistance and horrible faces, spite of my teeth and spite of myself, when I saw her pretty stained fingers come close to my mouth I must needs open it and suck them clean! When her little household was gathered in one room, to hear us all running about and shouting amidst screams of laughter, one would have thought a comedy was playing, and not that we were compounding elixirs and opiates." Charles Désiré Huc, who gives us this lively tableau, was born in Bossuet's city of Meaux, and instructed in painting by the elder Robert-Fleury. Mr. Donaldson's select little gallery contains sketches by Meissonier of a "Troubadour" and "Hussar," a "Prussian Soldier" by Detaille, a "Landscape" by Diaz, Doré's "Killing the Goose with Golden Eggs," Hill's "Mount Rainier," Bradford's "Polaris," Rothermel's "Titian and Charles V," Benike's fine "German Village at Twilight," and other tasteful selections.

Mr. WILLIAM SELLERS's collection embraces the masterpiece of William T. Richards, entitled "Mid-Ocean" (4½ × 2½ feet); this canvas was painted in 1859, and was one of the first to embody the exact and realistic study of wave-forms, in which this artist excels any marine painter who can be called to mind. The long swell of opaque leathery billows under a clouded sky, with no relief but the form of the distant laboring steamer, "dissipating its energy in a trailing fume which is its force," as Hugo says, altogether makes up a monotony that fascinates and almost paralyses the attention. The same collection comprises several forest and mountain scenes by Mr. Richards; "Arabs at Prayer" (12 × 16 inches) by Villegas, with six figures, painted in 1871; "A Boy with three Hunting Dogs" (8 × 13 inches) by Diaz; "A Heifer" (10 × 14 inches) by Auguste Bonheur; "The Game of Chess" by Escosura.

Mr. GEORGE WHITNEY, in a tasteful gallery built purposely for their reception, shows a very choice selection of pictures, both American and imported. Space is wanting to speak here with any fulness of his beautiful treasure, his gem by Merle, a subject of "A Good Sister" full of emotion; his Jules Breton, a coast-scene with female figures, his various specimens by Meyer von Bremen, including that universal favorite called "Grandmother's Pet," the photograph of which every girl buys for her album; his incomparable piece of painted sarcasm by Detaille, in his most incisive line, representing two Prussian spectacled soldiers pulling away at their pipes and mentally solving the problems of Hegel's metaphysics; his fine choice of American pictures, including many of the woodland and marine scenes of Wm. T. Richards, rivaling Hobbima for minute drawing and Claude for dimensions and open-air sentiment; the lively example of Eastman Johnson, a child's game in a dismantled carriage, known as "Stage-Coach;" and several of the most elaborate productions of Gay, including the tea-year-old rustic belle who trails an imaginary ball-dress about the garret in which she sleeps; from among these stores we are enabled to give in facsimile the artist's pen-sketch of "Grandfather's Favorite," by Louis Leloir, showing a good-natured old house-father who thoroughly understands "l'art

d'être grand-père." His pet granddaughter is installed in his easy chair, while he sits in a cushion in front of it, and allows the pretty mischief to run a comb through his thinning hair; the beautiful child thus engaged looks like a living allegory of taking Time by the forelock, and the figures are improved by being dressed and dated with the rich costumes of Henri IV's day. This picture, in water-colors, is by Louis, son of Auguste Leloir; its painter is also author of "The Temptation," in the Dousman gallery at St. Louis, and of the large "Fête du Grand-père," likewise owned in an American collection, that of Mr. O. D. MUNN.

A numerous and tasteful collection has been gathered by Mr. W. B. BEMENT, including the capital picture of Mouchot, "The Sortie of the Grand Council," representing the doge and senators and the Stairs of the Giants in their glory—a picture obtained from a great sale managed in this country by Evemrd after the Franco-Prussian war, and comprising some of the best things swept up out of Europe. Mr. BEMENT owns a Bouguereau of unusual excellence, having as much of technic as one may rightfully seek in a Bouguereau, and the advantage of an unusual charm thrown in; it is a life-size figure of a child plucking fruit: she looks cunningly up at the cherries on a fine branch above her head, which she pulls down as she stands upon the ground. One very red cherry, a match for her cherry-mouth, is already between her small finger and thumb, and in a moment will be ravished. Of her face, held sideways in a quizzical wise, one can but say that it is just the face of a child about to eat a tartish cherry: that interior operation of the arcana of Nature called watering of the mouth is here represented to a nicety in an external view. If ever a kissable face was painted it is this. Meyer von Bremen's "Grateful Invalid" is delineated leaning back in her chair to hear the Bible from the lips of her promising tow-headed boy, a fine little fellow, just old enough to spell out the sacred promises of the book.

Mr. G. F. TYLER has a considerable collection, including a well-known Bouguereau, a group full of plastic grace representing a happy scene of Arcady, and representing it with the elegant neatness of a chimney bronze: a baby leaps from its mother's arms towards its father, who enters bearing some fruit. E. Isabey, who never seems to sink below his own level, and among whose works there is small choice except for size and variety of detail, is well brought out with a group of gay figures in the costumes of Molière's comedies, emerging from church and forming a pompous cataract as they pour down the steps. By Troyon there is a fine cattle-scene, with an important foreground group of the animals relieved against a storm-cloud; by Diaz, five royal children of a wealthy seraglio playing with a splendid bird. Chaplin, painting as usual with pearl-powder and pomade, shows a modish type of the female Narcissus, a nude girl standing on the edge of a lake, in which her swan-colored limbs swim double, swan and shadow. From the easel of Meyerheim there is a conscientious picture, a dowager of the sixteenth century going primly to market attended by her maid.

A small collection of real value, mostly selected in France, belongs to the estate of the late General HECTOR

TYNDALE: among the finest pictures are the studies by Jouy for the "Martyrdom of Urbain Grandier," a canon of Loudon, burned by the monks in 1634 on an accusation of sorcery; one is a small sketch whereby the painter arranged his figures,

THE CELIBATE.

FAC-SIMILE OF A SKETCH FROM THE ORIGINAL PAINTING, BY T. ROUSSEAU.

showing the martyr sinking on the church pavement, robed in white, bound with cords, surrounded by priests with torches and penitents in masks, who sustain his failing body by the arms. The other and more considerable study shows the face of Grandier developed to the size of life, the shoulders covered with coarse white drapery and the rope knotted about the neck. The head is bent backward from the sinking shoulders with a divine impulse of Christian triumph, lifting itself toward heaven, as the dark eyes are lifted; we must go to Murillo himself, to his swarthy and ecstatic saints, for any such expression of victorious holiness; it seems the explosion of soul through the rents of the tortured body: from the very extremity of physical pain, from the face darkened and shining with agony, and the black hair glued with sweat, darts the live rapture of the sacred eyes—a revelation of religious passion such as it has but seldom been given to painting to portray. It is a loss to the world that this superb head has never been engraved, to repeat in every Christian household

the testimony of martyrdom and the advocacy of Art. The TYNDALE collection also possesses a water-color by Delacroix, a rude and satirical sketch showing a couple of profane monks lolling on a bench and smoking cigarettes beneath a gaunt and agonized crucifix. The pictures of Isabey were selected in considerable profusion by General TYNDALE during his lifetime, and in great measure introduced to American connoisseurs through his initiation.

Among these pages will be found illustrated, from the gallery of Mr. C. H. CLARK, "A Snow-Storm in Russia," by Schreyer, a harrowing scene of posting in a storm, where the traveler has to keep himself warm by picking off the wolves that infest the region. Also, from the gallery of Mr. C. H. ROGERS, "A Spanish Café," by F. Peralta, with the usual bull-fighters and manolas; it may be compared, for jewel-like glitter in the manner of the modern Spanish-Roman school, with FAIRMAN ROGERS'S "Interrupted Sitting," by the Neapolitan-Roman Oreste Cortazzo; or with Carl Hoff's "Unexpected Return," in the latter gallery too, if we choose to contrast brilliant costume-painting of the Romance races with the less impulsive but more velvety luxury of Düsseldorf.

Mr. A. PARTRIDGE has a gallery built expressly for pictures, and well filled, the finest being "The Choristers' Music Lesson," signed "M. B., Milan." Mr. WILLIAM WARNER, of North Broad Street, has a pair naturally considered by him to be among the very most valuable Fortuny's in existence— a couple of allegories, in water-color, one of which represents "Maidenhood as a Butterfly;" he also possesses, by Farina of Vienna, "Bulter and Piccolomini Planning the Assassination of Wallenstein," Buzze's "Sir Peter and Lady Teazle," Charles Felu's (the armless pede-artifex) picture of the "Widow Wadman and Uncle Toby," and Antonio's bust of the "Veiled Vestal." Mr. WARNER is a liberal and practical patron of art-education.—Mr. HARRISON EARL possesses a very fine collection of French, Belgian and German pictures, from among which is selected one of the most important works of Jules Worms, "Smugglers taking leave of their Female Companions to go on an Expedition," a large and admirable composition, over-brimming with Spanish character. The estate of the railroad monarch, the late Col. THOMAS A. SCOTT, possesses some excellent pictures, including Merle's "Marguerite, Martha and Mephistopheles," Heilbuth's "Meeting of Cardinals and Capucins on Monte Pincio," and Willems' "Judgment of Paris."—Knaus's famous "Golden Wedding" is owned here by Mrs. RUSSELL STURGES. Mr. ISAAC LEA has many "Old Masters."

Mr. C. H. WOLFF, whose time is divided between Philadelphia, Pittsburgh and Chambersburg, keeps partly in the first and partly in the last-named city a very fine gallery personally collected in Europe. We illustrate his grand Pasini, "A Persian Cavalcade," "At the Window," a truly admirable thing by F. Krause; "Good Morning," one of the loveliest conceptions of Carl Becker, and "The Commune," representing, in the form of monkeys, Courbet the painter, communistic minister of the Fine Arts, and Thiers, first President of the present Republic, wearing the embroidered coat of a Member of the Institute, with a star on the breast. Mr. M. E. SCHNERTZ.

Good Morning

ARTIST

CARL BECKER

COLLECTION OF

MR. C. H. WOLFF, PHILADELPHIA

of Pittsburgh, is an enlightened collector of art, the necessarily short tribute to whom can be brought in here better than in another place; one specimen of his collection is illustrated, "The Celibate," by the California prodigy, Toby Rosenthal, representing a young monastic devotee watching with irrepressible regrets the bridal excursion of a pair of butterflies.

Mr. JAMES L. CLAGHORN, the President of the Pennsylvania Academy of Fine Arts, is a collector of art treasures and a promoter of art second to none in the country. As a collector of engravings he is accorded among connoisseurs a celebrity that is literally world-wide. As a promoter of all worthy art interests at home his reputation is still more eminent and kindly. It was he who, in a day or two, by genially heading the list himself, collected a quantity of ten-thousand dollar subscriptions for building the new Academy. His gallery, built expressly for paintings, contains the remains of a once opulent collection, and still shows some choice gems, as an early figure-piece by Diaz, Flamm's "Twilight," etc., while in the neighboring rooms hang Maccari's "Fond Memories" and "Charm of Music." As a virtuoso in the collecting of engravings, Mr. CLAGHORN stands among the foremost private collectors living. His prints number more than fifty thousand, and include rare states of all the great masters. He has the "Hundred Guilder Print" both before and after it was retouched by Captain Baillie, a very rare impression of the "Three Crosses" (also by Rembrandt), "Christ and the Money-Changers" in the second state, an early state of the "Virgin's Death," and the "Angels and Shepherds" in a very bright state—more than one hundred and fifty Rembrandts, and two hundred Durers, including the Crucifixion engraved on the hilt of Maximilian's sword; in precious English mezzotints a great wealth, comprising Prince Rupert's "Executioner," sometimes called the first work in that style; and a very rare profusion of the early French engravers in fine states.

PHILADELPHIA, so long as the existence of the nation, has had collections of art. The ordinary disparaging remark of the newly-rich and of the dealers is, that until the present generation, people in this country did not collect pictures and statues. Whatever may have been true of other cities this was certainly not the case with the first metropolis of the republic. It is probable that the taste was partly due to the strong French tone observed in Philadelphia at different early epochs—as when the French allies of President Washington settled around his official residence in this city (Philadelphia being the national capital from 1787 to 1800), and later when the emigrants of the Revolution in France and in Santo Domingo chose the city so notoriously as their favorite refuge. At any rate we find the temper of the collector manifested at a date coeval with the existence of the United States. Lord Kames had given Franklin a portrait of Admiral Sir William Penn, which was presently lent for public exhibition; Joseph Allen Smith in 1807 and 1812 sent from Italy a fine donation of pictures to the Art Academy; the neighborhood of Joseph Bonaparte's galleries at Bordentown inspired the Philadelphians; in 1817 West's "Christ Healing the Sick" paid for the erection of an exhibition-hall and collected in fees fifteen thousand dollars besides. The Academy possessed *inter alia* a very fine Murillo, "The Roman Daughter," burned in 1845: this picture is historic, and known among the engravings of Murillo's works. The father of the Gettysburg conqueror, Gen. Meade, was our representative in Spain, and during the Peninsular troubles contrived to get hold of a large number of Spanish pictures. These formed a special collection, known as the Meade Gallery, in the Academy, where they were enshrined until the fire of 1845, and about that period were dispersed by auction. The sale of Joseph Bonaparte's collection by a Philadelphia auctioneer took place September 17, 1845, and further introduced the taste for collecting into many Philadelphia homes. Among the art treasures of the Academy of Fine Arts,—chartered in 1806 and erected the same year, (being thus the first chartered and first built American Art-Academy)—may be mentioned the following: Van der Helst's magnificent "Violinist;" Allston's "Dead Man Restored to Life" (bought in 1813, after receiving a hundred-guinea prize in London); one of Gilbert Stuart's full-length Washingtons, and his "Mrs. Blodgett;" B. West's "Christ Rejected," "Death on the Pale Horse" and "Paul at Athens;" W. E. West's original "Byron," painted at Leghorn; Vanderlyn's "Ariadne;" C. W. Peale's portrait of himself, from his famous Museum; Neagle's "Pat Lyon;" B. Wittkamp's colossal "Deliverance of Leyden;" Kaulbach's "King of Bavaria," "Parisina," by A. Gastaldi, and "Macchiavelli and Borgia" by Faruffini—two large Italian pictures (the last by an artist who afterwards committed suicide) both of which were medaled at Paris in 1867. Two unexcelled specimens of Joseph Vernet, "The Storm" and "The Cardinal and his Friends at Portici," are in the Academy, bought from the Joseph Bonaparte collection. The Carey Gallery, lately bequeathed, confers on the Academy various paintings collected to be engraved for the famous Carey and Hart Keepsakes —Huntington's original "Mercy's Dream" and "Christiana," Leslie's "Touchstone and Audrey" and "Olivia," Maclise's "Masaniello," Richard Wilson's "Tivoli" and Boddington's "Hayes Common." The Sculpture at the Academy includes the only important marble antique in America, a colossal headless figure called "Ceres," brought by Commodore Paterson from Megara early in the century; also, by Lough, (mentioned in Mrs. Browning's "Lady Geraldine") a colossal plaster group of "Fighting Centaurs;" and, among the casts for the school, what is not always found among such casts, Donatello's "St. George." The Academy possesses the Phillips Collection of about fifty thousand engravings, a very full representation for purposes of study.

Art-works of historical interest are distributed through the town, those of interest as relics being unusually abundant, and giving the metropolis its air of antique stability. The works of the first American sculptor, William Rush, who like

DEPARTURE OF THE SMUGGLERS.
FAC-SIMILE OF A SKETCH FROM THE ORIGINAL PAINTING BY JULES WORMS.

Puget was also a ship carver, abound in the city. His "Leda with the Swan," a portrait of Miss Vanuxem the belle, a work of 1820, is at Fairmount Park, as well as some allegorical groups over the wheel-houses, and statues of "Justice" and "Wisdom;" his "Tragedy" and "Comedy" are at the Forrest Home; his "Washington" (of 1821,) in the posturing French taste of the day, is at Independence Hall; a cast of the portrait of himself which he carved out of a pine-knot is seen at the Academy. A contemporary of his youth, John Bacon, R. A., (1740–1799) is represented by the leaden statue of William Penn, in the grounds of the old Hospital; Bacon was the father of English sculpture, as Rush of American, and received on the formation of the Royal Academy, in 1768, its first gold medal; his best works are in Westminster; the Penn statue, worthless artistically, was made for Lord Le Despencer, and set up by him at his seat of Wycomb in 1774; it was taken down by his successor in the estate, Sir John Dashwood, about 1800, condemned to be sold as old lead, bought by John Penn, the Founder's grandson, and presented to the Hospital, arriving in the city in 1804. The statue of Franklin (in a toga) at the Philadelphia Library was carved by Francesco Lazzarini of Carrara, and presented by William Bingham, the first U. S. senator from Pennsylvania. The marble figure of Stephen Girard, at his College, was made up by N. Gevelot in France about 1840, from old clothes and descriptions of friends, without the sculptor having the slightest acquaintance with his original, and considered a remarkable success. The monument to the Burd children, by Steinhauser, is at St. Stephen's church, in Tenth Street above Chestnut. At Fairmount Park are: Ezechiel's monument to Religious Freedom; an Italian Columbus monu-

ment; and one to Lincoln, by Randolph Rogers; there are also the bronze figures of Pegasus, led by History and Music, from the Vienna theatre. The Washington in front of Independence Hall is by Bailly; a monument to Gen. Meade has been projected, the prize for a design having been awarded to Mr. Calder; the Cincinnati Society's Washington monument, to cost two hundred thousand dollars, has been committed to a German artist, Prof. Siemering.

Pictures of public interest about the city are: the original portrait of William Penn, in armor, painted in Ireland, at the Historical Society's rooms; West's "Penn's Treaty," at Independence Hall, his early "Hercules," in the possession of John Jordan, Jr., his "James Hamilton" at the Spring Garden Institute,—at the Historical Society's hall, his "William Hamilton and Niece," and "Rev. William Smith, Provost of the College of Philadelphia;" at the Insane Asylum, his "Christ Healing the Sick;" it is a duplicate of that at Chelsea Hospital, painted in 1810, of which Haydon says, "nothing else was talked about in London;" in executing this replica, which he "determined should surpass the original," he conferred a very large pecuniary benefit on the Hospital, to which he presented it. Rothermel's "Gettysburg" is at Memorial Hall, in Fairmount Park, while at the Union League building

THE LETTER-BOX.
FAC-SIMILE OF A SKETCH FROM THE ORIGINAL PAINTING BY T. LOBRICHON.

is "Emigration," by Prof. Pauwells of Belgium, a picture in the taste of Yvon's "March of the States," at Saratoga.

ADDITIONAL ART TREASURES OF PHILADELPHIA.

MR. A. J. ANTELO'S COLLECTION.

MR. J. W. BATES' COLLECTION.

MR. W. B. BEMENT'S COLLECTION.

MR. C. H. CLARK'S COLLECTION.

MR. T. DOLAN'S COLLECTION.

MR. H. EARL'S COLLECTION.

MRS. J. G. FELL'S COLLECTION.

ADDITIONAL ART TREASURES OF PHILADELPHIA.

MRS. J. G. FELL'S COLLECTION.
Concluded.

MERLE, H.—La Folie.
MILLET, J. F.—Feeding Poultry.
PILOTY, C.—The Sick Mother.
ROUSSEAU, T.—The Plain of Barbizon.
STUART, G.—Portrait of Mrs. Greenleaf.
TROYON, C.—The Milkmaid.

MRS. T. A. SCOTT'S COLLECTION.

BOUGUEREAU, W. A.—Pastorale.
GÉRÔME, J. L.—Almehs Playing Checkers.
HEILBUTH, F.—Scene on the Pincian Hill, Rome.
LEYS, A.—Promenade, Vienna.
MERLE, H.—Marguerite, Martha and Mephistopheles.
   "   "   Fisherman's Family in a Storm.
MEYER VON BREMEN, J. G.—Threading Her Needle.
   "   "   "   Blind-Man's-Buff.
PASINI, A.—The Palanquin and its Guard.
SCHREYER, A.—Arab Ford.
VON SCHENDEL, P.—Candle-Light.
WILLEMS, F.—The Judgment of Paris.
ZAMACOÏS, E.—The Armorer's Shop.

MR. E. B. WARREN'S COLLECTION.

BOKER, G.—Early Friends.
BOUGUEREAU, W. A.—The Little Marauders.
BOUGES, L.—The Young Correspondent.
BOUTIBONNE, C. E.—What shall I say to Him?
BROMLEY, WM.—Landscape.
COMPTE-CALIX, F. C.—Returning from Market.
COROT, J. B. C.—Landscape.
DAGNAN-BOUVERET, P. A. J.—The Lovers' Quarrel.
DOUGLAS, H.—Kept In.
ERDMANN, O.—Lisette, the Pretty Waitress.
HART, WM.—White Mountains.
HERZOG, H.—Norwegian Scene.
JOHNSON, F.—Young Eyes and Old Eyes.
LAMBINET, E.—Landscape.
LASALLE, L.—Fagot Gatherers.
MACCARI, C.—The Reverie.
MEISSONIER, CH.—Outside Attractions.
MORRAU, A.—An Orchard.
PALMAROLI, V.—The Convalescent.
ROBBE, H.—Sheep and Lambs.
SCHREYER, A.—Algeria.
   "   "   Scene in Russia.
   "   "   Attelage.
SIMONETTI, A.—Proclamation in Front of Pantheon.
STORY, G. H.—An Art Student of Nature.
VIBERT, J. G.—Two Sous a Slice.
   "   "   The Serenade.
VERY, PAUL.—Lovers.
WEBER, PAUL.—The Shepherd's Return.

MR. G. WHITNEY'S COLLECTION.

BOKELMAN, L.—The Broken Bank.
BOUGHTON, G. N.—The March of Miles Standish.
   "   "   Going to Seek his Fortune.
BRETON, J.—The Departure for the Fields.
CHURCH, F. E.—Sunrise in the Catskills.

MR. G. WHITNEY'S COLLECTION.
Concluded.

DETAILLE, E.—Prussian Soldiers. Water-color.
GUY, S. J.—Making a Train.
JOHNSON, E.—The Stage-Coach.
KRAUS, L.—A City Girl.
LEJOUR, L.—Grandfather's Pet.
LOBRICHON, T.—The Letter-Box.
MERLE, H.—The Good Sister.
MEYER VON BREMEN, J. G.—Grandmother's Pet.
RICHARDS, W. T.—The Forest.
   "   "   The Wissahickon.
   "   "   Land's End—Cornwall.
   "   "   Sand Hills—Atlantic City.
   "   "   Paradise—Newport.
VAUTIER, B.—The Annual Dinner.
VIBERT, J. G.—A Theological Dispute.
   "   "   The Grasshopper and the Ant.

MRS. W. P. WILSTACH'S COLLECTION.

ACHENBACH, A.—The Old Mill after the Storm.
ACHENBACH, O.—The Staircase Street.
BECKER, C.—The Grandfather's Birthday.
BRETON, J.—Burning Brushwood.
   "   "   The Little Gleaner's Rest.
CARANEL, A.—The Italian Maiden.
COROT, J. B. C.—Le Batteux.
DIAL, N.—The Maiden and Cupid.
   "   "   The Words of Feminstheen.
FROMENTIN, E.—Arab Horsemen Nearing a City.
GÉRÔME, J. L.—An Armed Soldier.
LESSING, C. F.—The Monks' Repose.
LEYS, H.—The Guard-Room.
MAX, G.—Martyrdom of St. Ludmilla.
MUNKÁCSY, M.—Last Day of the Condemned.
RICHARDS, W. T.—Landscape.
RIEFFTAHL, W.—The Return from the Christening.
ROUSSEAU, P.—Peaches.
SCHLESINGER, R.—Alone in the Studio.
SCHREYER, A.—Russian Horses.
STEVENS, A.—Departing for the Promenade.
VAUTIER, B.—A Vocation for Art.
   "   "   Taking up the Collection. Crayon.
VOLLON, A.—Accessories of the Ball-Room.
VOLTZ, J. F.—Cattle.
WILLEMS, F.—"J'y suis!"
   "   "   Sealing the Love-Letter.
WYLIE, R.—Breton Group.
ZAMACOÏS, E.—Too Much Crimson!"
   "   "   The Useless Cavalry Boot.
   "   "   Trooper Attaching his Spurs.

MR. C. H. WOLFF'S COLLECTION.

ACHENBACH, O.—Storm in Roman Compagna.
   "   "   View Near Rome.
ALVAREZ, L.—The Amateurs.
AMBERG, W.—The Young Lace-Makers.
BARON, H. C. A.—The Archer's Rest.
BECKER, C.—Good Morning!
   "   "   Venetian Lady.
BUSCH, E.—Red-Riding-Hood.
BONANDIO, G. H.—Winter.
CASSAR, L.—First Lesson.

MR. C. H. WOLFF'S COLLECTION.
Concluded.

CHAPLIN, C.—The Bird's Nest.
COL, B.—The Wine Merchant.
CUBETTE, F. C.—Soldiers After a Carousal.
COMPTE-CALIX, F. C.—Field Oracle.
COROT, J. B. C.—Landscape.
DARGELAS, H.—The Gardener's Child.
DAUBIGNY, C. F.—Landscape.
   "   "   View on the Seine.
DE COCK, C.—View Near Paris.
DE JONGHE, G.—The Toilet.
DELORT, C.—Retrospect.
DE NITTIS, J.—Letter of Condolence.
FRÈRE, E.—Children and Fruit.
GLAIZE, L.—Stopping the Way.
GOUPIL, L.—The Commune.
HAMILTON, J.—Wreck off the Coast.
HENNESSY, W. J.—The Fagot Gatherer.
HERRNHOFFER, C.—The Polish Exile.
   "   "   The Fortune-Teller.
HERZOG, H.—Scene in Norway.
HILDEBRANDT, E.—The Frosty Morning.
KRAUS, F.—At the Window.
LANGLAIS, C.—Egyptian Fellah Girl.
LEON Y ESCOSURA, I.—The Appointment.
LÉPOITTEVIN, E.—Seaside Life.
LOBRICHON, T.—Forbidden Fruit.
MERLE, H.—The Angel's Prayer.
MICHEL, M.—The Young Botanist.
MICHETTI, F. P.—Driving the Duck.
   "   "   Through the Fields.
MIGNOT, L. R.—Autumn.
MOHRLAUEN, F. A.—The Linen Bleacher.
MOREAU, A.—Presents from Japan.
   "   "   The Storied Door.
NEHLIG, V.—Serenade.
NOTERMAN, Z.—The Watchful Mother.
ORTEL, J. A.—The Farmer's Return.
PAROTTI, A.—Leisure Hours.
PASINI, A.—Entering the Mosque.
   "   "   Persian Cavalcade.
PILLE, H.—The Music Lesson.
PITTARI, C.—Rainy Morning on the Road to Turin.
PORTAELS, J. F.—Jealousy.
RAFFAELLI, G. A.—Demanding Admission.
ROUBAUD, P.—Esmeralda's Window.
SALENTIN, H.—The Christening.
SCHLOESER, C.—The Puritan Lovers.
SCHREYER, A.—Arab Scouts.
SERGENT, A.—Sunday Morning.
SEIGNAC, P.—The Grandmother's Birthday.
SOHN, W.—The Mother's Pet.
SULLY, T.—Contemplation.
   "   "   Red-Riding-Hood.
TRAYER, C.—Mother and Child.
VAUTIER, B.—The Intercepted Letter.
VERNIER, E.—Old Mill Near Paris.
   "   "   Landscape and Cattle.
VERSCHUUR, W.—Interior of Stable.
VIBERT, J. G.—Armenian Officer.
WHITTREDGE, W.—The Meadow Brook.
WITTKAMP, J. B.—The Grandmother Instructing.
   "   "   Three Women of Crotewaer.
ZEZZOS, A.—Reading Death-Warrant to Queen Mary.
ZUBER-BUHLER, F.—The Award of Idleness.

Tarantella at Capri

ARTIST
E. ALEXANDRE SAIN

Born at Clent, France, 1830.   Pupil of Picot

COLLECTION OF

MRS. D. D. COLTON, SAN FRANCISCO, CAL.

COLLECTIONS IN SAN FRANCISCO.

HE (perhaps impertinent) astonishment of visitors who find on the extreme western end of the transcontinental road a community fully conversant with modern art and furnishing Goupil with his best customers, is simply a geographical astonishment. We cannot at once get used to the idea, only proper to this century, that considerations of space are now annihilated, and that Goupil has practically no more difficulty in placing a good picture on the coast of the Pacific than in the shadow of his own shop on the rue Chaptal. Before the invention of that powerful peace-maker and civilizer, the railroad, this suppression of distance did not enter into human calculations; but now knowledge flows over the earth freely without geographical barriers or distinction; gracious Art follows in its wake; and a painter who dismisses a masterpiece from his studio cannot tell whether he shall next hear of it in Siberia or in California. As should properly be the case, it is the railway kings, they who have made this diffusion of art-ideas possible, who are found the best patrons of art. A group of really enlightened patrons in California is one of railroad officers. Among their galleries, you forget that an ocean and a mighty continent intervene, and fancy yourself in the patchouli perfume characteristic of the Paris Salon. It is very old-fashioned, of course, to yield even for a moment to the emotion of surprise; but surely the late Decamps and

Couture would have been still more confounded than I was, to see their exquisite trivialities, "Pussy in Bed," and "Pierrot with the Moniteur" thoroughly at home in Mr. Mills's gallery, supported by other pictures their equals, and intelligently viewed by drawing-room throngs. These particular canvases have been removed to New York since my visit; but other works of the famous dead remain, in a locality where their painters would have felt such a representation to be like a translation to Prester John's country. Mr. Mills was certainly one of the earliest and best inspired of the California collectors. Mr. Milton S. Latham, whose collection was sold at New York in 1878, showed in all his treasures the most fastidious taste; his rarities and bric-à-brac, the dozen of superb tapestries hung round the dining-room of his country-seat, his audacity in buying the mighty "Samson" of the Austrian painter Jacobs, showed, in Art, the very courage of the pioneer who transfers mountains and plants foundations. Ex-Governor Leland Stanford has not only collected fine foreign works, but has done much to create a native school of painting, while his defrayal of the cost of Muybridge's photographic studies of horses and athletes in motion is unquestionably one of the most important contributions to art-anatomy made by this or any century. Mrs. Colton and Mrs. Mackey, though particularly eminent for collections of bric-à-brac, have not neglected the accumulation of pictures. Where could be found a more truly admirable and fitting piece of art-patronage than in the fact that the late Mr. Lick, when building one of those mighty inns characteristic of the West, chose to have the dining-room decorated with original views of California scenery by a landscape-artist of genius, and that when these were destroyed by a fire in 1877, the same Mr. Hill was charged by Mr. Lick's executors to renew the decorations with all possible speed?

Mr. CHARLES CROCKER's mansion is one of the splendid houses in that choice locality of San Francisco which the wits of the billiard-rooms, who respect nothing, call Nob Hill. On this hill, of really steep grade, the street is so inclined that the equipages of the wealthy residents would seem to be almost useless; the grade does not frighten the street-car, however, which simply puts down an iron claw and grasps an endless wire rope, forever traveling under the pavement of the street, and gets pulled along by that persuader. No sound can be more weird than the perpetual groaning of this never-resting underground wire, as heard when you are coming away from one of the genial parties of Nob Hill, in an utterly desert street during the small hours. The "nevermore" of the celebrated raven of one idea was cheerful to it. Mr. Crocker's personal explanations, delivered in a happy vein of reminiscence and cosmopolitanism, considerably increased my interest in his gallery. He told me how he had been struck, in the Trappenhaus of the New Museum at Berlin, with Kaulbach's allegorical borders to his great frescoes, and had caused them to be copied for the coves of his own picture-gallery. He compared the long bastion of Pelusium, in Lenoir's "Cambyses," with the equally long and exposed citadel-wall of the great fort at Cairo, where the massacre of the Mamelukes took place, and where he had wandered, and measured, and paced, to his heart's content as an insatiable American tourist. He was kind enough to be interested in my personal reminiscences of Lenoir, certainly one of the most cultured and witty of modern painters, the powers of whose mind undoubtedly culminated in the "Cambyses." The splendors of so magnificent a house obviously lost nothing of their brilliancy by the personal recollections, the thousand anecdotes of their selection, imparted by the host. In all the interior, furnished in the collector's most acquisitive spirit, nothing is more choice than the boudoir of the mansion's mistress, fitted up and as it were lined with that beautiful veined spar called Mexican onyx: in the room thus garnished, which resembled a fairy cave in a crystal mountain, I was charmed with a brilliant picture by Filosa, in water-color, representing "Ladies in the Fields," with a beautiful creature sitting on the autumnal grass,—a fair allegory of life's April extended over Nature's October!—and receiving an exquisite shower-bath of blossoms, which a playful comrade was represented as emptying over her. But the picture-gallery proper, containing Lenoir's "Cambyses," Cabanel's "Penelope," Vibert's "Monastery in Arms," and Lesrel's "Serenading the Chief"—to say nothing of Gérôme's "Sword-Dance," (introduced in 1881, since my visit)—certainly gives a more strictly art-feeling than the choicest of boudoirs trimmed with water-color pictures and precious stone. The cove of this gallery, which has been just alluded to, is faithfully copied in fresco after the friezes forming the bordering for Kaulbach's vast frescoes at Berlin. In this series of compositions—the child's-play of an ingenious mind—we see little genii indicating the world's progress; Architecture studying from the beaver and chimney-swallow, Music from the bird, with the attendance of asses for critics; Weaving from the spider,—as well as the philosophical dispute of Aristotle and Plato, the Egyptian mythology chased by the Greek torch of Neo-Platonism, and other clever caprices. As one of the

most interesting pictures of the gallery may be pointed out the "Cambyses at the Siege of Pelusium," painted by Paul-Marie Lenoir in 1867. This young artist was the son of the eminent Keeper of the Library of the Fine-Arts school, an antiquarian of distinction, and inherited a keen intellect and delicate taste, afterwards developed by all the resources of education. He was the pupil of Gérôme, and his companion in some of his Eastern travels: Lenoir's book on Le Fayoum, illustrated by Gérôme, is the record of this agreeable pilgrimage of master and pupil. Having penetrated as far as Persia, and recorded his recollections in some very promising paintings, he found himself too deeply bitten with the maggot of traveling to rest easily at home; but the taste he had imbibed proved fatal to him, and he died at Cairo in the spring of 1881, at the age of forty years. I have a vivid recollection of his pretty Paris studio, which he exhibited by opening the door whereon he had scrawled with charcoal "Ci git Paul Lenoir"—which graveyard inscription comes back to memory sadly enough with the thought of his untimely death; on the easel inside, in the year of the painting of this "Cambyses," but just before the journey which led to its

A VILLAGE OF ANTON.
FAC-SIMILE OF A SKETCH IN PENCIL FROM THE PAINTING BY A SKETCH.

production, was to be seen Lenoir's most ambitious subject, a crowded scene in the palace of Ulysses, with the suitors defending themselves, and in front Telemachus, like a young naked god, wrapping his garment over his left arm as a

THE CONVENT IN ARMS

ARTIST
JEHAN G. VIBERT

BORN AT PARIS, 1840.

PUPIL OF FÉLIX J. BARRIAS.

———

COLLECTION OF
MR. CHARLES CROCKER, SAN FRANCISCO, CAL.

shield, as he challenged the interlopers with the most flexible movement of the modern fencing-school. The subject of "Cambyses at the Siege of Pelusium" is drawn from the old story, narrating how the Persian monarch alarmed the religious fears of the Egyptians by confronting them with their sacred animal the cat; rather than risk any harm to these venerated beasts they delivered the city without fighting. The theme is here treated as a lively young Frenchman would naturally treat it, from its absurd and sarcastic side; the artist fills the air with the yelling divinities, before whom the Egyptian chivalry crouch in horror, fearful lest a cat should meet its death by contact with their unworthy bodies.

The artist when he painted this picture, at the age of twenty-six, was at the receptive period, and his style of paint-

wit's end for a bric-à-brac ornament; the Hathor heads are found on the caps of a particular temple colonnade, and that a late one of the Greek period of the Ptolemies. That they should have been set up, and exposed to assault, on an ancient Egyptian fort, transcends all belief; and the artist, in the act of showing how scrupulous the nation was in shrinking from an outrage towards Sekhet the sacred cat, exhibits it as exposing to slings and arrows the visage of its great goddess Isis-Hathor.

One of the best Paintings ever executed by Vibert is seen in Mr. CROCKER's Collection, "The Monastery under Arms." It represents a line of Spanish barefoot Capucin monks, in the cloister, being drilled by a truculent captain from the Spanish army, whose mouth is more used to oaths than to paternosters,

EXPECTATIONS FROM OUR AUNT.
ENGRAVED BY KRUELL FROM THE PAINTING BY JULES WORMS.

COLLECTION OF C. CROCKER.

ing showed, like most youthful work, an intelligent selection of artistic "standards" rather than originality. Anybody can see, in the posture and manner of each figure, how greatly the painter was preoccupied with Gérôme; the head of Cambyses, where the artist shows a sarcastic intention verging on caricature, proceeds from the same laboratory as the heads of the archons and areopagites in the "Phryne," and that of the weazened laugher in the "Augurs." Excessive general education kept Lenoir from being great in literature or in painting. His book on the Fayoum does not rise above the style of the feuilleton, and his "Cambyses" picture is a mosaic of clever bits. The imitation of the long stretch of the bastions, from the long stretch of the Casbah at Cairo, may be granted to be a clever thing; in the absence of documentary proof, the military architecture of modern Egypt may be the best thing to give a clever man the hint about the military architecture of Pelusium; but when he sets the heads of Hathor, with their cow's ears, on the battlements, he acts as a man at his

and whose uniform is as extravagantly warlike as the plumage of a fighting-cock. The friars cut the most risible figure imaginable, chiefly from the seriousness and good faith with which they drill. Their bare feet, shod only in the shuffling sole kept on the instep by a thong, have engaged in the mystery of the goose-step with punctuality and obedience. The most extraordinary effect is made by their brown frocks, gathered up in the shoulder-straps, compressed by the belt; the varied patterns of the muskets they carry form a valuable museum of artillery. Their sleek faces, filled out with many a meal of begged victuals, are now cheerfully sweating with the difficulties of military exercise. Such were the allies, or some of them, who helped Wellington defend the Peninsula from Napoleon. Spain, volatile and indifferent in time of war until the cause is nearly lost, always then arouses herself and offers the last drop of her last vein; then occur her prodigies of romantic or grotesque valor, then her maiden of Saragossa "mans" the cannon against the French, then the ranks of the army are beaten up from the very monastery, and legions of intensely vindictive Judiths wind down from the cities to the

SACKING A VILLAGE.

ENGRAVED BY G. VON OTTEN FROM THE PAINTING BY F. EBERLE

invading camps by night, patriotically bent on giving the enemy a more painful fate than that of Holofernes. If Vibert had always painted so well as in this picture, or as in the "Roll-Call" in Mr. H. C. Gibson's gallery, his technical reputation would be higher among artists, and instead of merely amusing, his painting would instruct. He is also shown in this collection by the witty picture of "Gulliver in Lilliput" (see also W. T. Walters' gallery), a conception exhibited by M. Vibert in the Salon of 1877.—"A Village of Artois," in this collection, is an admirable picture by Emile, brother of Jules Breton. It is a scene of the French winter. The sleet clinging to the trees is capitally expressed, and the soft spongy character of the snow in the village street is indicated by its rounded cohesive forms and by its tendency to give way over the puddled hollows of the gutters. A French winter, as different as may be from our bright and exhilarating Januaries, merely shows the lowest temperature at which snow can crystallize at all. French snow, to our notion, is abortive and miserable in the extreme, it does not even give sleighing. "Soggy," overshoe weather is all it affords. The painter finds his comfort in this extremity of discomfort. He exults in expressing the treachery of the snow, which gives way under foot. The slippery glazing on the trees gives him a fine opportunity to show off his glancing pencil, and the pellicles of crystal forming in the sky are distinctly accounted for by the peculiar tone and quality he has given to his firmament. One would say that the thermometer would fall before such a picture to the freezing point of Reaumur, constituting itself the most appreciative critic of the artist's success.—A most brilliant picture by the prince of German genre-painters, Ludwig Knaus, is sketched in these pages by the artist's own touches. "An Unwelcome Visitor" is a keen-set and lively dog, snatching his dinner from a butcher's shop. Knaus' favorite boy model, a lively curlypate, with his apron, his butcher-knife, and the steel whereon to sharpen the latter,

almost turns a somersault in his eagerness to pounce on the marauder. The admirable expression of movement in this urchin is the hit of the picture. Equally true, if less animated and galvanic, is the figure of the fat patroness who so accurately fills the doorway of her shop, and whose age and size prevent her from doing more than shaking her fist in a rage. Every part of this painting is worthy of admiration, and only to be looked for from a master; but the eye returns with greatest delight, after all, to the wonderful figure of the precipitated boy!—"Expectations from our Aunt" is a scene of manners by Jules Worms, the delightful Paris painter. It is capital comedy-painting. Like a queen on her throne, in front of the ruelle of her stately Louis Quatorze bed, an old lady of uncertain temper sits glowering. For fear of draughts she is wrapped in the old-fashioned hood and mantle, worn by dowagers when they play Molière at the Français. The expression shows that her intellect is concentrated on her own aches and pains, very much like the nurse's when Juliet tries to extract Romeo's message from her. Juliet's place in the present colloquy is taken by a fresh young girl, in a very charming Charlotte Corday costume, who has come in for inquiries and grasps a passive but royal hand, and who can get no answer. An abbé, a household familiar, sits in a chair,

FRA LIPPO LIPPI AND LUCREZIA.

FAC-SIMILE OF A SKETCH FROM THE ORIGINAL PAINTING BY G. CASTAGNOLA

the only suitor so honored, and takes snuff with an inimitably insolent air of having taken possession. It is improving and instructive to see the advantage thus accorded to holiness, as well as the livid hatred with which the nephew, approaching

THE TELEGRAM OF LOVE.
MARBLE STATUE BY E. CABURE.

with the dowager's chocolate, peers on the priest. Even the footman feels the sacred privilege of jealousy, and sweeps the group with an eye of impartial odium, while he opens the door as little as possible for the entry of another doffing and louting aspirant; why should not the footman get the legacy, as the expense of all the other sycophants?—F. Eberle's "Plunder" shows the sacking of a farm-house by hostile troops, in the seventeenth century or thereabouts. The women have given the alarm, and a body of farmers with pitch-forks burst over the hill, just as the troopers have tied to their sumpter-horse the murdered geese, and the goats, and the slain lamb. Making a stand to defend the booty, an arquebusier in a helmet cocks his flintlock, the leader draws his sword, one pillager climbs out of the granary, and the expectancy of an exciting encounter enlivens the lawless

scene. Eberle is again represented by the "Truants," a crowded schoolroom tableau with a couple of young deserters caught in the act.—Gérôme's "Sword-Dance in a Café" is among his more celebrated subjects, distinguished by one of those unforgetable and daring poses—for the dancer, of course —which when once invented by this master and stamped in his adamant become permanent gains and additions to the wealth of art in the world. The scene takes place in a gloomy café, with a miscellaneous cluster of onlookers. Among these spectators, poised like a perching stork in one of the dusty beams which come through the skylight, a curly Turkish scimetar balanced on her head, postures the Almeh. A statuette has been made after this lifelike figure. Though the Almeh who dances is ably designed and in admirable equilibrium, the tone and color of this picture are more offensive than is usual even with Gérôme, who indeed is no colorist; the style is hard, and the indication of the beams of light unsuccessful simply because impossible. Ever since Girodet placed a painted moonbeam in the "Psyche and Zephyr" of the Louvre, there has been a mad ambition among the French artists to paint beams of light; they might as well attempt to carve them. "The Sword-Dance" has been again painted by Gérôme, with the addition of a proud Pacha and his suite as spectators, and in this form is seen in the New York gallery of Mr. W. H. Vanderbilt.—Cabanel is represented in the CROCKER gallery by a picture of considerable importance, a "Penelope." One arm hangs in lassitude as she stands, and is finely modeled. A black veil, representing Penelope's supposition of widowhood, covers the head, and the interminable tapestry, woven by day and unraveled by night, is depicted as a web in a primitive weaving-frame, the prototype loom of Ithaca, at the right of the picture. Boldini's "Morning Visit" (34 × 26 inches) shows a fair dame sitting on a canapé, playing the mandolin, with another lady reclining on the lounge alongside, an arm thrown over the back, and her pretty head reclining in her friend's lap. Altogether, none of the palaces on California Street can show a richer gallery than this of Mr. CROCKER's.

INITIAL FROM A DESIGN BY ARCHAMBAULT.

PON California Street also, at the corner of Taylor street, in another palace, is the gallery of Mrs. General D. D. COLTON. The paintings in this collection, without being of less merit for that, are distinguished for size and imposing effect, the true "gallery" quality. E. Benner furnishes a large and striking picture, not in the least cheerful, of "The Suicide," a grisette dying of charcoal fumes in a Paris *grenier*. This life-size corpse, all alone with the spectator, is far from being a reassuring comrade. The

THE TEMPTATION OF MARGUERITE
FAC-SIMILE OF A SKETCH FROM THE ORIGINAL PAINTING BY W. A. BOUGUEREAU

hapless girl, whose form has not lost its beauty, lies on a poor cot, in a writhing posture full of grace, her linen contorted with her movements, a clay furnace and bellows on the floor beneath her nostrils, poverty telling its stern tale in the carpetless boards and raveled rush chair, on the seat of which lies the ink-stand and the letter—desertion's last appeal to the absconder. "Temptation," a Faust and Marguerite group, by Bouguereau, shows, in a pair of life-size figures, the appeal of young love. The importunate suitor looking in at the window exhibits that power of influence, that inexplicable magnetic quality, which leads to full mesmeric possession of another's will, and which in a work of this topic must be authoritatively expressed by the artist or the theme is meaningless. Shakespeare, in his *Passionate Pilgrim*, is the only one who has done this to perfection, but the painter is not far behind the writer in conveying the sense of irresistible control. The spinning maiden, in the simple old German costume, looks rapt and impressible, and the dialogue, so long as the present harmony of interests continues, is attractive and pleasing.—Mr. Harry Thompson contributes three genre pictures, of which the most amusing represents a family of eighteenth-century ladies receiving the visit of an agent from the silk-mercer's, who brings into their boudoir his shining rolls of flowered brocade. One adorable pattern, with a sprig and a dot, and a twill and a stripe, and every desirable thing,

is thrown for exhibition upon the shoulders of a bony gigantic skeleton of a negro footman; the flattered creature wraps his gaunt bones in the courtly stuff, and smiles with immense complacency at his impromptu costume.—The "Dance at Capri" is by E. Sain, an agreeable young artist who for ten years made himself the younger brother and traveling companion and fidus Achates of Hamon, the unequaled painter of tender allegories. All the joy of Capri life, the serene gold of the evening sky, the delight of sport after the close of fishing-toil, the gentleness of soft and complaisant maidens, the antique grace of a half-stripped young boatman, whose flannel scapular or talisman beats upon his breast as he dances, and the consenting harmony of a female coryphæus who times the dance by clashing with the triple wooden hammers—all this delicious vagabondage respires in a thoroughly pleasant composition. Perhaps I indulge the picture rather too much, from having met and liked M. Sain in Italy, in the midst of these Capri studies, when he was representing whole bevies of the most fascinating female descendants of the victims of Tiberius's island, bright and uncontaminated on fadeless canvases, radiantly finding the prettiest bronzes of Pompeii, or dancing with all the zest of the most inspiring spider of Naples. But the painting, even more harshly judged, is a capable and careful work, as honest in technical execution as it is illustrative of the purest happiness of

THE LOVE-SONG.
FAC-SIMILE OF A SKETCH FROM THE ORIGINAL PAINTING BY J. VICHER

Arcady left upon our sordid earth.—Van Lerius' "Cinderella" is a picture so well known from the large German engraving that one wonders to find the original canvas, not in a Berlin or Munich Museum, but quite at home in the rolling fog that rises every evening from the Pacific. The favorite treatment of this nursery theme by the veteran artist shows Cinderella in the ashes, and the two proud sisters, haughtily beautiful too in their own way, arraying themselves in the splendid robes and pearled wimples of the sixteenth century. There is always something positive, full-blooded, distinct to the imagination, real, responsive to the mental grasp, in a conception of Van Lerius; you are sure to remember and to form an opinion about it, whether he shows you Paul holding the big banana-leaf over Virginia, or Godiva stealing like a Rubens goddess down the castle stair.—By A. Guerra there is in this collection "The Studio," a scene where the artist, painting from a nude male model, is visited by a lady and gentleman in the fullest and correctest ceremonial costume of the last century. By Hippolyte Delaunoy, of Paris, there is the "Art Critic" (5 × 3 feet,) recalling the fable of Xeuxis and the grapes, the allusion being applied to a masterly treatment of plums, peaches and flowers. By Ernest Zimmerman, of Munich, is a lively anecdote-picture, "The Traveling Menagerie." Between the acts of the regular circus performance we detect the young bear-leader training bruin to allow a monkey to dance on his back, while the other members of the company look on. Henriette Ronner contributes "Coming

from Market,"—two dogs driven in their cart by a German huckster's boy. There are some very large and admirable

THE SILK MERCHANT

pictures by James Hamilton, the best among the American marine painters of the last generation, whose intense and often magical effects are by no means defeated by the more realistic work now usual in landscape or marine art. Mr. Hamilton, a Pennsylvania Academician, died lately in San Francisco, having removed thither from Philadelphia and dedicated the last few years of his life's labor to Pacific aspects of his favorite element. Blackwood's Magazine grew enthusiastic over Hamilton's wonderful illustrations in mezzotint to Dr. Kane's voyages; one of his smallest sketches, presented to Dickens, sold for sixty pounds at the sale of that author's effects. It was for the late Gen. COLTON to secure what after all is perhaps the masterpiece left by Hamilton, a composition where the marine painter most victoriously invades the domain of the historical painter,—the immense canvas showing the "Fight between the Bonhomme Richard and Serapis." Here we see the ship of John Paul Jones lashed to her enemy, while the explosion of the store of grenades on the British frigate crowds a great square-shaped tower of sooty smoke into the heavens. The cohesion and intensity of this cubical monument of fume, caught before it has had time to scatter, is a lucky bit of fancy or observation, and makes the picture memorable and alive. In future days, when San Francisco has her schools of art, some pupil of engraving from the Sandwich Islands may make his reputation by translating this effective historical picture with the burin. Another very large painting by Hamilton, perhaps equally fine in quality, represents the "Escape of the Smugglers." It is one of his powerful sunset effects, with a play of vermilion and orange in the sky worthy of the courage of Turner, and representing, at this hour suggestive of the last judgment, the escape of criminals in their smuggling vessels, which creep and fly among the sea-birds along the beetling cliffs of the Welsh coast. E. Lesrel is represented by an amusing scene, where a squad of swashbucklers are "Serenading the Chief" —none other than a saucy vivandière, who accepts the homage by leaping upon a table, striking a military attitude, and smilingly drinking in the tribute of flattery. The costumes of this rollicking scene are of the sixteenth century,

Ex-Governor LELAND STANFORD has a fine gallery of pictures, some of them well enough known to the world of

WAITING FOR MONTÉLEONE.
FAC-SIMILE OF A SKETCH FROM THE ORIGINAL PAINTING BY J. FAVRETTO.

collectors. For instance, "Feeding the Carps at Fontaine-bleau," by P. C. Comte, is an agreeable and artistic composition, made popular by engraving. The scene is at the fish-pond in front of the old palace, whose steep roofs slant upward in the background. King Francis' favorite carps form a tumultuous group in front, and their food is thrown to them by a proud smiling dame—perhaps the very lady who cast her glove to the same king's lions, for a test of her lover's constancy. A maid of honor, carrying a square fan, descends the terrace steps, pulling at a reluctant King Charles spaniel—for the King Charles may be supposed to exist in France before Charles himself existed to give it a name in England. The pedestal with its copy of the Boar of Florence supports the leaning figure of a gay carpet knight, and ladies of the court cluster on the steps or over the balustrade. The costumes are scrupulously suitable to the period, and the tightly laced and braced figures give an aspect of external

decorum to that witty court which entertained its leisure hours with the tales of the Queen of Navarre.—Auguste Leloir's picture of "The Christian Martyr," with figures nearly life-size, shows a fair girl, whom a jailer pushes by the shoulder into the arena of the Coliseum. The wild beasts glare at her from their cages as she passes them; an ancient bearded martyr comes behind, and the contrast between her seraphic face and the venerable countenance of the older sufferer is emphatic. He seems to regret that he can give to heaven such a few remaining years, while the maiden can offer the whole rich treasure of her life.—Bouguereau's large picture is well known from the photographs—"Purloining the Grapes;" an Italian contadina mother, who holds a fine boy in her arms, is prettily harassed by a pet goat, determined to filch the clusters which the baby whimperingly clings to.— His smaller contribution represents a "Flower-Girl." Meyer von Bremen is found contributing "The New Arrival," a grandmother presenting the recently-born baby to its little sister. Toulmouche shows "Three Ladies," discussing the modes. Gérôme, with "The Veil," gives one of his smooth-skinned oriental women at half-length, lightly covered as far as the countenance goes with the coquettish yashmak. Bouvier, a Milanese artist, shows "Salvator Rosa's Reception." The American contingent of pictures ranges from comedy to tragedy and from religious sublimity to landscape grandeur. Benjamin West's life-size "Resurrection of Christ" heads the list of American representatives with a name of dignity; of more modern painters of this country there are the famous landscape artists, Bierstadt, with "The Happy Hunting Grounds," Thomas Hill with "Donner Lake," William Keith with "The Summit of the Sierras," and Bradford with an "Arctic Scene." E. Wood Perry is represented by "Words of Comfort" and "Hospitality," and William H. Beard by "The Court of Law," a diverting scene where all the contestants are monkeys. One of the most striking American subjects is the "Richelieu" of the late J. Beaufain Irving,

SUICIDE BY CHARCOAL.
FAC-SIMILE OF A SKETCH FROM THE ORIGINAL PAINTING BY E. SERVER.

representing that most popular scene of Bulwer's play, where the Cardinal defends his niece from the minions of Louis

Cambyses at Pelusium

ARTIST

PAUL LENOIR

Born at Paris, 1843. Died, 1881.

Pupil of Cabanel

COLLECTION OF

MR. CHARLES CROCKER, SAN FRANCISCO, CAL.

XIII. The collection contains Meissonier's portrait of the proprietor, that of his wife by Bonnat, and his son's by Carolus Duran.

AN UNWELCOME VISITOR.
FAC-SIMILE FROM A SKETCH FOR THE ORIGINAL PAINTING BY S. KNUT.

Mr. IRVING M. SCOTT has an excellent collection, including a most spirited Schreyer, "The Bursting Bomb;" J. G. Brown's "Dress Parade," showing a boot-black who drills his comrades, armed with brooms; "The Love-Song," by Richter of Paris, an Alhambra scene with a beautiful improvisatrice; a Munich-painted subject from *Marsción*, by Rosenthal, representing the trial of Constance; and "Awaiting Montezuma," by Jules Tavernier, an excellent French artist settled in California; this depicts the Arizona village-building Indians, of Aztec origin, gathering on their housetops to greet their Messiah, the returning Montezuma, in the person of the June sunrise.—Mr. A. E. HEAD possesses a valuable gallery, from which there are selected for illustration "The Room of the Bears," a clever restoration of the Pompeii chamber frescoed with bears,— those rare animals in ancient art,—with enlivenment of natural and probable Roman figures, by Scifoni; and an ingenious statue by Caroni, "The Telegram of Love."—Mrs. G. HEARST has a statue-gallery and numerous pictures—among them "Fra Lippo Lippi," the monkish painter who fell in love with the nun-model of his Madonnas,—a pair represented by C. Castagnola, as a nun in her robes and an artist already tired of his monastic dress and appearing as a full-fledged world-ling.—The Hon. J. W. MACKAY, among other paintings, has the portrait of his wife painted by Meissonier, in a black costume of what drapers call *merveilleuse*; the price for this treasure, about a foot in height, is stated to have been eighty thousand francs.—Mrs. R. C. JOHNSON has Toby Rosenthal's fine Germanesque picture of "Elaine," W. Bradford's large "Ship caught in a Floe, under the Midnight Sun," and Thomas Hill's "Picnickers on a Rocky Coast," and a mountain scene.—Mrs. DENNISON, who married a son of the author of "The Old Oaken Bucket," has the painting of this title, copied after that by Jerome Thompson; also Jerome Thompson's "Coming through the Rye," the original of Marshall's engraving; James Hamilton's "The Glory of Egypt shall pass Away," in water-color; and many pictures by Thomas Welsh, a young artist of genius studying at Munich. Mr. TIBURCIO PARROTT, the gentleman who originally ordered Rosenthal's "Elaine," has secured an "Elaine" by Tojetti, of small artistic value, and the same painter's "Venus and Cupid."

THE "ROOM OF THE BEARS" AT POMPEII.
FAC-SIMILE OF A SKETCH FROM THE ORIGINAL PAINTING BY A. SCIFONI.

COLLECTIONS IN SAN FRANCISCO.

MR. CHAS. CROCKER'S COLLECTION.

BAUGNIET, CH.—Art Studies.
BICHI, L.—Roman Peasants.
BENLLINI, —The Sale of Loves. Marble.
BOLDINI, G.—Morning Visit.
BEATON, E.—A Village of Artists in Winter.
"   "   Snow-Scene in Holland.
CABANEL, A.—Penelope.
CHAUVET, E.—Cup-and-Ball Game.
COOMANS, J.—Pompeian Girl.
DESGOFFE, B.—Vase of Flowers.
DULLOR, S.—The Letter.
DURAND, S.—Strolling Menagerie.
EBERLE, V.—Seeking a Village.
"   "   The Truants.
"   "   The Alarmed Villagers.
FILDES, G. B.—Ladies in the Fields.
GARDNER, E. J.—Cinderella.
GÉRÔME, J. L.—Sword-Dance in the Café.
GRISON, V.—Delayed Travelers.
GUES, A.—The King's Guard.
HAGBORG, A.—The Fisher-Woman.
HAMMEL, J. E.—The Peasant.
HARPER, J.—The Music-Lesson.
HERBOR, H.—The Rapids.   [Saco Valley.
JOHNSTONE, H. J.—An Australian Billabong—Col.
KNAUS, L.—The Unwelcome Visitor.
KOBERT, J.—Wedding Fête.
LENOIR, PAUL.—Gondynas at Siege of Pelusium.
LEON Y ESCOSURA, D. I.—Marie Antoinette at Versailles.
LIESEL, E.—Serenading the Chief.
MADRAZO, R.—Tourist.
MARCHETTI, L.—Wounded Prisoner.
MEYER VON BREMEN.—Pay Toll.
PALLIÈRE, J. L.—The Confession.
ROBIE, J.—Flowers.
SCHENCK, A. F.—Sheep in a Storm.
TOULMOUCHE, A.—Confidence.
VERBOECKHOVEN, E.—Cattle.
"   "   Sheep.
VIBERT, J. G.—Gulliver and the Lilliputians.
"   "   The Monastery in Arms.
WILLEMS, F.—The Love-Letter.
WORMS, J.—Expectations from our Aunt.

MRS. D. D. COLTON'S COLLECTION.

BENNER, E.—The Suicide.
BOUGUEREAU, W. A.—Persuasion of Marguerite.
BRILLOUIN, C.—Going to School.
"   "   The Surprise.
BURGERS, H. J.—A Girl Fishing.
CALITHEAU, —Bacchanalian.
COUMANT, C.—Harvest Scene.
DELAUNAY, H. P.—The Art Critic.
FABRE, T.—Island of Philæ.
"   "   The Pyramids of Ghizeh.
GUAY, G.—The Birth of Spring.
GUERRA, A.—The Studio.
HAMILTON, J.—The Escape of the Smugglers.
"   "   Engagement between the Bonhomme
Richard and Serapis.
MARTIN, W.—The Kitchen.

MRS. D. D. COLTON'S COLLECTION.
Concluded

MECKLENBURG, L.—The Grand Canal, Venice.
MUHLIG, M.—The Coal Vendors.
ORTLIEB, F.—The Monk's Visit.
RICHWOESS, J.—Ignorance is Bliss.
RIDGEY, E. F. W.—The Connoisseur.
RONNER, H.—Coming from Market.
SAIN, E. A.—Recreations in Capri.
SCHAEFFELS, H.—The Fountain of Love.
THOMPSON, HARRY.—The Introduction.
"   "   The Silk Merchant.
"   "   The Tambourine Girl
TRIPET, A.—The Spirit Bride, "Belle in fin pendant
ta vie."
"   "   The Morning Walk.
VAN LERIUS, J. H. F.—Cinderella.
VERBOECKHOVEN, E.—Sheep.
ZIMMERMAN, E.—The Traveling Menagerie.

MR. A. E. HEAD'S COLLECTION.

ANGIOLINI, LEO.—Group. Marble.
BODENER, ROSA.—Sheep.
BONNEFRAY, W. A.—Two Portraits.
CARSON, E.—The Messenger of Love. Marble.
CARROW, A. H.—Scene on the Adriatic.
"   "   Balcony Scene.
"   "   The Tryst at the Gate.
FRIEDLEBEN, E.—Children Gathering Wild Flowers.
GIOJA, B.—An Interior.
GUARNERIO, P.—The Forced Prayer. Marble.
"   "   Beggar Boy. Marble.
KOPF, T.—Cramp. Marble.
POLIZZI, FELIX.—Italian Girl and Goats.
ROBIE, H.—Cattle in Meadow.
ROBIE, J.—Red and White Roses.
SCHIOPPO, ANTONIO.—Room of the Roses, Pompeii.
TADOLINI, S.—Eve Reclining. Marble.
VERBOECKHOVEN, E.—Sheep.
"   "   Cows and Sheep.
"   "   Barn-Yard.

MRS. GEO. HEARST'S COLLECTION.

ANGIOLINI, LEO.—Flora. Marble.
"   "   Hunting Boy. "
"   "   Boy and Girl. "
"   "   Fruit. "
"   "   Galatea. "
CANDIDA, A.—Italian Sentinel.
CASTAGNOLA, G.—Philippo Lippi and Lucretia.
CHARLEMONT, HUGO.—Still-Life.
COULDERTE, J. H.—Cats in an Attic.
MOORE, H. H.—Moorish Water-Carrier.
"   "   Reverie.
"   "   Good News.
PERRY, E. W.—Old Lady.
SCHREYER, AD.—Horsemen at a Well in the Desert.
TAVERNIER, JULES.—Indian Encampment.
"   "   Indian Burial Ground.
TOFT, —Water-colors—Various.
WAYNE, E.—Peasant Girl at Dinner.

MR. I. M. SCOTT'S COLLECTION.

BETZGER, H.—Harvest Luncheon.
BOUGUEREAU, W. A.—Pensive.
BOFFEY, F.—Hot Weather in Spain.
BROWN, J. G.—A Sure Thing.
"   "   A Dress Parade.
EDELFELT, A.—Courting.
GUY, S. J.—Cash in Hand.
"   "   First Up.
HILL, T.—Early Morning—Yosemite.
HINDE, J.—Game of Chess.
"   "   Endangered Lunch.
KEITH, W.—Autumn—Mount Lyell.
"   "   Spring—Tamalpais.
"   "   Summer—St. Helena.
"   "   Winter—San Francisco Bay.
MICHIS, P.—The Double Indiscretion.
MOORE, H. H.—Child of Wealth.
NARJOT, E.—The Oracle of the Fields.
NOEMANN, E.—Norman Horses.
PILTY, B.—Child of Poverty.
RICHTER, E.—The Song of Love.
ROESSLER, L. C.—Spiritual Consolation.
ROOKE, N.—Leaving Home.
ROSENTHAL, T.—Chapter of St. Benedict.
SAVRY, H.—Cattle Nooning.
SCHREYER, A.—The Bursting Bomb.
TAVERNIER, J.—The Broken Bridge.
"   "   Awaiting Montezuma.
THOMPSON, H.—Alms.
VAN DER VENNE, A.—Gipsy Tent.
VIBERT, J. G.—Duet of Love.

EX-GOV. L. STANFORD'S COLLECTION

BEARD, W. H.—The Court of Law.
BELLY, —Fighting with Easter Eggs.
BIERSTADT, A.—The Happy Hunting-Grounds.
BISPHAM, H. C.—Two Trotters.
BOUGUEREAU, W. A.—Purloining the Grapes.
BOUVIER, —Salvator Rosa's Reception.
BRADFORD, W.—Arctic Scene.
CHARNEAU, —Cattle.
COMTE, P. C.—Fording Corps at Fontainebleau.
DE HAAS, W. F. H.—Gras-Nez Castle, Isle of
Jersey.
GÉRÔME, J. I.—Oriental Woman.
HILL, T.—Donner Lake.
IRVING, J. B.—Richelieu Protecting Julie—Bulwer's
Play.
KAEMMERER, F. H.—Winter Sport.
KEITH, WM.—Summit of the Sierras.
KNAUS, L.—German Subject.
LELOIR, AUGUSTE.—A Maiden Martyr.
MEYER VON BREMEN.—The New Arrival.
PERRY, E. W.—Words of Comfort.
"   "   Hospitality.
PIOT, A.—Italian Girl.
TOULMOUCHE, A.—Three Ladies Conversing.
VERBOECKHOVEN, E.—Sheep and Poultry.
WEST, BENJAMIN.—Resurrection of Christ.

TRUTH

ARTIST
JULES J. LEFEBVRE

BORN AT TOURNAN, FRANCE, 1876.

PUPIL OF CORNOBET

COLLECTION OF
MR. SAMUEL A. COALE, ST. LOUIS, MO.

CHRISTIAN WOMEN ENTERING THE CHAPEL OF THE VIRGIN.
FAC-SIMILE OF A SKETCH FROM THE ORIGINAL PAINTING BY J. J. L. LECOMTE-DU-NOÜY.

COLLECTIONS IN THE CITY OF SAINT LOUIS.

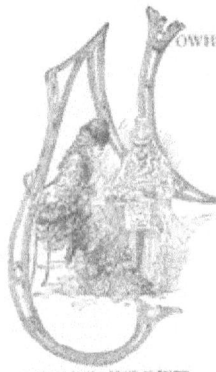

OWHERE on the banks of the Mississippi does the love of art flourish so conspicuously as in Saint Louis, that admirable meeting-place of Southern luxury and Northern enterprise. Among the splendid galleries which here attract the visitor, that of Mr. S. A. COALE, junior, is unsurpassed; a description of its accumulations to the date of this work will be welcome. Of Jules Lefebvre's great picture in the Luxembourg, the grand nude figure called "Truth,"

Mr. COALE possesses a small replica by the hand of the artist, 7 by 18 inches in dimensions. The divinity is represented in a superb attitude, standing, yet seeming to soar, and lifting on high, with a glorious and energetic impulse, the mirror which accuses all the world. The face has the intent look of one who detects. In the dark, rocky cell where she abides, and which forms the artistic equivalent for the symbolic well, is seen a flash of water and a growth of flags in bloom; the embracing rock encloses the white form of Truth like a hollow shaft, her celestial flesh shining against the dark

enclosure like the marble of some divinity in its niche. Many an artist's conception, primarily intended for execution in life-size, is greatly changed for the worse when copied in miniature; the forms become "lumpy," the details get "liney" or "thready;" the compression of the component parts beyond what was intended, even when accurately made to scale, ruins the repose, the serenity and breadth of style proper to the idea. This is not at all the case with Lefebvre's "Truth." The planes of modeling are so large, simple, and discerningly partitioned off, that the work endures a scientifically accurate reduction without loss of its original dignity. —"The Repose in Egypt" (4 × 2 feet) is a novel treatment of an old subject by the French artist Luc-Olivier Merson. The flight from Herod's massacre into the neighboring Roman dependency of Egypt, suggests a thought of the general safety of Roman subjects under the powerful government of Augustus. Except in Judea, where the Herods, by basest sycophancy, had attained a power which they usurped to vile designs, the proconsulates of the great empire were asylums of security; and Joseph felt a fuller confidence in the police regulations of the more dependent nation by the Nile than in the government of his own race and people. The painter represents the little group of three as straying into the full plenitude of the spells of ancient Egypt. The stars, which the priests of Thebes had interpreted, are over their heads; the Sphinx, which Cheops had worshiped, stares at the sky; the illimitable sands are all around, and the flat and muddy

Nile forms a thread in the distance, as different as possible from bowery Jordan. Against this mighty theocracy, still recognized by many a Roman subject as superior to his own, the new religion is sent in the form of a little babe. Cradled on the very breast of the Sphinx, the divine child reposes and slumbers in his mother's arms, biding his time. The sentiment of Mr. Merson's very novel and striking representation of the Flight has been quite fancifully expressed by A. Dézamy in a little poem of five stanzas inspired by this picture. "The Sphinx interrogates the stars: 'Why do I tremble from head to base before this infant?' A voice replies: 'The true God is revealed; thy kings only sowed

of imagination seems to expand to a boundless horizon, and becomes a true poem which it is a privilege to investigate. Very tender is the physical insignificance of the divine infant lying in the Virgin's arms between the paws of the Sphinx, glowing in the light of his own aureole, in the serene night of Africa, and symbolizing the new revelation in the grasp of antique paganism. Saint Joseph, representing ordinary and feeble humanity, lies powerless on the ground. He is worn out with fatigue, but a hopeful dream consoles him—a repetition of that inspired vision which had counseled him to retire into Egypt with the divine ward for whose safety he was responsible; his thoughts, even in slumber,

THE REPOSE IN EGYPT

FAC-SIMILE OF AN ENGRAVING OF ANGRAU FROM THE ORIGINAL PAINTING BY L. O. MERSON.

hatred; love must now be planted; be proud to shelter this bright head which will shine for the whole world!' Thus spoke the star to this stony soul, and the monster felt two granite tears roll from its inflexible eyelids." It is to be observed, however, that this invasion of Egypt by the God of Christendom has never been effectual; and from that day to this the country of the Nile has been occupied by rulers who did not accept the authority of the Son of Man now seated upon the Sphinx. Egypt has always been a pagan country, and the Sphinx in the long-run has held its own. This strange and thoughtful subject was exhibited by M. Merson in the Paris Salon of 1879, where it held crowds in irresistible and unaccustomed fascination. The most frivolous lounger from the boulevards could not help a tribute of thoughtfulness to the picture, attracted by its popularity and spell-bound by its suggestiveness. The "Flight" or "Repose in Egypt" is of no grand dimension; it is a simple page taken from the Bible, but which under the influence

communicate with heaven, like the white flame of the watch-fire which rises to the firmament from beside him. External nature is shown waiting for the more perfect revelation, utterly comfortless, silent, unconscious, and uneventful; one would say that the pressure of four thousand years of human misery had reduced the landscape to this abject level. One of nature's faithful creatures, the dumb ass—who may survive to bear one day the Messiah with hosannas to the gates of Jerusalem,—peacefully browses on the sparse herbage of the desert. The Nile is almost lost in the distance, but its drowsy current repeats the dial of the constellations, even as the patriarch's slumber mirrors the calculations of heaven. In this thoughtful composition all is filled with purpose, and the influence upon the heart and the imagination is a lasting one.

Luminais, so valuable for his romantic interpretations of the life of wild Gaul, contributes a small picture of "The Pursuit," in which his rich color and loaded brush play with the greatest freedom and breadth. A prisoner is retreating.

TEMPTATION OF ST. ANTHONY

ARTIST

LOUIS A. LELOIR

BORN AT PARIS, 1843.   PUPIL OF HIS FATHER, J. B. A. LELOIR.

COLLECTION OF

MR. HERCULES L. DOUSMAN, ST. LOUIS

and as he lets himself down a precipice, by a crackling branch, the muscles of his herculean body and thong-bound legs swell desperately in his mighty effort of escape. Over the brow of the cliff are seen his wild pursuers, almost sure of their prey, and eager to follow him down the terrible path he has chosen. "Love's Defiance," a graceful water-color picture by Jules Worms, shows one of his neat satirical fancies. A pretty modern flirt interrogates a statue of Cupid, which lifts its marble finger as a challenge and asserts its power. Let Love only come out of his stony envelope, exchange the symbol for the reality, and assume the warmth of living flesh and blood, and the damsel will have little left of her saucy security.—Cabanel is represented by a picture of considerable importance, a conception which the artist himself esteems representative of his talent, for he selected the group of which this is one of the figures to stand for him at the Paris Exposition of 1867; the conception alluded to is the "Eve," repeated by the artist from a very large group in which Adam and the Eternal Father are represented besides. This central figure of the Fall gives the painter a good opportunity to develop his science of the human female body in its typical presentment. An Eve should be the central model and matrix of the whole race. The Paris painter represents her

head, while her feet trail off to the left with a pronounced lack of volition and power. The strong torso, that is the envelope

LOVE'S DEFIANCE.
FAC-SIMILE OF A SKETCH FROM THE ORIGINAL PAINTING BY JULES WORMS.

of all humanity, is supported against a rock, cushioned with an abundant fall of sunny hair. While acknowledging a suitable amount of conventional beauty for this figure, and a skill in the technical part of the picture which only a master of the craft can possess, it may be demurred that the conception is trivial and undignified, and that the piercing glance of Michael Angelo was needed to incise a few tendons and articulations in this rather limp and rubbery castaway.—One of Henner's nude figures, so admirable for their expression of flesh-texture and sharp impinging light—a strange unity of Correggio softness with Ribera definition—is included in the collection, and gives proof of a genius that must always rank among the masters; "The Nymph" this time,—more supine than some others of Henner's large nymph-family—is delicately reposing on the margin of a lake.—Edouard Toudouze is represented in Mr. Coale's collection by a large canvas of 6 by 4 feet, representing the "Beach at Yport" (Manche). It is a successfully sunny picture from the Salon of 1878, with costumes of the date of painting. The usual groups of a French watering-place are distributed in a life-like manner over a pebbly beach that slopes down to a stretch of warm sea to the left. The French rustic seats—convenient X-shaped chairs—are overthrown here and there; one playful lady, who can sit on anything with grace, occupies at the left a seat in its overthrown condition. A pretty idler looks out at the ships with an opera glass, another works at an inter-

GAULISH FUGITIVE.
FAC-SIMILE OF A SKETCH FROM THE ORIGINAL PAINTING BY E. V. LUMINAIS.

as cast along upon the ground, her forehead supported by her elbow and hand, the other arm despairingly thrown over her

minable piece of tapestry, while her children play with their dolls behind a Japanese parasol. A male figure would spoil

ORIENTAL WOMAN
FAC-SIMILE OF A SKETCH FROM THE ORIGINAL PAINTING BY CAROLUS DURAN.

the harmony, and the picture gains in piquancy by being altogether confined to the ways and works of fashionable women, contrasting their beauty with the rudeness of the ocean. The skillful picture, beheld in a capital so far inland, beside the mighty river that creases the continent down the middle like the fold in a letter-sheet, has an almost magical effect. It seems to fill the gallery, which certainly never heard the murmur of the sea, with salt perfume and a dash of spray.—Adolphe Jourdain is author of a large picture of "Leda." The beautiful queen sits nude upon her draperies, showing a graceful posture nearly in profile, half supported on the knuckles of one hand thrown behind her. At her feet flows the Eurotas, by a bank fringed with morning-glories, and the celestial swan caresses her ankle with his supple neck. The white limbs of the beauty are so grouped with the approaching bird that the two figures form a combination of singular grace, relieved like silver repoussé upon a dark background made of the primitive forest.—By Alvarez, one of the witty Spanish painters of the day, is the famous cherry-picking scene from the memoirs of Rousseau, where the young enthusiast indulges in that Arcadian employment with Mme. de Warens and Mme. de Wolmar; it is unnecessary to explain what sport the lively compatriot of Sancho Panza and Gil Blas makes of this incident. Courbet is shown in one of the studies he made after his retirement to Switzerland— an "Evening in the Jura"—the small-change of a bankrupt career, of uncommon abundance and interest, forming a distinct and individual gallery. The water-colors in this collection are Diego Martin Rico, who is finely represented by "The House of Pilate at Seville" and "Washerwomen by the Seine." Vibert's "Spanish Water-Carrier" is very lively and characteristic. Lucio Rossi's "Cocotte" and "Thirteenth

Century Cavalier" are painted with infinite chic. Michetti's "Olive Gatherers of the Abruzzi" shows his rare power of placing figures unmistakably in the open air and sunshine. A Madrid painter, Jose Casado del Alisal, shows "Zaida the Favorite," an aquarelle of which the life-size original in oil is owned by Col. R. C. Hawkins of New York. Boldini contributes a "Bois de Boulogne." Count Zichi of Cracow, so bepraised in Théophile Gautier's Russia, is seen with "A Fantasia." "The Sentinel" is an exquisitely-finished Turkish subject in the style of Gérôme by Charles Bargue, whose delicate lithographs for drawing-schools are such miracles of precision. G. Clairin shows Mlle. Sarah Bernhardt dressed for her part of the American adventuress, Mrs. Clarkson. Maurice Leloir, in "The Toilet of the Fields," exhibits a lovely butterfly-catcher, her net lying on the ground, sitting and attaching the splendid insects all over an enormous bonnet of the Directoire period. Doré is easily recognized in a "Transfiguration."—Among the paintings of greater age we notice "The Court of Death" by Rembrandt Peale, a canvas of no less than 24 x 13 feet, which has covered almost the whole country in its peregrinations during the sixty years or thereabouts that it has existed. It was suggested by Bishop Porteus' poem on death, and painted as an effort to improve on West's "Death on the Pale Horse" and Rou- billiac's skeleton "Death" on a famous Westminster tomb. In this large group the figure personifying Age is the artist's father, the admirable Charles Wilson Peale, one of the first and best American artists. John Neal, the author, imperso- nated the Warrior; the corpse, lying under the foot of Death and in the waves of oblivion, has the head of Mr. Smith, founder of the Baltimore Hospital; Franklin Peale, a painter and a brother to the artist, stood (without demur, it seems,) for Inebriation; and the author's daughters personified the allegorical females. Altogether the COALE collection not only gives a high idea of the spread of refinement and culture in

EVE AFTER THE FALL
FAC-SIMILE OF A SKETCH FROM THE ORIGINAL PAINTING BY A. CABANEL.

the heart of the continent, but shows how much a single example will do in influencing the civilization of a whole

Between Friends

ARTIST
VINCENT CHEVILLIARD

Born at Ronen, 1875

Pupil of Cabanel

COLLECTION OF
MR. DANIEL CATLIN, ST. LOUIS, MO.

community. Mr. COALE is justly regarded as the pioneer of picture-collecting in his city; and the noble impulse given by him has not only stimulated a number of his fellow-townsmen in the formation of rival galleries of imported works, but has led to the encouragement and support of several local American artists of merit.

Mr. D. CATLIN has a select and variously-interesting collection, in which, for central jewel, we find the "Cigale" (3×8 feet) of Lefebvre, from the gallery of Mr. Latham of San Francisco. This "Cigale," having journeyed from Paris to California, thence to New York, and thence to the Mississippi, must be acknowledged as a very great traveler, considering that she is such a radically unprotected female. Of a picture so widely known a very slight sketch suffices to recall the character to any reader; the posture is one of the most graceful and sympathetic yet discovered, even by Lefebvre, whose elegant heroines are like a statue-gallery of well-considered poses. The pettish sullenness of the poor musician, as she bites her finger when the first breeze of autumn whistles; her implied defiance of Fate, as if certain that a being so in harmony with nature will not be quite bereft of natural protection; her choice of pouting instead of whining, are quite in harmony with the careless courage of the Bohemian race. As a study of a beautiful figure, at the first budding period of development, the "Cigale" is singularly happy in design, and its author's masterpiece; it is certainly thin in style, however, and without any suggestion of the richer qualities of flesh-painting as found in the works of Velasquez, Rembrandt or Rubens. By Lefebvre, Mr. CATLIN has also a lovely creation, "The Morning-Glory;" it is a half-length life-size figure of a maiden, in a transparent classical drapery of white, rising among the pale mists of dawn, and looking at you full-face with the half-puzzled and inquiring air of a being just born: a spray of morning-glory, wreathed around the forehead and falling on the shoulder, opens a score of delicate trumpets to play the pæan of daybreak.—Of a very different character is the side-splitting scene depicted in

A LESSON IN HARMONY.
FAC-SIMILE OF A SKETCH FROM THE ORIGINAL PAINTING, BY J. M. AUBERT.

1880 by Casanova, "The Sick Monk" (3×2 feet.) Three Franciscans are seen in a handsomely furnished room of a

monastery: the doctor of the brotherhood, barefoot and cowled, holds his old-fashioned turnip watch and counts the

THE CUP OF FRIENDSHIP.
FAC-SIMILE FROM A SKETCH FOR THE ORIGINAL PAINTING BY J. CHARLES.

pulse of his holy patient,—a sitting monk with the most woe-begone expression,—who not only submits his wrist, but holds out his tongue as far as it will possibly go, with an overweening sense of the importance of his symptoms. It is evident that his mind clings to the physician as to the last branch in a deluge. His head is tied in a flowery kerchief, his bony feet are drawn under the arm-chair, and he supports with his hand the arm that the doctor is feeling, less from weakness than from self-pity. To this ethereal pair enters by the doorway a fat monk, of the male-nurse type,—greasy, gossipy and bustling,—his arms loaded with half-a-dozen bottles of sweet-oil and a syringe, his eyes shining with the zest of immediate application to business. The composition is a bit of low comedy, the figures are out of proportion, the color is not good, but the farce-instinct of the author is so neat and brilliant that the picture drowns criticism in laughter. "The Lesson in Astronomy," by Aubert, is graceful as a little poem by Heine. An old philosopher sits at dusk, pointing with his lean arm to each star as it uncloses flower-like in the mighty parterre of the sky. Behind him are seated Daphnis and Chloe, his hopeful pupils, seeing stars in "mutual eyes," and printing their lips upon each other; thus they take their lesson. It is difficult in painting such a scene to relieve the pedagogue figure—the individual who is so completely out of the game—from the aspect of ridiculousness; but Aubert has found a rapt and solemn expression for his astronomer which gives him as high an interest, though of another kind, as that of the dreaming lovers. This picture was painted in 1878.— Adrien Moreau is represented by "The Stepping-Stones" (18 ×30 inches), a merry group in Rabelais costumes, crossing a stream. F. Indoni is seen contributing a pleasant scene "In the Garden," with three ladies and a cavalier in eighteenth-century costumes, and a tomb in the background. A very fine Jules Breton, less champêtre than his wont, shows "The Sea-Bird" (3×4 feet); it is a life-size half-length figure of a brown fisher-maiden with a captured sea-mew. Here again, as with Mr. COALE's "Toudouze," the most refreshing, most stinging sort of an ocean breeze is wafted by painter's magic into the very interior of the continent.—Perrault's "Prayer"

THE HEART AWAKENED.
FAC-SIMILE OF A SKETCH FROM THE ORIGINAL PAINTING BY A. VÉLY

(2 × 4 feet) reveals an Italian girl, life-size, in a suitable attitude.—Schreyer's "The Standard" (36 × 18 inches) shows Arabs in a back view.—A subject of a "Flock of Sheep" (5 × 3 feet), by Schenck of Ecouen, delineates his ordinary sitters in natural and vigorous attitudes, their dog among them for schoolmaster.—Jacque's "Sheep" (2 × 3 feet) shows the same creatures in shadowy groves, an enormous oak spreading above them.—"After the Shower" (36 × 24), by Van Marcke, delineates half-a-dozen cattle in a landscape of deeply-calculated light-and-shade, well adapted to contrast and set off their picturesqueness.—De Neuville's "Reconnoissance" shows, at the left, two mounted scouts, and, at the right, three standing infantrymen reaping the advantage of their investigations.—There is a landscape of 1874, by Daubigny, showing that the close of his fruitful career still found him in full force; and a "Boats on the Seine," by Diego Martin Rico, painted with address and felicity.—"The Roses' Scent," by Toulmouche, shows the full-length figure of a young lady in profile, looking to the left, her face protruded towards the flowers, her arm thrown decisively behind her back as she strides among the rose-bushes; this rather grenadier-like attitude is applied simply to a greenhouse reconnaissance.—Chevilliard, the witty Juvenal of the clergy, shows "A Good Bottle," and one of the pampered race indulging in the secure, homelike, intimate pleasures of the palate; the chamber is furnished in the choicest style of bachelor comfort; a map on the wall takes the place of

the Marc Antonio or Volpato of a more intellectual kind of dilettante; and the old woman in attendance is a house-keeper who mingles the respect of the disciple with the drill of the trained servant. The good bottle is yielding its cork to the persuasion of the comfortable gourmand, who eases it out gently as he sits, and we may be assured that a vintage of unusual quality is enshrined in the crystal spire. Although we cannot distinctly perceive the aroma which is just beginning to tickle the experienced nostril of the priest, we can be perfectly certain that the liquor of his domestic communion is of a very, very different quality from that which is dispensed to an ordinary congregation in church.

Mr. H. L. Dousman has built a very beautiful picture-gallery in connection with his residence, where every picture, however large, is seen under glass; the canvases are thus protected from the floating impurities of an atmosphere which is sometimes too much enamored with the sooty bosom of a fire of bituminous coal. One of the most striking pictures in the collection is "The Temptation," by Louis Leloir. Saint Anthony—a monk of most refined and intelligent profile—kneels before his cross and makes fight against the bewildering female visions; his attitude is that of a shipwrecked man, battling in waves of suffocating temptation, at which his fine nostril quivers with disgust and horror; his only branch of safety is the cross, which breaks as he catches at it. The alluring feminine shapes beset him before and behind,—one young importunate creature clinging to the shoulders, another more mature and impudent character laying her head in his lap and quite securely laughing in his face. It is a curious thing that the painters seem to know so little what sort of type would be a real allurement to a hermit of education and intelligence. The consolation which these recluses actually missed was the peace and security of home; they had resisted the tears of their sisters, the white locks of their mothers, and the vows of faithful wives. What tempted them was a vision

A LESSON IN ASTRONOMY.
FAC-SIMILE OF A SKETCH FROM THE ORIGINAL PAINTING BY J. E. AUBERT

of the rest, the permanence of home; matrimony was what they renounced, and its loss was what separated them from

THE LOVE FEAST

ARTIST

A. J. MAZEROLLE

BORN AT PARIS, 1832.   PUPIL OF OUDOT AND GLEYRE.

COLLECTION OF

MR. CHARLES PARSONS, ST. LOUIS, MO.

other men. The image which would have seriously attracted them would have been the image of a modest and tranquil woman, promising joys of attachment unchangeable. Instead, the artists always present in such scenes of temptation the conception of woman in her most fickle and untrustworthy aspect, for whom could be felt only an attraction too transitory to engage a thinking man. The artist of this picture has not escaped the pitfall into which every painter of a Saint Anthony seems to sink. In presence of this important example of a very skillful artist it is well to recall that he comes from an artistic race, his father, Auguste Leloir, being author of a "Homer" in the Luxembourg Gallery, and himself (born at Paris in 1843) being the painter of "The Grandfather's Fête" and "The Slave,"—both owned in America,—besides the present canvas.—The large painting of "The Heart Awakened," which looks very imposing in its central position and under the crystal honors of an immense sheet of plate-glass, is by Anatole Vély, a young painter who died unexpectedly January 11, 1882. A beautiful girl, dressed in the close and modest costume of the middle ages, sits at the feet of an aged duenna, who has been reading out of a cumbrous volume. The thoughts of the fair châtelaine have strayed from the text, and she looks up with the rapt expression of day-dreams. The inattention of the young girl has excited the old dame's curiosity, and she looks down suspiciously at the fair face, so alive with hope and anticipation. The young heart has awakened. A handsome hound curls round the feet of his beautiful mistress. This painting was exhibited at the Paris Salon of 1880.—Aubert's "Lesson in Harmony" corresponds with his "Lesson in Astronomy," just seen in the Catlin collection. It represents a Greek maiden sitting beside a

THE SICK MONK.
FAC-SIMILE OF A SKETCH FROM THE ORIGINAL PAINTING BY ARTURO CASANOVA.

pipe of his own, which forms the real example of the melody. —Coomans, the Belgian painter, is represented by an elaborate

example of some fifteen or sixteen figures, "The Cup of Friendship." It is a feast in a classical banquet-hall. The banqueting guests are stretched on soft cushions in the midst of flute-girls and dancers and children, and the moment has arrived when the host, dropping into his cup a rose or a pearl, drinks to the health of the assembled company.—Carolus Duran's "Oriental Woman" is a sumptuous little color-study, representing an odalisque standing, with a large salver in her hands. There is great beauty in the association of rich tints composing the costume, and the work has the freshness of a sketch combined with the surety of taste conferred by consummate art and experienced calculation.—Lecomte Du Nouy takes us to the Holy Land with a large and highly-finished composition of "Christian Women Entering the Chapel of the Virgin." A Turkish sentinel, standing impassive at the portal, smokes a disrespectful pipe amid the ecstasy of these ardent Coptic and Albanian Christians, who kneel in the doorway or lean their heads in prayer against the external wall, fearing to enter until they have prayed away their sins and expiated their unworthiness. This picture is executed in palpable imitation of the style of Gérôme, but lacks that painter's lucidity of arrangement and purity of expression.— Victor Bachereau is represented by a death-bed scene of many figures, "The Last Hours of François de Lorraine." This brave general, a member of the famous family of Guise, died at the siege of Orléans, in 1663, shot by the Protestant, Poltrot.— Jacquet is seen in a very delicate conception, a "Cinderella;" the picture, of some 26 by 36 inches, represents the neglected beauty musing by the hearth.—Luis Alvarez contributes a dazzling and bewildering piece of pageantry, in the style of the modern Spanish-Roman school, representing the "Marriage of Pauline Bonaparte and Prince Borghese." Camille Borghese was the last heir of the old and noble Sienese family, whose palace is one of the sights of modern Rome. He was charged by Napoleon with the government of

LA CIGALE.
FAC-SIMILE OF A SKETCH FROM THE ORIGINAL PAINTING BY J. LEFEBVRE.

shepherd-boy, who teaches her to play upon the pipe. Behind her, as a familiar spirit, stands Cupid, blowing softly into a

Piedmont. In 1803 he espoused the most beautiful of the Bonaparte sisters, the enthusiastic and impulsive Pauline, at that time widow of General Leclerc, who died in the expedition against Santo Domingo. Pauline gave up her diamonds to help defray the cost of Waterloo. This singular and fascinating creature, whose true portrait has been published for his peculiar style of flash and glitter.—Mr. Dousman's collection contains three of the voluptuous pictures of Kray, the gorgeous Vienna painter; of these "Lorelei," a nude enchantress sitting on a precipice of the Rhine, is the most celebrated; the others, respectively a "Swimming-Lesson" and "Fishing," can sufficiently be imagined when it is said

THE ELDER SISTER.
FAC-SIMILE OF AN ENGRAVING BY SALVE FROM THE ORIGINAL PAINTING BY W. BOUGUEREAU.

in the account of Judge Hilton's collection, is represented by the Spanish painter as introduced into the fairy-like Borghese Villa as its mistress. The high company are banqueting on a raised platform, from golden dishes, under a starry chandelier. A balcony filled with musicians bears the insignia of "Carolus III, Rex." In the foreground the marble floors are covered with tapestries, and the handsomest young chevaliers of Rome stand as sentinels to guard the steps leading to the princely tables, or keep off the crowd of holiday-dressed contadinas who press up to the railing. The last of the really splendid feasts of the Villa Borghese gives the artist a rare opportunity

that they contain all that heart can imagine of graceful grouping divested of drapery.—C. L. Muller's large color-study for "The Last Roll-Call in the Conciergerie" is similar to that described in the collection of Mr. J. J. Astor, which was illustrated with that gentleman's gallery. Of the two repetitions, the present study looks more like a sketch, and is slighter in execution; Mr. Astor's copy has the aspect of an elaborate reduction made après coup, and perhaps does not profess to be a first thought for the picture.

In the gallery of Mr. Charles Parsons, made homelike by the assemblage of works on art, is a collection of well-

CHURCH AND STATE

ARTIST
JEHAN G. VIBERT

BORN AT PARIS, 1840.   PUPIL OF FÉLIX J. BARRIAS

COLLECTION OF
MR. JOHN J. O'FALLON, ST. LOUIS, MO.

selected pictures,—gathered slowly and with critical taste. The Italian painter, growing in American favor, Luis Alvarez,

THE INTERRUPTED READING.
THE WIDTH OF A SKETCH FROM THE ORIGINAL PAINTING BY V. PALMAROLI.

is represented in Mr. Parson's collection by a very recent painting, "The Introduction of the Betrothed," which exhibits

all the traits of that artist's *chic*. Mazerolle, the decorator of rooms in municipal buildings in Paris, the artist of the superb frieze which adorns the parlor of the D. O. Mills palace in Fifth Avenue, is here with his masterpiece in serious work, "*Les Agapes*," "The Love-Feast," representing a party of early Christians partaking of that periodical repast, which is continued to the present day in all churches under the name of "Communion." A careful study by Steinheil—called "The Antiquary"—indicates the future of this artist if he chooses to follow in the track of his father-in-law, M. Meissonier. Mr. Parsons in his gathering has a few choice examples of great men of the past generation:—Calame, in a landscape, exhibiting his force; N. de Keyser, in an "Old Man Reading;" Brion, in one of his best-known works, "The Invasion."

The nuclei of two very charming collections are in the parlors of Mr. J. A. Scudder of St. Louis, and of Mr. J. J. O'Fallon in his residence about ten miles west of St. Louis. With correct taste and ample means to gratify it, we see the seed of rivals to many collections—now larger, and certainly older. To look at these necessary family adornments and educators, domiciled twelve or thirteen hundred miles from the seaboard, one is impelled to the thought that art belongs to no nation, but is universal in its teachings and command of admiration.

COLLECTIONS IN THE CITY OF SAINT LOUIS.

MR. DANIEL CATLIN'S COLLECTION.

ALVAREZ, L.—*Flirtation.*
AUBERT, J. E.—*The Lesson in Astronomy.*
BRETON, JULES.—*The Sea-Bird.*
CASANOVA, A.—*The Sick Monk.*
CHEVILLIARD, V.—*A Good Battle.*
COROT, J. B. C.—*Washerwomen at the Stream.*
DAUBIGNY, KARL.—*Washerwomen on the Seine.*
DE NEUVILLE, A.—*The Reconnaissance.*
INDONI, G.—*The Gallant.*
JACQUE, CH.—*Landscape and Sheep.*
JORIS, PIO.—*Summer Reading.*
LEFEBVRE, J.—*Morning-Glory.*
"   "   *La Cigale.*
LELOIR, L.—*The Bouquet.*
MENELER, C. A.—*Study.*
MOREAU, A.—*The Stepping-Stones.*
PERRAULT, L.—*Prayer.*
PONCHART, L.—*The Cage.*
RICHARDS, W. T.—*Sea-Shore.*
RICO, D. M.—*Village of Bougival.*
SCHREYER, A.—*Standard-Bearer.*
SCHENCK, A. F. A.—*The Flock.*
TOULMOUCHE, A.—*The Rust's Secret.*
VAN MARCKE, E.—*After the Shower.*
VOILLEMOT, CH.—*An Odalisque.*

MR. J. A. SCUDDER'S COLLECTION.

ALVAREZ, L.—*The New Baby.*
BERTRAND, J.—*Mignon.*
BOLDINI, G.—*The Café Pigalle.*
HAMMON, N.—*The First Quarrel.*
INNESS, GEORGE.—*A Passing Storm.*
LEFEBVRE, J. J.—*Evening.*
MEYER VON BREMEN, J. G.—*Crossing the Bridge.*
POIRSON, M.—*Pier at Trouville.*
SAINTPAIN, J. E.—*The Miniature.*
SCHOBERGENBERG, J.—*A Cup of Tea.*
TAPIRO, J.—*In the Garden.*
VAN THOREN, O.—*At the Sea-Shore.*

MR. CHAS. PARSON'S COLLECTION.

ALVAREZ, LUIS.—*The Introduction of the Betrothed.*
AMBERG, W.—*On the Sea-Shore.*
BELLOWS, A. F.—*Landscape and Cattle.*
BÉRANGER, E.—*The Bouquet.*
BILLET, P.—*On the Sea-Shore.*
BRION, G.—*The Invasion.*
CALAME, A.—*Landscape.*
CHURCH, F. E.—*Sunset at Mount Desert.*
COL. DAVID.—*The Perilous Leap.*
COOMANS, JOS.—*The Panic.*

MR. CHAS. PARSON'S COLLECTION.
Concluded.

DAUBIGNY, C.—*Landscape.*
DE COCK, C.—*Springtime.*
DE KEYSER, N.—*Old Man Reading.*
DE NEUVILLE, A.—*Soldier on Guard.*
FRÈRE, E.—*Cavalier and Lady (Louis XIII.)*
GIFFORD, S. R.—*Venetian Sails.*
JAZET, V.—*The Favorite.*
JORIS, PIO.—*At the Wine-Shop.*
KAEMMERER, F. H.—*The Garden.*
KOEKKOEK, C. B.—*The Zuyder Zee.*
LAMBINET, E.—*Boy Fishers.*
LELOIR, L.—*The Kitten Merchant.*
LOBBET, A.—*Halberdier.*
MAZEROLLE, A. J.—*The Love-Feast.*
PALMAROLI, V.—*Hiding Abelard.*
RICHARDS, W. T.—*Sea-Shore.*
SCHREYER, A.—*Retreating Arabs.*
SEITZ, A.—*Reflection.*
SIMONETTI, E.—*Monk Reading.   Water-color.*
STEINHEIL, A.—*The Antiquarian.*
TAPIRO, J.—*Woodcutter.*
TROYON, C.—*Landscape and Cattle.*
VELY, A.—*The First Step.*
VERBOECKHOVEN, E.—*Goat and Sheep.*
VIBERT, J. G.—*Maître's Welcome.   Water-color.*
VOLTZ, F.—*Cattle at a Stream.*
ZIEM, F.—*The Arsenal, Venice.*

COLLECTIONS IN THE CITY OF SAINT LOUIS.

(CONTINUED.)

MR. S. A. COALE'S COLLECTION.

ALVAREZ, LUIS.—*Rousseau and Mesdames de Warens and de Wilmar in the Garden.*
BRUGUNET, C.—*Autumn.* Water-color.
BELLOWS, A. F.—*The Old Mill.* Water-color.
BIANCHI, L.—*The Knitter.*
BOURGOIN, DÉSIRÉ.—*Sara Bernhardt's Studio.* Water-color.
BOUTIER, AUG.—*Pompeian Maiden.* Water-color.
BROWNE, H. K.—*The Good Little Sister.* Cartoon.
CABANEL, A.—*Eve after the Expulsion.*
CAMOS, VICTOR.—*Landscape.* Water-color.
CAMPOTOSTA, W.—*The Noonside Rest.*
CAPRIANI, R.—*Cavalier of the Fourteenth Century.*
CAZADO DEL ALISAL, JOSE.—*Zaida.* Water-color.
CHAPPELAT, L.—*Spring.*
CLAIRIN, GEORGE.—*Sara Bernhardt.*
COOPER, T. S.—*Landscape and Cattle.*
"   "
COROT, J. B. C.—*Landscape—Evening.*
"   "
COUSSET, GUSTAVE.—*Evening in the Jura.*
DALBANO, L.—*A Spanish Beauty.* Water-color.
"   " —*Naples.*
DAUBIGNY, C. F.—*Landscape—Morning.*
DE BEAUMONT, C. E.—*The Knight and the Maid.*
DEFREGGER, F.—*Head of a Girl.*
DELORT, C. E.—*In the Antechamber.*
DE NEUVILLE, A.—*On Guard.*
DIAZ, N.—*Landscape.*
DORÉ, G.—*The Transfiguration.* Cartoon.
FERES, C.—*St. Cecilia.*
FOSTER, BIRKET.—*Children at Play.* Water-color.
"   " —*The Little Romps.*
GERLER, OTTO.—*Cattle.*
GIRARD, A.—*Landscape.* Water-color.
HAMILTON, JAMES.—*Salem Flats.* Water-color.
HAMMAN, E.—*Pretty as a Picture.*
HENNER, J. J.—*The Nymph.*
INGHAM, P.—*The Promenade.* Water-color.
"   " —*Confidence.* Water-color.
ITTENBACH, F.—*The Holy Family.*
JACQUET, J. G.—*Ophelia.*
JOHN, PIO.—*Why Comes He Not?* Water-color.
"   " —*A Japanese Lady.*
JOURDAN, AD.—*Leda and the Swan.*
KAUFFMAN, ANGELICA.—*Head of Minerva.*
KLIESCH, EUGENE.—*An Episode from Boccaccio.*
"   " —*The Parting Pledge.*
"   " —*The Olden Time.*
KNAUS, LUDWIG.—*The Wood-Chopper.*
KURZBAUER, C.—*Head of a Boy.*
LEFEBVRE, J. J.—*Truth.*
LELOIR, LOUIS.—*The Odalisque.* Water-color.
LELOIR, MAURICE.—*The Toilet of the Fields.* Water-color.
LUMINAIS, E. V.—*The Pursuit.*
MAX, GABRIEL.—*Faust and Marguerite.*
MAZEROLLE, A. J.—*La Charmeuse.*
"   " —*La Source.*
McENTEE, J.—*Landscape.*
MERSON, L. O.—*The Repose in Egypt.* [color.
MEYER VON BREMEN.—*The Little Sister.* Water-
MICHETTI, F. P.—*Olive-Gatherers of the Abruzzi.* Water-color.

MR. S. A. COALE'S COLLECTION.

Concluded.

MULLER, CARL.—*The Saviour.*
MURRAY, ELIZABETH.—*A Greek Betrothal.*
NATIVY, L.—*Ready for the Bath.*
PALMAROLI, V.—*Reverie.*
"   " —*The Beautiful Marchioness.*
PEALE, REMBRANDT.—*The Court of Death.*
PERRAULT, LEON.—*Poverty.*
POLLET, VICTOR.—*Venus Victrix.* Water-color.
"   " —*Age of Innocence.* "
"   " —*Venus and Cupid.* "
"   " —*The Convalescent.* "
PILOTY, CARL.—*Scene from Castle.* Cartoon.
ROSSI, L.—*Une Gavotte.* Water-color.
"   " —*A Cavalier.*
SIMONETTI, A.—*La Femme Galante.*
"   " —*Reverie.* Water-color.
SIMSON, P.—*Madame De Maintenon.* Water-color.
SOHN, WILLIAM.—*Female Study.*
SUTTER, J.—*The Belle of Thune.*
TOUDOUZE, E.—*The Beach at Yport.*
VAUTIER, B.—*An Interior.*
VIBERT, J. G.—*A Spanish Water-Carrier.* Water-color.
VOILLEMOT, A. C.—*A Fantasy.*
VOLTE, F.—*Landscape and Cattle.*
WIMAR, CHARLES.—*On the War-Path.*
WORMS, JULES.—*Love's Defiance.* Water-color.
ZICHY, THE COUNT.—*Fantaisie.* Water-color.

MR. H. L. DOUSMAN'S COLLECTION.

ALVAREZ, LUIS.—*Marriage of Pauline Bonaparte to Prince Borghese.*
ARRER, W.—*Dolce far niente.*
"   " —*The Young Mother.*
AUBERT, E. J.—*The Lesson in Harmony.*
BACHEREAU, V.—*Last Hours of the Duke of Guise.*
BOUGUEREAU, W. A.—*The Guardian Angel.*
"   " —*Young Bohemians.*
CABANEL, A.—*Eve After the Fall.*
CARANOVA, A.—*La Vieta.*
CHELMONSKI, J.—*Mail Carrier.*
CHLEBOWSKI, ST.—*Arab Women at the Carpet-Merchant's.*
CLAUS, P. J.—*Port of Ostend.*
CONSTANT, B.—*The Daughter of Cæsar.*
"   " —*The Sultan's Favorite.*
COOMANS, P. O. J.—*The Cup of Friendship.*
COROT, J. B. C.—*Morning.*
CRACKARAEL.—*The Turk's War Booty.*
DE HAAS, J. H. L.—*Cattle in the Meadows of Holland.*
DE NEUVILLE, A.—*Bivouac.*
DIAZ DE LA PENA, N.—*La Tristesse.*
DUPRÉ, JULES.—*Autumn Morning.*
DURAN.—*Oriental Woman.*
"   " —*Head of a Girl.*
GROS, L. A.—*Seigneur—Time of Henri II.*
GRÜS, A.—*Courtship.*
HAGBORG, A.—*L'Attendant.*
HEILBUTH, F.—*Morning Mail.*

MR. H. L. DOUSMAN'S COLLECTION.

Concluded.

INDONI, P.—*Borghese Villa.*
JACQUET, J. G.—*Cinderella.*
JOURDAN, A.—*Virginity.*
KRAY, W.—*Lorki.*
"   " —*The Fishers.*
"   " —*The Swimming-Lesson.*
LAGYE, V.—*The Departure.*
LECOMTE, PH.—*A Servant.*
LECOMTE DU NOÜY, J. J. A.—*Christian Women at the Chapel of the Virgin.*
LELOIR, A. L.—*Temptation of St. Anthony.*
MADRAZO, R.—*Spanish Dance.*
"   " —*Bal Masqué.*
MAX, G.—*Maternal Happiness.*
"   " —*Study—Head.*
MEISSONIER, J. L. E.—*Musketeer.*
MORGHONT, F.—*Environs of Lagny.*
MEYER VON BREMEN.—*Leaving Home.*
MORRAU, A.—*Strolling through the Woods.*
MULLER, C. L.—*The Roll-Call of the Condemned.*
ODINI, P.—*Femme Marocain.*
PALMAROLI, V.—*Pompeian Woman's Toilet.*
"   " —*The Pretty Model.*
"   " —*Sketching on the Seaside.*
PERRAULT, L.—*The Prayer.*
POSCHART, L.—*Chrysalis.*
PLOCKHORST, B.—*Christ taking Leave of his Mother.*
"   " —*Christ on the Way to Emmaus.*
RICHTER, G.—*The Bayadère.*
RICO, D. M.—*Entrance to the Grand Canal, Venice.*
ROSSI, L.—*Garden of Fontainebleau.*
SCHAEFELS, H. F.—*Return from Hawking.*
SCHENCK, A. F. A.—*Snow Storm in the Pyrenees.*
SCHINDEL, P. VAN.—*Market-Woman.*
SCHREYER, A.—*Wallachian Horses on the Lower Danube.*
SIMONI, G.—*A Court-Jester.*
SJAMAAR, —*Interior.*
TERRADA, G. H.—*Fortuny's Atelier.*
TOULMOUCHE, A.—*The Flowers.*
VELY, A.—*The Heart Awakened.*
VERBOECKHOVEN, E. J.—*Sheep and Lambs.*
VILLEGAS, —*Le Connoisseur de Faïence.*
VOILLEMOT, A. C.—*Spring.*
"   " —*Summer.*
WAGNER, F.—*Evening Devotions.*
ZIEM, F.—*Grand Canal, Venice.*

MR. J. J. O'FALLON'S COLLECTION.

BOUGUEREAU, W. A.—*The Elder Sister.*
BRENAUNE, FRANCISCO.—*Marguerite.* Marble.
COOMANS, JOS.—*The Future Emperor's Education.*
JACQUET, G.—*Lady of the Directoire.*
LINGLAR, A.—*The Jungfrau.*
MORRAU, A.—*Looking Out.*
ROSSI, J.—*Fruit and Flowers.*
SCHREYER, A.—*The Attack by Arabs.*
STROEBEL, A.—*Dutch Interior.*
VERBOECKHOVEN, E.—*Flemish Bull.*
VIBERT, J. G.—*A State Secret.*

LE HÉRO DE LA FÊTE

ARTIST

ANTONIO CASANOVA

BORN AT TORDERA, SPAIN . . . . PUPIL OF F. DE MADRAZO

COLLECTION OF

MR. VICTOR NEWCOMB, LOUISVILLE, KY.

MARRIAGE OF THE ADRIATIC.
FAC-SIMILE OF A SKETCH FROM THE ORIGINAL PAINTING BY F. GUBL.

INLAND ART TREASURES.

N important picture gallery has been partly inherited and partly collected by Mr. H. Victor Newcomb, of Louisville, Kentucky. The selection of pictures is characteristic of the highest taste, and the best modern artists are represented. A beautiful little specimen of Alma-Tadema's early style, before his removal to London, represents "A Lady of Ancient Rome Returning Home." A placid, imperious dame, with the great bunch of forehead curls worn in the time of the later emperors, returns from a promenade, accompanied by her little boy who has brought home a wreath for his father's bust, and a domestic bondwoman. The slave who acts as porter opens the portal reverentially, holding in his hand a great hoop or ring, on which are the household keys. The usual inscriptions of welcome or warning are seen on the door-sill, "Salve," and "Cave Canem," both borrowed from existing Mosaics, at Pompeii. One of the painter's objects in this picture seems to be to combat the idea we are apt to derive from the statues

and ruins, that the ancients wore bleak, white garments, and lived in an architecture that was square, monumental and unrelieved. On the contrary, as he here shows us, their houses were softened with hangings and garlands, and their robes were sprigged and checkered as gaily as the Japanese. This precious little panel was exhibited at Gambart's, London, in 1871, as a recent picture. It shows that studious antiquarianism in which Alma-Tadema leads all the world of artists, along with his unexceptionable qualities as a highly-chastened, fastidious master of technic. Laurent Alma-Tadema, the reader may need to be reminded, is a Dutchman, born at Droonaryp in 1836; at the age of sixteen, in 1852, he entered the studio of Baron Leys, whose style he follows, changing the mediæval antiquarianism of his master for a classical antiquarianism. His pictures were for a long time the gems of the Paris and Belgian exhibitions, but it is a remarkable thing that the English journalists were in those days quite insensible to his uncommon merit. When he became a Londoner, at the Prussian war epoch of 1871, British criticism instantly discovered that he was the most exquisite artist living—a singular instance of the impartiality and penetration of the experts of Albion.—The large canvas by L. Courtat (8 x 5 feet), representing "Hagar and Ishmael," was painted in 1877. The story of the thirst that was nigh consuming the Arab race in its inception, forms a powerful motive for this young and ambitious painter. He places the scene among the sand-mountains, where nothing grows but the aloe—emblem of aridity. A horror of solitude and desolation encloses the two figures; the boy, destined to found the tribes of Ishmael, lies naked on the hot sand, hardly able to drink from the jar of miraculous water which the mother anxiously presses to his lips; the angel has disappeared. The slave Hagar has the vulgar type of the bondwoman, and her maternal tenderness is for the present only shown in unbeautiful anxiety: she will do her part, she will save the race, but she shows no sweetness in her expression, no beauty in her features. The painter is not very archæological, for he represents Hagar's head encircled with coins, like a modern almeh's, though it may most reasonably be doubted whether stamped coinage was invented in Abraham's time.—"Marie de Médicis Receiving the Nuptial Gifts of Henri IV" is a courtly bit of painting by Lesrel, executed in 1879. Lesrel is a careful finisher, but he is not an inspired master of composition, and singular infelicities sometimes escape him. For instance, in this arrangement of his, there are four hands, all pointing to the left, and reminding the spectator of guide-boards at the cross-roads. The picture is sumptuous in its material, though dry in its technic. Cellini's richest gold ewer and plateau have been chosen to plead the cause of the gallant king; an envoy as pretty as a troubadour, in very new gloves and boots, points out their merits to the daughter of the Médici, who sits in gala dress and lays a hand on her heart. Marie has the pinched lips and presumably reddish nose of her coins, struck with all haste after her coveted regency; it will be remembered that she insisted with great energy on having a special coronation, and that Henri was assassinated next day. The pompous glories of her mid-career are painted with all the splendor of Rubens' brush in the long gallery of the Louvre. On the day of her coronation she looked so rosy and handsome that the dissolute king was for the first time struck, and said he could really love her if she were his mistress instead of his wife. Her patronage of Rubens was returned when the great painter gave her a refuge in his house at Antwerp, where she crept to shelter in age and poverty, harshly exiled by Louis XIII.—By Gallait, the venerable and powerful emotional painter of Brussels, the Newcomb gallery contains a fine picture of "Mendicants" (3 x 4 feet). The old beggar is blind; his guide is dying;—who so lost as they! The world must indeed seem pathless, as the aged wanderer, turning his sightless eyes in vain for succor, cherishes in his lap the feeble boy, whose almost lifeless hand the dog is licking. Misery has no more complete image.—That satirist of clerical things, Casanova, in "The Hero of the Fête," represents a gigantic Franciscan, whom some lively dames of the court of Carlo IV have tempted into their saloon, made tipsy with grapes of Xeres, and persuaded to dance in his bare, sandal-clattering feet. He complies with a will, and a slender girl, delicate as an insect, malicious as an ogress, catches her flower-like skirts in front of him and executes with him the contra-danse. This persistent sarcasm against the church, this resolute degradation of its ministers, until one fancies they are all guzzlers and bibbers, leaves an aftertaste of disgust in the critical mouth, however clever the witticism. Antonio Casanova y Estorach,

we may recall, was born at Tortosa, in Spain, August 9, 1847. His early years were clouded by the indigence of his family, and he was only thirteen when, abandoning a literary education, he began to cultivate his marketable quality of natural draughtsmanship at the Fine-Arts School of Barcelona. He afterwards took lessons of Claudio Lorenzale and of Federico Madrazo, father of the more famous Ramon. In 1871, at the age of twenty-four, the goal of his young ambition was reached by the attainment of the prize of Rome, enabling him to work and study in Italy at government charge. A few years later, in 1875, he brought his talents to market in Paris, exposed "The Victims of a Pillage" in the Salon of 1876, and has since resided, full of business and honors, at the French capital.—Schreyer contributes the "Wallachian Teamsters fast in the Snow" (6 x 4 feet), painted with his usual energy and power. Several shrinking horses, stalled in the snow-storm, put their noses together in deepest discouragement; one would never think that these dejected heads could bridle and toss in the delights of racing; the fur-capped visage of the groom emerges from among their hanging skulls and draggled manes; at the left the driver works with a crowbar to extricate the wheel from the frozen rut.— Probably the most important name in the gallery is that of Paul Delaroche, by whose hand is an exquisite color-study of "Christ at Gethsemane" (4 x 6 inches); it shows the clear, felicitous sense of arrangement with which Delaroche distributed the personages of his groups, and the principal figure, even in this sketch, expresses a great deal by a simple attitude.—By Edouard Frère is "The Little Flageolet-Player" (7 x 8 inches); in this tranquil theme a rustic boy, in a round country hat, sits on a stone at the right, and a standing younger child at the left watches and listens; the subject is treated with all of Frère's usual quiet pastoral tenderness.—R. Sorbi is shown in a subject of "A Pompeian Girl" (3 x 4 feet) a standing maiden in simple antique tunic, who with both hands holds a little cluster of carnation-flowers to her bosom. —By Meissonier is seen a very good specimen, a "Halberdier" (6 x 8 inches), wonderfully polished and finished from his steel helmet to his rawhide shoes; he stands erect, in a soldierly attitude, in the military costume of that period dear to painters—the Louis XIII period in France, the Cromwell period in England.—Bruck-Lajos is the painter of a "Fruit-Girl and Boy" (3 x 4 feet); a pair of lively life-size figures painted with a good deal of skill, in Paris, in 1878.—"Temptation," by the frank Scotch humorist Erskine Nicol, shows a boy and a jam-pot. It was painted in 1877.—Bouguereau contributes "The Little Reader," a canvas of 1879, showing in profile view the figure of a female child, turned to the spectator's right, and bending over a volume.—L. Jiminez has a "Young Lady of the Directoire," perched on a garden wall. —V. Palmaroli shows a "Girl Reading;" Sonderland, "The Dispute"—two little children quarreling; C. de Chirico, "The Steep Street," one of the staircase streets common in Naples, with peasants coming down towards the spectator; it was painted at Naples in 1878.—Ziem shows a fine stretch of "The Grand Canal" (6 x 4 feet), including the Salute Church on the left and Ducal Palace at the right, with a liberal stretch of the wider part of the Canal between them. O. Meyer's "Tambourine Girl," painted at Rome in 1863, is a piquant vision of a saucy Bohemian beauty. Sidney Cooper, the very popular English cattle-painter, is seen to advantage in a canvas entitled "Early Morning in the Highlands" (5×3 feet). It has been thus charmingly described by the late John R. Thompson, the southern poet-writer, whose polished pen dropped from his hand in New York a few years since, in a death-scene soothed by the company of Bryant and the best of the literary guild. "The distance slowly fills with light, the mist sweeping away before the morning sun. The cow risen to her feet, but still inactive, dreamily awaits the accustomed milking. On the left, some goats having taken refuge in the glen from the damps of night, now climb the hill to meet the genial warmth. The foreground group lends unwilling ears to morning's 'summons to fresh fields' of 'verdure dewed.' One of the number, while assenting with one eye, settles his head comfortably for a second nap; another resumes the cud, as if declining breakfast. Those risen to their feet have the air of sleepy soldiers at reveille, roused, perhaps, by a wholesome fear of the sheep-dog, for they have strayed from the flock in the darkness. The whole band protests by attitude and expression against such hours."

E. Leutze is represented by a picture certainly possessing a strong interest, and an interest destined to increase vastly with time. It depicts "A Western Emigrant Train, bound for California, Across the Plains, alarmed by the approach of Hostile Indians." Leutze was not the great artist that he

THE NUPTIAL GIFTS OF MARIE DE MÉDICIS.
FACSIMILE OF A SKETCH FROM THE ORIGINAL PAINTING BY A. LOREL.

perhaps thought himself; but in pictures like this, and like the "Westward Ho!" of the Capitol at Washington, he

has accumulated a mass of notes, of types, of characteristic details, for which the coming historical painter will one day bless his memory.

FIGURES FROM "THE HERO OF THE FÊTE."
FACSIMILE OF A SKETCH FROM THE ORIGINAL PAINTING BY A. CASANOVA.

A precious picture, likewise in the Newcomb gallery, is J. F. Millet's "Milk-Jar," a subject of a girl returned from milking; she poises her jar on her head by means of a cord held by her extended hand. This Millet has been illustrated in the article on Mr. J. C. Runkle's collection in this work, being essentially a replica of Mr. Runkle's example and also of one owned by Mrs. A. E. Borie.

Mr. W. H. Fosdick, of Louisville, has a collection which was largely gathered together under those circumstances desired by every purchaser for himself—discerning selections made when cheap, of artists' work destined to become dear. No compliment that can be paid a connoisseur is so eloquent as this rhetoric of facts, proving an unusual and enviable discrimination and an eye for merit before its acknowledgment by the world. By Chelmonski is seen the "Sleighing in Russia" (6½×3 feet); it shows a pair of very spirited black horses, galloping as if possessed by a fiend, and dragging, over a frightful road—about as rough as a natural glacier—the sleigh in which are a cowering lady and an excited driver; the coachman's cloak lifts in the wind and violently thrashes his head and shoulders, and he as energetically thrashes the team with his long whip.—"The Orange Girl" by Félix Henri Giacomotti (3×4 feet), is an unique treasure by an artist otherwise hardly known in America, and whose works we have not previously encountered in the course of these researches. In Paris he is considered one of the blue-blooded princes of portraiture, his female likenesses combining in rare degree the sterling qualities that artists demand, along with the sense of social graces demanded by sitters. The "Orange Girl" is reposing with ease and grace on the steps of a portico, a plate of Sorrento fruit by her side; her tattered shoes and humble costume bespeak poverty, but the wealth of beauty is opulently displayed in her face and in the fine Roman modeling of her hands and frame. The color is very rich, the distinction of posture and temperament is clearly asserted through the indigence of the subject, and every beauty who contemplates the picture must needs sigh to have her portrait executed by an artist who comprehends so well how to make the points of a fair woman tell in painting. Giacomotti was born in France, at Quingey, Doubs, attained the prize of Rome in Paris, in 1854, and, after various medals, received the cross of the Legion of Honor in 1867.—"Rabbits at Play" (4 x 2 feet), in Mr. Fosdick's collection, is by no less a celebrity than Mr. Tom Taylor, the late editor of *Punch*,

Mr. F. D. Corley, also of Louisville, has a curiosity of a house in the modern decorative style, the parlor-floor being inlaid with the musical notes of *Home, Sweet Home* and the cabinets and cupboards overflowing with *virtù*. His most important picture is an excellent "Tambourine Girl," by Arthur Hill, an oriental figure in long clinging robe; his remaining pictures, such as Quartley's illustration of Edgar Fawcett's poem, *The White Gulls Float*, and Meyer's "Ring-around-a-Rosy" are well chosen and valuable.—Mr. George N. Moore, of the same city, possesses a numerous collection of modern pictures, including "The Joint Investment," a lively boot-black incident by Wood, of New York.—Also in

ROMAN LADY RETURNING FROM SHOPPING.
FAC-SIMILE OF A SKETCH FROM THE ORIGINAL PAINTING BY L. ALMA-TADEMA

biographer of Reynolds and Leslie, and playwright of *The Fool's Revenge*. It is certainly unexpected to see so much technical excellence in an amateur, and the picture is justly regarded as an object of *haute curiosité*. A company of well-painted rabbits, life-size, are playing blind-man's-buff in a forest dell. The texture of fur and the knowledge of animal anatomy would not shame Landseer, and the soft moonlight stealing through the foliage, over the crisp and dewy turf, shows landscape merit of a high order. The picture was executed in 1864.—Carl Becker shows "The Farewell," a handsome girl leaving an apartment with a gesture of adieu. By Coomans is "Nydia," a standing figure, with a nude boy seated alongside, and the blindness of the heroine asserted without offensiveness. A small painting by Kaemmerer, with two figures, "The Amanuensis;" Comte's "Don Quixotte;" E. De Beaumont's "Vandyke Painting;" and the American Hamilton's grand and tumultuous "Storm-Scene from 'David Copperfield'" (4 x 3 feet) also deserves notice in Mr. Fosdick's collection.

Louisville is the interesting collection of Mr. Jouett Menifee, a grandson of one of Gilbert Stuart's best pupils, the western prodigy, Matthew Jouett. This collection, being composed more especially of "Old Masters," does not come entirely within the scope of the present work, the adjudication of the rights of such claimants requiring ample time and great caution; the catalogue titles include an "Ecce Homo" by Carlo Dolci, a "Saint Sebastian" by Guercino, an "Annunciation" by Paoli Farinati, "Hercules and Diana" by Santo Creara; and a "St. Michael," by Solimena. Mr. Menifee owns several portraits by Matthew Jouett, a considerable one representing a "Mother and Child;" the works of this artist, who settled in Kentucky, are of great interest in the history of American art; some of them are engraved in the *National Portrait Gallery*, and hold their own with the portraits of Stuart and Neagle. Mr. Menifee's collection likewise contains a large and brilliant scheme for decorating the new State Capitol of Kentucky with the adventures of Daniel Boone—

VIRGINIA

ARTIST
JAMES BERTRAND

BORN AT LYONS, FRANCE   . PUPIL OF PLAIN,

COLLECTION OF
MR. RUFUS B. KELLOGG, GREEN BAY, WIS.

an enterprise into which the French artist, Victor Nehlig, threw himself heart and soul, without succeeding in obtaining the commission for the work. In this complicated color-study are seen an elaborate centre-piece, showing Boone and his men viewing the plains of Kentucky from the Alleghanies, and adjacent subjects, such as the wounding of Boone's son by Indians in the father's presence, an Indian village fired by whites, and an Indian attack on a block fort.—Capt. S. F. MILLER, in Louisville, owns among others two large pictures, "The Haymakers" by C. Raupp, and "Lauterbrunnen" by August Hoeter.—At the house of Mr. A. R. COOPER are seen many pictures by his relative, Eugene Benson, including "Worship at Cadore" (exhibited in 1876 at the Royal Academy), "Sunset during a Sirocco, Venice," "Afternoon on the Lagoon," "Interior of St. Marks," "Renunciation," and "The Reverential Anatomist."—In the Roman Catholic Cathedral of Louisville is to be seen a large and highly interesting picture, claimed with reason to be an original Vandyke, and representing, in a great crowd, a warrior receiving extreme unction on the battle-field.

In the city of Chicago, Mr. LEITER, of the firm of Field, Leiter & Co., owns a collection that forms one of the important galleries of the West. Among Mr. LEITER's paintings is an important example of Cabanel, representing "Phædra," the queen of Theseus, enduring the torments of Venus in a mad passion for the boy Hippolytus.—Mr. CHAUNCEY J. BLAIR, likewise of the city of Chicago, owns some interesting

TONING THE BELL.
ENGRAVED BY MEISENBACH FROM THE ORIGINAL PAINTING, BY WALTER SHIRLAW.

THE MENDICANTS.
ENGRAVED BY A SKETCH FROM THE ORIGINAL PAINTING, BY A. MALLAT.

pictures, including the admirable subject by De Nittis, called "Isn't it Cold?" On a freezing winter day some ladies have descended from their carriage, in a public park, and are creeping, with timid steps, along through the snow and ice, with a vast sense of their own courage. The feeling of frosty atmosphere is admirably conveyed in this canvas. Mr. BLAIR's collection also comprises an "Oriental Fountain" by Pasini, "The Hague" by César de Cock, and "The Coquette" by Jules Worms.—Mr. H. J. WILLING, also of Chicago, includes among his collection of pictures "The Toning of the Bell" by Walter Shirlaw, a painter born in Scotland and educated in Munich, but classed among American artists from his long residence in the United States. The cut gives an excellent idea of this picture. A bell for the carillon of some church of the old faith has just been cast, and lies proudly on its side, decorated with bass-reliefs of the crucifixion; the founder strikes its rim with a hammer, to exhibit its sound to the *kappelmeister*, who touches his violin with the needed note. The heads of the two men skillfully indicate two methods of careful listening, on the part of a person of high education and one of natural good sense respectively. The picture is crowded with very happy accessories; the child bringing up its doll, cradled in a wooden shoe, with the urchin who mocks the violinist by a performance on the bellows, and the gravity of a listening bull-dog, adding variously to the life of the scene. "The Grandmother's Surprise," a vivacious picture by the Munich artist, Vollmar, may be mentioned as another noticeable work in Mr. WILLING's collection.

Mr. J. RUSSELL JONES, also of Chicago, owns a full representation of the modern Belgian school, including Clays,

WALLACHIAN TEAMSTERS FAST IN THE SNOW.
FAC-SIMILE OF A SKETCH FROM THE ORIGINAL PAINTING BY J. SCHREYER.

who contributes a fine "Marine," Burnier with a "Coming from the Pasture," Louis Robbe with a cattle-piece, Verlat, and Verboeckhoven; Schreyer's "Watering the Horses," and "Deer in the Frost," by Charles Jacque, are also comprised in this interesting collection.

Mr. S. M. NICKERSON, another resident of Chicago, owns an art collection, represented by such specimens as Gustave Doré's "Loch Katrine," Escosura's "Before the Departure," Madou's "Old Cronies," D. Neal's "Interior of St. Mark's, at Venice," and E. Vedder's "Landscape near Rome."

Ex-Minister RUFUS B. KELLOGG, of Green Bay, Wisconsin, includes in his collection of paintings the large and favorite picture of "Virginia," by James Bertrand, of which we have noted the smaller color-study in the New York gallery of Mr. J. Wolfe; it illustrates the closing scene from the immortal story by Bernardin de Saint-Pierre. "One of the first objects I saw upon the beach was the body of Virginia. The features were not changed, her eyes were closed, but the brow still retained its expression of serenity, and on her cheeks was the livid hue of death, blended with the blush of virgin modesty." A specimen by the well-known landscape painter Bierstadt, "King's River, California," is likewise shown among the honorable collector's treasures.

Also in Wisconsin, is to be noticed the tasteful collection of Mrs. ALEXANDER MITCHELL, of Milwaukee, consisting of about ninety pictures, in oil or aquarelle. A water-color by Sir John Gilbert, "The Cavalier," Vertunni's "View of Boulak" and "Stone Pines," a "Breton Boy" by Lanfant de Metz, Mrs. Jerichau's "Egyptian Water-Carrier," and Bierstadt's "Camp Fire" may be mentioned among the contents.

In the city of Cleveland, Ohio, is found the collection of Mr. H. B. HURLBUT, the president of the Cincinnati, Cleveland, Columbus and Indianapolis Railroad. This collector possesses a fine specimen of Félix Ziem, the most celebrated of the modern illustrators of Venice. It represents "The Marriage of the Adriatic," and shows the Doge, in the good old days, about to embark in a skiff, at the Quai dei Schiavoni, to take his place in the bucentaur, and steer into the open

channel, where he will drop the wedding-ring into the liquid lap of his political bride. This consort, by the by, needed a deal of marrying, the ceremony having to be renewed year by year. The same gallery contains, among many well-chosen canvases, "The Betrothal" by De Vriendt, the excellent Belgian painter. It represents an innocent and fair girl, in the modest dress and white wimple of the Middle Ages, standing at a latticed casement and gazing down dreamily at the betrothment-ring.

Mr. HURLBUT's gallery in fact contains a fair showing of the more prominent celebrities of the day, in all the continental schools, whether French, Belgian or German, not to speak of the American. Even the modern Spanish-Roman school, *dernier mot* of unorthodox art, is shown in such samples as Palmaroli's "In a Garden," and, by Escosura— that perfunctory continuation of the dead and gone genius Zamacois—the "Return from the Hunt." One of Cabanel's refined, evaporated types is the "Ginevra Amieri" in this collection. Cabanel has a singular fondness for introducing the character of modern valetudinarian and nervous refinement into his studies of antique traditions. To look at his languid and emaciated heroines, all oppressed with fancied

THE BETROTHAL.
FAC-SIMILE OF A SKETCH FROM THE ORIGINAL PAINTING BY A. DE VRIENDT.

woes,—derived apparently from reading Chateaubriand and Senancourt,—you would fancy the personages of a modern

"Isn't it Cold?"

ARTIST

GIUSEPPE DE NITTIS

Born at Barletta, Italy   Pupil of Gérôme

COLLECTION OF

MR. CHAUNCEY J. BLAIR, CHICAGO

æsthetic salon carried back into the costumes and situations of legendary epochs. Bouguereau shows his polished and marble-cutting style—too fine for daily life but undeniably exquisite—in a subject of "Italian Mother and Children." Jules Breton exhibits a manlier method and a more thoughtful depth of true feeling in a pastoral figure designated as "The Tired Gleaner." Edouard Frère shows one of his simple, Burns-like scenes of cottage-life in the group of "Mother and Children." Jacquet's "Study of a Head" gives at least an *échantillon* of his subtle refinement and poem-like grace. The late Hugues Merle—in whose death Bouguereau gets rid of his closest rival—bequeathes a subject called "Contemplation." Toulmouche's crisp and enameled finish is characteristically seen in a figure known as "Reverie." Schreyer's "Scene in Wallachia" takes us, for the hundredth time, among the rough horses and primitive civilization of the provinces by the Danube. With these examples, the brilliant painters of the Paris exhibitions may be held to have a fair showing in the city of Cleveland. The modern emancipated group of Munich is also shown with effect; Fritz Kaulbach, who has struck out a line of novel originality and beauty in his delicate heroines and châtelaines—a series holding affinity rather with Makart and Siemiradski than with the old official allegorical style of the elder Kaulbach,—is represented by two pictures, "A Shady Place," and a "Study of a Head," more highly finished than the apologetic term of a "study" need necessarily imply. Beyschlag's "Before the Wedding" is young Germany again, and shows a style not unlike Fritz Kaulbach's. Gabriel Max, with another "Head," brings into the collection a breath of that intellectual and rather morbid imagination which has invented so many tragedies and celebrated so many fair martyrs. Altogether, the HURLBUT gallery is eclectic and cosmopolitan.

Mr. GEORGE WORTHINGTON, also of Cleveland, distinguishes with special favor, among his pictures, the "Expecta-

SLEIGHING IN RUSSIA.
FAC-SIMILE OF A SKETCH FROM THE ORIGINAL PAINTING BY J. CHELMINSKI.

tion" (5 × 3½ feet), considered as the masterpiece of Professor Bianchi, of Milan. It represents three Italian girls standing just without a gateway, in the rear of a country house of northern Italy, on the lookout for the arrival of the lover of one or another of them. The look of expectancy in the exquisite face of the maiden more immediately interested is most expressive and fascinating. This important canvas was executed in 1878, and shown in its freshness at the Paris Universal Exposition of that year.

Having gotten into the commonwealth of Ohio with the gallery just considered, the collections of Cincinnati, in that State, might be added to the contents of the present chapter. It would be hardly suitable, however, to consider the wealth of such an art-centre as Cincinnati at the end of a scattered selection of Western galleries, and its opulent treasures of painting and statuary will therefore be described in the ensuing article.

HAGAR AND ISHMAEL.
FAC-SIMILE OF A SKETCH FROM THE ORIGINAL PAINTING BY L. COGNIET.

COLLECTIONS IN THE CITY OF LOUISVILLE.

MR. W. H. FOSDICK'S COLLECTION.

Becker, Carl.—*The Farewell.*
Brissot, F.—*Cattle.*
Castiglioni, G.—*Plucking the Rose.*
Coelmonska, J.—*Sleighing in Russia.*
Comte, E.—*Don Quixote.*
Coomans, J.—*Nydia.*
De Beaumont, Ed.—*Vandyck Painting.*
Giacomotti, F. H.—*The Orange Girl.*
Hamilton, James.—*Death of Stonefroth.*
Henry, Col. Alfred.—*Genevieve.*
Hubner, E.—*Peasant Girls Playing with Rabbit.*
Humbert, Chas.—*Cattle.*
Kaemmerer, F. H.—*The Amusement.*
Lebel, Edouard.—*The Dancer.*
Morrau, A.—*Pompeian Girl with Parrot.*
Noel, Jules.—*On the Bosphorus.*
Robie, J.—*Straw Hat and Roses.*
Signac, P.—*The Lesson.*
Taylor, Tom.—*Rabbits Playing Blindman's-Buff.*
Toulmouche, A.—*Reverie.*
Weber, Paul.—*River Landscape.*

MR. GEO. N. MOORE'S COLLECTION.

Beard, W. H.—*The Tramp.*
Castan, E.—*The Evening Prayer.*

MR. GEO. N. MOORE'S COLLECTION.

Concluded.

De Beul, L.—*Shepherd and Flock.*
Delaroche, L.—*Council Cemetery.*
Gernac, L. A.—*Italian Refugees.*
Kuwasseg, C., Fils.—*View at Cernac.*
Lautheimer, A.—*The Memorandum Book.*
Maes, E. R.—*Group of Chickens.*
Percy, S. R.—*Near Dodgeport, North Wales.*
Rousseau, J.—*Interior.*
Rossenboom, A.—*The Latest Acquisition.*
Roy, Y.—*Grand Square et Bruges.*
Toussaint, L.—*The Tourist.*
Vertisson, A.—*Chickens.*
Volkers, E.—*The Brown Mare.*
Vooguerd, W. J.—*Horses.*
Wickstead, R.—*On the Beach at Trouville.*
Wood, T. W.—*The Joint Investment.*

MR. H. V. NEWCOMB'S COLLECTION.

Alma Tadema, L.—*Roman Lady Returning Home.*
Bouguereau, W. A.—*The Little Reader.*
Brown, J. G.—*Nautilack Munching on Apple.*
Bruck-Lajos, L.—*Fruit-Girl.*
Chisco, C.—*The Steep Street, Naples.*

MR. H. V. NEWCOMB'S COLLECTION.

Concluded.

Cooper, Sidney.—*The Herd in the Mountains.*
Courtat, L.—*Hagar and Ishmael.*
Delaroche, Paul.—*Gethsemane.*
Frere, E.—*The Little Flute-Player.*
Gallait, L.—*The Mendicants.*
Gerome, J. L.—*Circassian Girl.*
Lambinet, Eugene.—*Landscape.*
Leibel, A.—*Marie de Medicis Receiving Nuptial Gifts from Henri IV.*
Meisner, E.—*Sheep and Poultry.*
Meissonier, Charles.—*A Courtier.*
Meissonier, J. L. E.—*Halberdier.*
Meyer, O.—*Three Little Smokers.*
   "   " —*Tambourine Girl.*
Mulley, J. F.—*The Milk-Jar.*
Nicol, Erskine.—*Temptation.*
Palmaroli, V.—*Girl Reading.*
Salmon, Charles.—*Shepherdess and Sheep.*
Schrayer, A.—*Wallachian Teamsters Fast in the Snow.*
Shayer, W.—*The Oracle of the Fields.*
Sinderland, V.—*Two Children Disputing.*
Sorel, R.—*Pompeian Girl.*
Watson, J.—*Sitting Counselor.*
Ziem, V.—*Grand Canal, Venice.*

THE CITY OF CLEVELAND.

MR. H. B. HURLBUT'S COLLECTION.

Adan, Emile.—*Room at Fontainebleau.*
Baugniet, C.—*After the Ball.* [color.
Bellows, A. F.—*Sunday in New England.* Water-
Beyschlag, R.—*Before the Wedding.*
Bocher, Otto.—*Objects of Art.*
Bouguereau, W. A.—*Italian Mother and Children.*
Breton, Jules.—*The Tired Gleaner.*
Daichis, A. T.—*Landscape.*
Brown, J. G.—*Cold Comfort.*
Carabel, A.—*Ginevra Amieri.*
Cassat, E.—*Feeding the Kitten.*
Chapman, John G.—*Returning from the Vintage.*
   "   "   —*The Seasons.*
   "   "   —*Threshing Wheat on the Campagna.*
Church, F. E.—*Monastery—"Our Lady of the Snow."*
De Haas, M. F. H.—*Moonlight at Sea.*
De Vroemt, A.—*The Betrothal.*
Demotte, Blaise.—*Flowers and Objects of Art.*
Diaz, N.—*A Forest Scene.*
Durand, A. B.—*Berkshire Hills.*
Fichel, E.—*Lunch Time.*

MR. H. B. HURLBUT'S COLLECTION.

Continued.

Frere, Edward.—*Mother and Children.*
Frere, Theodore.—*Scene on the Nile.*
Gifford, S. R.—*View in Venice.*
Hart, J. M.—*Morning in New England.*
Hart, William.—*Autumn Scene in the Adirondacks.*
Heade, M. J.—*High Tide on the Marshes.*
   "   " —*South American Scene.*
   "   " —*Apple-Blossoms.*
Irving, J. B.—*A Cavalier.*
Jacquet, J. G.—*Study of a Head.*
Johnson, Eastman.—*Interior of a Nantucket Kitchen.*
   "   "   —*Boy Fishing.*
Kaulbach, F. A.—*Study of a Head.*
   "   "   —*A Shady Place.*
Knaus, L.—*Head of a Madonna.*
Lalky Escosura, I.—*Return from the Hunt.*
Max, Gabriel.—*Study of a Head.*
McEntee, Jervis.—*Autumn in the Catskills.*
Merle, H.—*Contemplation.*
Meyer von Bremen, J. G.—*Saying Grace.*
Meyerheim, F.—*Present Children.*
Moran, Thomas.—*St. George's Island.*

MR. H. B. HURLBUT'S COLLECTION.

Concluded.

Palmaroli, V.—*Garden Scene.*
Peale, Rembrandt.—*Head of Washington.*
Preyer, E.—*Fruit-Piece.*
Robie, J.—*Flowers.*
Rogers, R.—*Nydia.* Sculpture.
Schreyer, Ad.—*Winter Scene in Wallachia.*
Seitz, Anton.—*Charity.*
Smith, Henry P.—*An English Cottage.*
Stentt, Arthur J.—*Roman Aqueduct.*
   "   "   —*Appian Way.*
Tait, A. F.—*Historical Solitude.*
Terry, Luther.—*Ruth and Naomi.*
Tilton, J. R.—*Lake Como.*
   "   " —*Venice.*
Toulmouche, A.—*Reverie.*
Van Elten, K.—*Windmills in Holland.*
   "   " —*Landscape.*
Verboeckhoven, Eugene.—*Sheep and Chickens.*
Volte, Francis.—*Cattle and Landscape.*
Webb, Carl M.—*Wine-Tasters.*
Wood, T. W.—*No Smoking Here!*
Ziem, Felix.—*Marriage of the Adriatic.*

The Women and the Secret

(LA FONTAINE)

ARTIST

HUGUES MERLE

BORN AT SAINT-MARCELLIN, FRANCE, 1823   ·   ·   PUPIL OF COGNIET.

COLLECTION OF

MR. HENRY PROBASCO, CINCINNATI

FEEDING THE SHEEP.
FAC-SIMILE OF A SKETCH FROM THE ORIGINAL PAINTING BY C. JACQUE.

COLLECTIONS IN CINCINNATI.

LETTING our scrutiny begin with the magnificent picture-gallery of HENRY PROBASCO, Esq., we find ourselves at a suburban villa conveniently near the city, in the midst of a shady park, with the pugnacious group of Kiss's Amazon, in bronze, at the angle of the portico, to guard the portal of a house resembling a Genoese palazzo. The interior, with carved doors, stairways and panels, is chiefly a resumé of the different styles of carving in wood; but there are some very rare marbles in addition, among the columns and pedestals. Several of these pedestals or plinths are curiosities as well as ornaments, being derived from the most gorgeous times of antique or mediæval Rome. They must sometimes wonder, like Gautier's "Obelisk," how they got into the heart of a strange continent. Many of the paintings in this collection are quite famous in the annals of modern art, so that it is hardly needful in Mr. PROBASCO's case to illustrate the text with those fac-similes from the artists' drawings, which have been habitually used as aids to memory in other parts of this work, and the plates of his Kaulbach and Merle will suffice to sample the treasures of elegance and beauty. The celebrated

Kaulbach, "Mother-Love," is well known to the public from photographs, but the possession of the authentic work in the expansive majesty of its mighty size is naturally considered a high privilege by the proprietor. The figures in this original would seem to be somewhat larger than nature, and the group appears in its broad treatment a sort of altar-piece of the cultus of family piety. To give his subject the spacious effect designed, the painter found it necessary to add additional canvas for the background, and the joining, which can just be perceived in certain lights, impresses the eye with a sense of how his work grew on him as the artist proceeded, and as its capacity for monumental expansion became more evident. Seen in place, as the wall-picture of a dignified staircase-landing, it can be contemplated devoutly from below like a chancel-fresco, and doubtless yields for the faithful admirers of the German school a greater pleasure than any canvas in the country can bestow. It represents a mother, in vaguely classical draperies, nursing four children at once; but description here is unnecessary, as these pages have already alluded to its smaller replica in colors in the Gibson gallery, and to its cartoon in Governor Morgan's collection.—"The Secret," from the fable of La Fontaine, is one of the best pictures left by the late Hugues Merle, who when at his highest pitch of excellence may be granted the equal of Cabanel, Jalabert and Dubufe. The scene, of course, is at the village fountain, where the woman who has been made the guardian of the confidence is imparting it to her neighbor with strictest injunctions of privacy; the mighty matter will be as privately conveyed to a third party, and thence scattered like the ashes of Wicliffe; in fact "keeping a secret" may be termed the newspaper-press of primitive and provincial communities. Merle makes these prudent women young and beautiful,—the finest ideal of village comeliness. In the foreground he paints an urchin, who like all his childish figures is remarkably sturdy, handsome, and felicitous; the child is trying to pull away from his handsome blonde mother, whose attention is conscientiously bent on the fulfillment of her carrier-dove mission.—The great bulk of Mr. Probasco's art treasures, constituting undoubtedly the finest gallery of the West, can only be touched upon here in a cursory manner, though in no other case would it be so fascinating or so fruitful to

its article contained a beautiful pastoral bit of description, a peasant-scene, in the manner of George Sand, in her *Little Fadette*. Millet himself entered the field with a letter published since his death, in which he asks: "Apropos of what Jean Rousseau says about my men carrying a calf as if it were the sacrament of the bull Apis, how does he expect them to carry it? If he admits that they carry well, I need no more to be satisfied, and I would tell him that the expression of a couple of men carrying something on a litter depends upon the weight which hangs from their arms. Even if they were filled with admiration and reverence for what they were carrying, still they would be subject to the law of weight, and their expression could only be that of the

CLIFFS AT SCARBOROUGH.
ENGRAVED ON A SKETCH FROM THE ORIGINAL WATER-COLOR BY J. M. W. TURNER.

linger. The example of Jules Breton is most exquisite— "The Gleaners," a canvas in which he has garnered his treasures of light, color and grace; behind the stooping women the red sun sets, full in the middle of the horizon, while the sickle of the moon, faint as a cicatrice, marks the sky over the head of the standing woman at the left of the picture. This canvas was executed in 1866.—The example of Millet is a central type of his genius, the "Peasants Carrying a New-born Calf," of the year 1864. On the first exhibition of this picture the Paris press was almost unanimous in condemnation or ridicule of its serious treatment and solemnity; it was declared that the farmers bore the calf on its litter as if they were carrying the Host. Millet had witnessed this rustic scene at his birthplace, on one of his infrequent visits, and sketched and colored the whole incident from nature; the bearers of the calf were even members of his own family. The *Indépendance Belge*, in a criticism written by Thoré, was almost alone in praising the picture;

weight. The more they care to save the object carried, the more careful will be their manner of walking, and they will keep step. They must, in every case and always, keep step, and if they do not their fatigue will be more than doubled. And this is the secret of all this solemnity so much decried. But it is easy enough to find two porters carrying a bureau on a litter in Paris. Any one can see how they keep step. Let M. Jean Rousseau and any of his friends try to do the same and still keep a common gait; do they not know that a false step may make the burden jostle off?" Such were the discussions, such the hair-splitting arguments, on the first appearance of this noble picture.—The example of Delacroix is of a size, an importance, and a splendor of color that make it unique among the master's works owned in this country. It represents "Clotilda Delivering the Martyrs," from Tasso's *Jerusalem*. The lady knight is seen at the left, amid a cloud of chivalry, while lifted high at the right are the victims and the stake. It is hardly necessary to point out what a rainbow

Mother-Love

ARTIST
WILHELM VON KAULBACH

GERMANY, 1805.   DIED, 1874.   PUPIL OF CORNELIUS

COLLECTION OF
MR. HENRY PROBASCO, CINCINNATI, O.

of glory Delacroix would make of the subject, set in its Eastern sunshine. Clotilda, the tigress-nurtured Ethiopian

JOHN HUSS BEFORE THE COUNCIL OF CONSTANCE.
FAC-SIMILE OF A SKETCH FROM THE ORIGINAL PAINTING BY C. F. LESSING.

woman-general of the paynim troops, will receive Christian baptism ere she meets her death-blow, delivered by mishap by her lover in the night.—Couture's "Daydreams" is nearly a replica of the same subject already described and highly praised, in the article on Miss Wolfe's collection: it is likewise of life-size; the slate is turned the other way, however, and the dreaming scholar is more slightly painted. A white card stuck in the slate-frame has a gibing motto fit for a dunce-cap—"*haute aux paresseux*," or the like.—The small specimen of Alfred Stevens is thoroughly good—"The New Robe;" it was painted in 1866, and shows a standing lady, her face turned a little to the left, who parades a splendid silk spread over the expansive *cage* of that period.—The Fromentin is particularly fine, and is heralded among other Fromentins by the peculiarity of having "no horse in it." We see a per-spective of some Eastern street, with its passers-by, in a vista of white walls; in the foreground is an unusual throng, and therein, a little to the left, a group of three or four dancing jugglers; they flourish their bare arms, which Fromentin has been particularly careful in modeling.—By Gérôme is "Le Berger Syrien;" this reminiscence is devoted to the delinea-tion of a flock of black goats, with a shepherd standing near the mid-scene, all collected among the desolation of the desert sand-hills. The hot blast sweeps the sand in clouds in a cradle-shaped form, making a hollow vortex in the midst of which the dark shapes of the diabolical-looking goats are placed. The picture is unusually low in key for a landscape-effect of Gérôme's.—In the German school of art, Piloty is represented by a subject of "Elizabeth, Queen of Bohemia, Re-ceiving News of the Defeat at Prague." Elizabeth—offspring of the first Scotch king of England, and granddaughter of Mary Queen of Scots—prevailed on her husband, the Elector Palatine Frederick V, to take the proffered crown of Bohemia; but her ambition caused her husband's ruin, his acceptance involving him in war and leading to his defeat in the battle of Prague, in 1620, after which he lost even his hereditary estates, and died in exile. The picture is one of Piloty's

skillful fifth-act tableaus, with a banquet, a throng of gaudy courtiers, and a pale queen starting to her feet as the bad news is brought from the battle-field by a man in armor, who stands phantom-like at the left of the scene, to proclaim the defeat of ambition and the inevitable failure of any enterprise undertaken by one of the ill-fated Stuarts.—Baron Wappers is seen with a touching composition in the best style of the Belgian school, showing "Count Egmont's Family doing propitiatory Penance in the Streets of Brussels on the Eve of his Execution." In the midst of a crowd of sympathizing citizens are seen two or three drooping ladies, draped in black, slowly moving in a sad cortège of propitiatory suppli-cation.—Nicaise de Keyser is recognized in an ambitious and interesting composition, representing "Francis I at Fontaine-bleau," with the wits and beauties who gave lustre to his court. Here, in a splendid hall of his favorite palace, the magnificent king is grouped with an arbitrary assemblage of the heroes or the heroines of that golden age of the French renaissance. At the right of the indolent and splendid figure of the King are seen Diane de Poitiers and the Duchess d'Estampes, with Philibert Delorme, the architect of the Louvre, behind them. The monarch's sister,—the Queen of Navarre, and authoress of the famous *Tales*,—is near by; and the Prince—afterwards Henry II—comes next, near whom attend the Cardinal du Bellay and Pierre Ronsard the poet. On the left-hand side of the picture is seen Bernard Palissy, holding one of his beautiful dishes, and the gloomy Catharine de Médicis sits between him and the sovereign, in the per-petual black of her widowhood.—By Oswald Achenbach is seen one of his merry, crowded views, a "Naples," brilliant as the stage-setting of the fish-market scene in *Masaniello*, when they play the piece at San Carlo's; in the foreground a fisherman hauls along a great dolphin, dying in a hundred colors; the crowd in front contains half-dressed *pescatori*, and girls arrayed in peasant-costume; a monk, inseparable from his umbrella, catches the eye in front, at the right; and, over all, the sky is indented with the eaves of the tall white houses, forming a curved line around the Bay.—Returning to the French painters, we find Aubert's "Reverie," a sitting

MARTYRDOM OF JOHN HUSS.
FAC-SIMILE OF A SKETCH FROM THE ORIGINAL PAINTING BY C. F. LESSING.

maiden, well-known from the engraving; and the "Penelope" of Marchal, the suicide-artist, the engraving of which is equally popular, a painting representing a modern faithful wife, occupied with her sewing, which she stands to finish by the last fading rays of twilight; this figure is about half the size of nature.—"The Little Savoyard," by the exquisite artist Hébert, whose works are so rarely seen outside of France, is found here; a sitting form of weary boyhood and vagabondage, musing beside a pair of dancing marionettes, with the dance all taken out of them by the lassitude or dejection of their little master; this copy of the picture is more highly finished than the corresponding one of the same subject in the Belmont gallery at New York.—By Eugène Isabey is a group in an unusual scale, representing "The Three Graces," half the size of life; a trinity of maidens, in white vesture, stand in a cluster, while overhead, at the right, a swarm of genii shower roses, and a single Cupid, on the left, at the summit of the composition, shoots smartly at his predestined prey.—By Edouard de Beaumont is to be noticed "The Torturers of Cupid," a sanguinary satire on feminine treachery, where some nymphs are actually preparing to roast a bound love-god upon an altar.—The French landscape school is represented by some radiant examples. A rich and satisfying specimen of Théodore Rousseau is the "Oak-Tree of Barbizon," a picture of considerable size, showing a gigantic and quite globular oak at the right, some water to the left, and Rousseau's own heart-warming mantle of sunlight spread over the middle distance. His "Fontainebleau Birch-Trees," one of two smaller pictures by him, reveals the white stems of a line of birches, against some dark foliage behind; the trees crest an eminence in a rolling country, where a valley divides the composition at the centre.—Birch-trees are found again, but this time close in a forest interior, occupying with

OLD AGE AND CHILDHOOD.
FAC-SIMILE OF A SKETCH FROM THE ORIGINAL PAINTING BY L. KNAUS.

their sun-spotted silver stems a station to the left in a sylvan tangle of trees, in Diaz's "Fontainebleau Woods." One of

the same artist's figure-groups, a company of "Bohemians," an upright-shaped composition, shows the Franco-Spaniard's

LE JOUR DES MORTS.
FAC-SIMILE OF A SKETCH FROM THE ORIGINAL PAINTING BY W. A. BOUGUEREAU.

gorgeous application of flower-like colors.—Rosa Bonheur contributes a "Cow and Dog," the canine reclining at the right, and the bovine, standing at the left, contemplating him critically; one is fain to ask why is the cow watching the watch-dog, instead of the dog watching the cow?—Auguste Bonheur is found presenting his "Cattle at Fontainebleau," a small color-study for that masterpiece of his life, the superb cattle-piece in Mrs. A. T. Stewart's New York gallery.—Bellangé, a battle-painter who died in 1867, and who was of sufficient repute to justify the posthumous collection of his works which I remember seeing at the Beaux-Arts School, is represented by a historical scene of "Napoleon's Return from Elba." The hero of the hundred days, surrounded by a few trusty officers, is found in a great throng in the market-place of a French village. A crowd of his old grenadiers cluster at the left, the foremost one bringing out his old father to be presented to the Little Corporal.—A Troyon in this collection is unusually large and fine; it is thought to be a match in quality for the splendid Troyon sold in the Taylor Johnston collection. The present example was painted in 1859. It is a group of strongly-patched black and white cattle, as vivid in contrast as the most ambitious effects with which Van Marcke has more recently tried to improve on his master. The eye is caught by some unusually vigorous cows' heads towards the right of the middle, standing out in their decided modeling and energetic color with all the emphasis of the heads of the divine Hathor in a collection of monumental Egyptian bronzes. There are few finer Troyons in the galleries of the world than Mr. Probasco's "Herd of Cattle."—"The Russian Inn," by Schreyer, a canvas of 1867, shows a traveler arriving at a shed with a covered four-horse wagon; at the right the driver enters the little rustic portico; spits

Pompeian Dance

ARTIST

P. O. JOSEPH COOMANS

Born at Brussels, 1816.   Pupil of Baron Wappers

COLLECTION OF

JUDGE GEORGE HOADLEY, CINCINNATI, O.

of snow drift over the ground without entirely obscuring it. Schreyer's "Arabs in Egypt" is a fine loosely-painted bit of orientalism, bathed in lustre and glister.—By Mélin is a subject of "Stag and Hounds," dated 1865; the deer, almost buried in a dozen dogs, is crossing a stream, which spreads off to the left of the picture, and in which is a fine figure of a wounded dog; the hounds are varied and excellent, while the bounding stag is the conventional animal of Landseer's studies.—Toulmouche is found in an unprecedented mood of tenderness and pure domestic sentiment, which shines out in all the faces of his group of "The Card Castle." A lovely young mother faces the spectator as she sits at a table, adjusting the last card that crowns the edifice, and her pretty bevy of three or four little architects surround her ecstatic.

gesture of repudiation. Over his shoulder leans Gerson, the supposed author of the *Imitation of Christ*, who was not without sympathy for Huss, and who endeavors to soften the nuncio's wrath. In front of the pope's representative sits the oldest envoy present, D'Ailly, Cardinal of Cambrai, who showed the greatest ingenuity in trying to entangle Huss in theological subtleties. His enemies are all around the doomed reformer—the Archbishop of Prague, Michael de Causis, who wrote the act of accusation, Stephen Paletz, and the Bishop of Lodi, who preached an impassioned sermon against him at the last sitting of the Council, July 6, 1414.—"The Martyrdom of Huss" is a smaller replica of the great picture long admired at the old Düsseldorf Gallery in New York, and now in the Berlin Gallery. The Elector Palatine

HUSS BAKING HAY.
FAC-SIMILE OF A SKETCH FROM THE ORIGINAL PAINTING BY W. DIEFFTAHL.

Mr. Probasco has a hall filled with marble sculpture. The favorite work in this kind is Magni's famous "Leggitrice" or Reading Girl, a peasant-maiden gracefully sitting sideways on a rustic chair, whose back supports her volume; this universally beloved figure has conquered the affections of the whole world at a series of Universal Expositions; near by are Randolph Rogers' kneeling "Ruth," Tantardini's standing "Reading Girl," seen at the Centennial Exposition, Powers' bust of "Charity," with a flame on the forehead, and that of his "Diana;" and Connolly's bust of "Cordelia."

Mr. Joseph Longworth has a collection of great variety and interest, including several works by the famous Silesian artist Charles F. Lessing, born 1808, the grand-nephew of the author of *Nathan the Wise*. "Huss before the Council of Constance" is a replica diminished for the engraving, of the large canvas retained in Germany. It was painted in 1845. Huss has marched to the trap of his free will, confiding in the safe-conduct of Sigismund, who so quickly betrays him. The legate from Rome, armed with the pope's *bulla*, sits in the midst, and listens to the defence of Huss with an emphatic

having invited him to abjure, and Huss refusing, a yellow cap, painted with devils and inscribed with the word "heresiarch," is pressed upon his forehead by the man-at-arms, while the martyr kneels with seraphic upturned face. Ziska stands near by, grasping a staff, and the Reformer's converts—John of Duba and John of Chlum—watch the scene with painful sympathy. Lessing's accidental reading of a *History of Bohemia* changed the whole current of his art, and the fame of the martyr, whose death kindled the flames of terrible wars among his faithful Bohemians, has been carried by his pencil further than the Rhine carried the reformer's ashes. Three other Lessings are in the collection, with Knaus's "Age and Childhood," which we illustrate, a splendid "Man-at-Arms" by Spagnoletto, and Riefstahl's pen-drawing of "A Mountain Church," with an open-air congregation showing the quaintest head-dresses.

Judge George Hoadly has an interesting collection, embracing our illustrated Chialiva, "Feeding the Sheep," and Turner's "Scarborough," whose authenticity is sufficiently certified to by Mr. Moncure D. Conway, "Soyer's "Baby's

Meal," and Sauvage's "Children and Canary," a superb sunset Corot, "The Goatherd," and Coomans' graceful "Pompeian Dance."—Mr. W. S. GROESBECK's paintings include our illustrated "Jour des Morts," by Bouguereau, Merle's "L'Ange Intercesseur," and Salentin's "The Little Preacher."—Mr. J. L. STETTINIUS has the "Nuns Raking Hay" (4×2 feet) of Riefstahl (cut page 73), a quaint and piquant incident; H. Lommon's "Among the Factories" (1878, 5×3½ feet); and Fortuny's "Sentinel."—Mr. W. W. SCARBOROUGH's Lessing, "A Scene in the Thirty Years' War" must not be forgotten, nor Mr. I. B. HARRISON's Turner, "Mist on the Thames," from the Gillott sale, nor Mr. W. HOOPER's "Shepherd" by Millet, nor Mr. CARMAN's collection of engravings.

The public "Tyler-Davidson" fountain in bronze, given to the city by Mr. Probasco, is the finest in the country; it is of German workmanship; Mr. Müller, who made it, having come over to America to participate in its dedication. Benjamin West's "Ophelia" (14×12 feet) was bequeathed by N. LONGWORTH to the city, and has been placed in the Music Hall; it is a *pendant* to the "Lear" in the Boston Museum,

both brought over by Robert Fulton. Murillo's "Deliverance of Peter," in the Cathedral, was one of the Spanish acquisitions of Marshal Soult, and was presented by Cardinal Fesch to Bishop Kenwick. A much talked-of picture is Haydon's "Christ Entering Jerusalem" (16×14 feet), to be seen at the Cathedral. While exhibiting at Philadelphia it was injured by the Academy fire of 1845, restored, and bought for a few hundred dollars. It was presented to Archbishop Purcell, for the Cathedral, by Mrs. Reuben Springer. The picture on its first exhibition made a profound sensation; Mrs. Siddons deciding the merit of the Christ with her announcement, "It is perfection," and discovering its "supernatural paleness." The latest English Life of Haydon is full of the story of it, and contains an illustration for the head of Wordsworth,—for the wise painter introduced Voltaire, "Mr. Hazlitt looking at the Saviour as an investigator, Keats in the background, and Woodsworth bowing in reverence and awe." His own wife and child are portrayed at the left. The donkey is said to be by Landseer, then his pupil, and there are unkind critics who say it is the only good thing in the picture.

COLLECTIONS IN CINCINNATI.

JUDGE G. HOADLY'S COLLECTION.

ACHENBACH, O.—*Night at Capri.*
CHIALIVA, L.—*Feeding the Sheep.*
COOMANS, J.—*Pompeian Dance.*
COROT, J. B. C.—*The Goatherd.*
COURBET, G.—*Solitude.*
   "   "   *Lake Leman.*
DAHL, HANS.—*Norwegian Fishermen.*
DARGELAS, H.—*The Little Faggot-Gatherers.*
DAUBIGNY, C.—*River Scene.*
DE BEAKALAER, F.—*Picking the Grapes.*
FRÈRE, E.—*At Last.*
   "   *The Captain's First Ship.*
KOEKKOEK, B. C.—*Study in Light, Air and Water.*
                         Water-color.
   "   "   *Cattle and Landscape.* Sepia.
LEON Y ESCOSURA, I.—*Ancient Régime.*
LANSING, C. V.—*The Ambush.*
MADRAZO, R.—*Flirtation in a Spanish Court-Yard.*
MERLE, H.—*The Good Sister.*
PREYER, J. W.—*Fruit.*
RICO, M.—*Canal of St. Barnabas, Venice.*
ROYBET, F.—*Ludovic Lesly, (called Le Balafré.)*
SOYER, PAUL.—*Ruby's Meal.*
TROÏ, JULES.—*Landscape.*
TOFT, PETER.—*Cottage at Hastings.*   [color.
TURNER, J. M. W.—*Gifts at Scarborough.* Water-
VERNET, H.—*Wounded Soldier in Algiers.*
ZAMACOÏS, E.—*A Spanish Notary.*
ZIEM, F.—*The Tyrrhenian Sea.*

MR. H. PROBASCO'S COLLECTION.

ACHENBACH, O.—*The Fish Market, Naples.*
ANSDELL, RICHARD.—*Multeers and Alhambra.*
AUBERT, E. J.—*Reverie.*

MR. H. PROBASCO'S COLLECTION.

Continued.

BEAUMONT, E. DE.—*The Torturers of Cupid.*
BELLANGÉ, J. L. H.—*Napoleon's Return from Elba.*
BOOCKER, ROSA.—*Cattle and Dog.*
BONHEUR, A.—*Cattle at Fontainebleau.*
BRETON, J.—*The Gleaners.*
COLE, VICAT.—*Autumn's Golden Crown.*
COUTURE, T.—*Day-Dreams.*
DE KNYFF, NICAISE.—*Francis I at Fontainebleau.*
DELACROIX, E.—*Clotilde Delivering the Martyrs.*
DIAZ, N.—*Dark Wood Interior.*
   "   "   *The Bohemians.*
FROMENTIN, E.—*Street-Scene in Algiers.*
GÉRÔME, J. L.—*La Danger Syrien.*
GOODENSTAERL.—*The Flower-Girl.*
HÉBERT, E.—*The Savoyard.*
ISABEY, E.—*The Three Graces.*
KAULBACH, W.—*Mother-Love.*
LINNELL, J.—*Harvest-Time.*
MARCHAL, C.—*Penelope.*
MELIN, JOSEPH.—*Stag and Hounds.*
MERLE, H.—*The Secret.*
MEYER VON BREMEN, J. G.—*Old Letters.*
MILLET, J. F.—*The Birth of the Calf.*
PILOTY, CARL.—*Elisabeth of Bohemia.*
ROUSSEAU, TH.—*Oak Tree of Barbizon.*
   "   "   *Birch Trees at Fontainebleau.*
   "   "   *Landscape.*
SCHREYER, A.—*Arabs in Egypt.*
   "   "   *Russian Inn.*
STEVENS, ALFRED.—*The New Robe.*
TOULMOUCHE, A.—*The Card Castle.*
   "   "   *Lady and Several Children.*
TROYON, C.—*Cattle.*
WAPPERS, BARON G.—*Count Egmont's Family Doing Propitiatory Penance.*

MR. H. PROBASCO'S COLLECTION.

Concluded.

STATUARY.

CONNOLLY, F. V.—*Cordelia.* Bust.
KISS, AUGUST.—*Amazon.*
MAGNI, E.—*La Leggiera.*
POWERS, H.—*Charity.* Bust.
   "   "   *Diana.* Bust.
ROGERS, R.—*Ruth.*
TANTARDINI, A.—*Reading Girl.*

MR. J. LONGWORTH'S COLLECTION.

ACHENBACH, A.—*The Swedish Cataract.*
   "   "   *Interior Church, St. Carlos, Rome.*
                Water-color.
   "   "   *Iron District of Westphalia.*
   "   "   *Marine.*
   "   "   *Sudden Squall.*
   "   "   *The Wreck.*
CHIALIVA, I.—*Children and Cattle.*
DE KNYFF, N.—*The Returned Crusader.*
GUDE, HANS.—*Autumn in the Hills of Norway.*
   "   "   *Spring in the Hills of Norway.*
KNAUS, I.—*Old Age and Childhood.*
KOEKKOEK, B. C.—*Skaters.*
KUHN, CARL.—*Cattle.*
LESSING, C. F.—*After a Summer Shower.*
   "   "   *Martyrdom of Huss.*
   "   "   *Huss Before the Council of Constance.*
   "   "   *The Hymn of the Ages.*
   "   "   *Sunrise in the Hartz Mountains.*
   "   "   *Landscape with Peaches.*
RIBERA, J. (SPAGNOLETTO).—*Soldier.*
RIEFSTAHL, W.—*A Mountain Church.* Pen drawing.

ART AND LITERATURE

ARTIST
WILLIAM A. BOUGUEREAU

BORN AT LA ROCHELLE, FRANCE, 1825.

PUPIL OF PICOT.

COLLECTION OF
THE LATE COL. J. STRICKER JENKINS, BALTIMORE

BRITTANY PEASANTS AT PRAYER.
FAC-SIMILE OF A SKETCH FROM THE ORIGINAL PAINTING BY G. BRION.

ADDITIONAL COLLECTIONS IN THE CITY OF BALTIMORE.

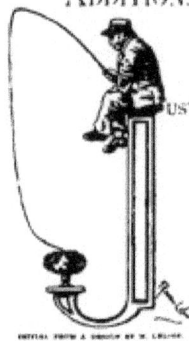

USTICE demands that a short article should be devoted to the additional collections preserved in the Monument City, whose principal gallery has been already described in the chapter consecrated to Mr. W. T. WALTERS' paintings. There are several parlor collections of great interest among the splendid homes of this ancient and beautiful city, where the warm enthusiasm of the South finds itself hospitable to every form and development of art, in distinction from the dilettante clannishness of the North,—too prone to make fetishes of its Millets or its Corots.

The illustrations to this article are the photogravure plates of Holman Hunt's "Isabella" and Bouguereau's "Art and Literature," and sketches of Brion's "Peasants at Prayer," Gérôme's "Bashi-Bazouk," and Muraton's "Bread of the Poor." The Holman Hunt—the first specimen we have encountered on our search of an English artist who has attained a surprising celebrity—merits particular attention. In size it is about 14 by 24 inches. I am unable to concede that the artist has fairly chosen his type of the wealthy Florentine inamorata; but an advanced criticism asks simply whether a painter has studied his model with skill and ability, not whether the model itself is applicable: to demand the latter is to confine art too much to the illustrative function—the bane or quicksand of technical painting. Let an artist produce a work, well-wrought in its pure aspect of nature-study, faithful to its own ideal, or conception, or entity, and it may be as faultily illustrative as a Venus of Rembrandt's, and still be a great thing. So, it is not very important to consider whether the ardor of the "Isabella" is truly the ardor of an Italian, made constant by a long hot gust of rapture and passion, and not rather the opinionated, headstrong determination of a Northern strong-minded woman; nor whether her stubby fingers and feet are suitable to a Florentine of condition. The figure remains a monument of English pre-Raphaelite study, in its mood of most inexorable, insistant, implacable adherence to fact. Facts are piled up and accumulated in this thorough-going piece of painting; the pores of the skin seem to be counted, the trim of the nails and the enamel of the eyes are insisted on, as Desgoffe insists on the gloss of his articles of *virtù*. So far as dogged attention and industry go, there is not one more touch of the paint-brush to lay on. If tenacious trying will make a perfect picture, Mr. Hunt has no shortcoming to reproach himself with. The painting contains a wonderful accumulation of *bric-à-brac*, besides its human interest; the curious majolica pot, in which the heroine has planted her murdered lover's head, the lettered embroidery which her patience has achieved to cover its pedestal, and the opalescent watering-jar of faïence in front, are all elaborated by the artist with perfectly impartial enthusiasm. The whole composition, which Mr. Hunt has finished with the devotion of a monk illuminating a missal, is a scheme of bright primitive colors, which have not faded or changed in the twenty years of the picture's existence, and, however misjudged the labor, forms a tender tribute to the lovelorn heroine of Keats and Boccaccio, who nourished her basil-plant from the brain of the lover assassinated by her merciless brothers. The picture pertains to the collection of Mr. JOHN W. GARRETT, President of the Baltimore and Ohio Railroad, to whom also belongs Brion's "Brittany Peasants at Prayer" (60 × 50 inches,) at the head of the preceding page. The latter canvas is one of the noblest and profoundest of the extant specimens of the dead Alsatian painter, showing that when he chose he could rise to the full height of Millet, and catch for his canvas the most subtle aroma of pastoral poetry and charm; the "Peasants at Prayer" indeed deserves to be set beside Millet's "Angelus," for a penetrating thoughtfulness and a religious serenity, in setting of pure country seclusion. Nobody can have wandered through the primitive recesses of Brittany, and found some lost chapel in a wilderness on the day of the *pardon* of its tutelary saint, without perceiving the sentiment of antique devotion and *sana fides* recorded by the painter on this canvas. None can have seen the God's acre around the church filled with the overflow of a thronging congregation, its sacred graves pressed by kneeling figures who pray upon the very bosoms of their dead, beside the reliquaries containing the skulls of past generations, and in the shadow of the elaborate stone Calvaries, without feeling the solemn poetry of this rustic adoration, and the conviction that here was a subject for the pencil either of Millet or of Brion.—The "Bashi-Bazouk" (8 × 10 inches), likewise in Mr. GARRETT's collection, is one of the better class of Gérôme's studies of travel; a head modeled with exhaustive knowledge and skill, solid and real as any bronze, hard and rigid in its watchful immobility, but over-clouded and softened with voluptuous Eastern draperies and fringes. The face clearly bespeaks the cruelties and atrocities which made the irresponsible Bashi-Bazouks, the mercenaries of the unspeakable Turk, to be so execrated during the late revolutions in the various Turkish dependencies of the Danube. The famous artist seems to have especially enjoyed painting one of those high felt caps, wound about with a scarf whose body twists into a rope, and whose dangling fringe forms a cage for the fly-tormented face —coiffures which he has introduced into his Eastern scenes with every caprice of spiral twist and blinding pendents, but has seldom represented in such scale and with such realism as here.—Georges Clairin's "Feeding the Flamingo" (24 × 30 inches) shows a squatting Moor in a chamber of the Alhambra handing food on a rod, from the platter before him, to a stalking flamingo that writes S with his long crooked neck; a saddle and gun are seen on the heaped-up rug on the ground. Mr. GARRETT's collection also contains "The Japanese Mask-Painter" (38 × 30 inches), painted in 1872. An old native, in round spectacles, squats in his booth, busily painting a horrible mask, of the kind used in festivals and dances; the rows of the masks already done afford an infinite study of these unimaginable grotesques,—more inventive, and often more

realistic, than those of any country, and accordingly much sought after by modern collectors. A beautiful lady of Yeddo passing the bazaar, attended by a couple of maids, stops to watch the artist, and three laughing children creep perilously near to his elbow.—Willems shows a picture of "Reading" (18 × 28 inches); a young lady in the usual dress of alabaster satin folds her hands on a table, whose carvings are partly concealed by the cover of gold and crimson velvet, while her companion, in a broad lace collar, reads from an antique folio.—"The Egyptian Girl, Thebes," by Landelle, is an unnaturally comely fellah-woman, seen to the knees, poising a water-jar on her hand.—Ziem contributes the "Entrance to the Grand Canal, Venice," a sunset scene, almost all sky, with the two square campanili at opposite sides, the darting gondola, the market-boat, which make up the budget of the usual Venice view, here painted with a charm and fluency that are not usual.—A. Achenbach shows "Fishing-Boats at Sunset" (24 × 14 inches).—Vetter, the excellent Alsatian painter, gives us "The Refreshing Draught," reminding us once more that drinking is the soldier's pleasure, and that sweet is pleasure after pain, as a serving-maid at a country inn pours a measure of beer for a sitting man-at-arms, from the troops of Louis XIII and Richelieu.—Eastman Johnson's "Wandering Fiddler" (30 × 25 inches) is a composition of nine figures, showing a negro in a country house, and a young mother holding up her baby before him.—E. L. Henry's "Railway Station" (24 × 12 inches), from the J. Taylor Johnston sale, gives a good idea of the citizen-haunted railway at a point near the large capitals, and reminds a great railway monarch of the tide of travel over which he bears despotic sway. W. H. Beard's "Santa Claus" (3 × 2 feet), T. Cole's small "Kenilworth," and F. E. Church's "Twilight in the Wilderness" (50 × 40 inches) and "Sunset in Vermont" also belong to the collection.

"Art and Literature" is one of the larger compositions of the faultily faultless painter Bouguereau, and its ample dimension simply affords the impeccable painter the more room to be infallible in. The smoothness and finish of this group are equal to that of the most highly-polished sculpture, and whoever loves exalted refinement for its own sake, divested of imagination and originality, will have a feast in this effort of Bouguereau's at allegory. The sister muses are depicted as young Greeks, who have additionally acquired, by some happy anachronism, the modern repose of the Paris drawing-room,—a repose not depending upon ignorance of doubt, but rather a calculated repose prepared for emergencies. Painting, however, has a rather dissatisfied and perplexed expression as she stands searching the horizon for a subject, while Literature, sitting with tablet and stylus, is severely calm, and will evidently turn out sophomore verses as correct as Bouguereau's pictures. The topic was proposed to, not originated by, the artist, who expressed unusual delight to his American patron for a chance to give a loose to his classical feeling and idealism in a kind of theme which the dealers, enamored of his accomplished peasant-girls, seldom allow him to attempt. This large and typical Bouguereau has always been known, since its stay in America, as the property of Col. J. STRICKER JENKINS, of Baltimore; but the executors of that gentleman, now deceased, caused the picture to be sold at auction, in the latter part of the year 1881, while the present work was in press, and since the preparation of the plate representing it. It was bought by Mr. E. WALTER, N. Y.

"The Bread of the Poor" is a subject by A. Muraton, in the collection of M. C. MORTON. It represents that ordinary donation of food from the monasteries practised wherever the Church of Rome holds sway. The most picturesque example

In the collection of Mr. JAMES CAREY COALE is an exquisite specimen of the art of Jules Breton, the "Fleur de Sable" or Beach-Blossom (24 × 40 inches). It is a full-length figure of a lovely budding fisher-maiden of fourteen years, who walks along the edge of the tide, holding up her skirt of brown stuff, and letting the sea ripple over her insteps. Her profile is bent down, so that she can see her graceful brown ankles, while the horizon line, crossing the composition on a level with her face, the faint distance and a far-off promontory,

BASHI-BAZOUK WARRIOR.
FACSIMILE OF A SKETCH FROM THE ORIGINAL PAINTING BY J. L. GÉRÔME.

of this eleemosynary distribution is doubtless that of the Ara Cœli Church at Rome, because there the mendicants come for it up the interminable flight of steps leading to the edifice, covering the Hill of the Capitol with their variegated beggary. The present painter chooses two figures, in some Benedictine monastery,—the disburser and the recipient. A venerable and intellectual friar, his limbs draped in the white Benedictine frock, breaks the bread and glances at the crucified image, remembering the words of the original,—"The poor ye have always with you." A little basket-carrying girl stands ready to receive the fragment to be chiseled from the loaf, marked on its floury surface with the intaglio of the cross. Alphonse Muraton, a native of Tours, instructed at Paris in the studio of Drolling, and the recipient of a medal in 1868, has not previously been mentioned in this publication.

the foggy afternoon sky and tender blonde field of the ocean, form altogether a light relief for her delicate but richly vital figure. The picture was executed in 1874.

A lovely poem was written on the "Fleur de Sable" by Jules Breton, who is himself a pastoral poet of no mean order. It was printed in the *Gazette des Beaux-Arts.*

By C. Delort, in Mr. J. CAREY COALE's collection, is a picture which may be called "Impudence and Innocence," (36 × 24 inches). A brace of roaring swashbucklers, in the gayest costumes of Francis I, swagger past a sweet girl who knits in a doorway. The father of the *ingénue*—a burgher, marked by an unmistakable air of guarding forbidden fruit—stands in front of her, with his hands clasped over his paternal entrails, which are strongly moved at the thought of such innocence and such danger.—Mme. Juliette Peyrol-Bonheur, sister of Rosa Bonheur, contributes a "Sheep-Farm" (40 × 24 inches). A French grange, backed by the ordinary one-story thatched cottage among its trees, is the theatre of a quiet, sunny little drama of country noons and leisures. A group of nine sheep occupies the foreground, one of them reaching up to crop the young leaves from the tree which canopies the scene; the ewe and lamb lying down in front are regarded by the black ram who, while browsing, turns his head towards his offspring; these figures are relieved against the green of the fields, and the whole composition is curtained with verdure.— G. Brion shows an "Alsatian Peasant-Girl," an ancient compatriot of his; in a gaudy dress and flaunting coiffure, she takes old letters from a painted box in her lap, and looks through a leaded window at the gaieties of a village fair— where perhaps the author of the letters is dancing with another.—Bouguereau's "La Rosière" (24 × 36 inches) or winner of the prize of virtue, is seen at half-length and of life-size, kneeling in church; the white gauze falls from her head over the shoulders, and over the village neck-kerchief of checked gingham; her hands are clasped on the *prie-Dieu*, and her musing face, turned away so as to show the profile, is, of course, more refined than would be natural in the girl's condition.—G. Brillouin shows "The Card-Players," a half-dozen of soldiers, in the costume of Louis XIII, playing cards on a bench outside a castle.—Meyer von Bremen has a small picture, "The Faggot," a little girl of ten carrying home a bundle of sticks.—By R. S. Zimmermann is "Discussing the War-News" (20 × 16 inches), showing a village debate. The country schoolmaster drives his forefinger like a nail into the war-map spread on the table, and looks up toward the priest, who will not be convinced, but emits a determined negation along with a wisp of straight horizontal smoke coming out of his mouth. A third figure, with trumpet, holds up a newspaper.—Schlesinger contributes "Reverie," painted in 1869, a girl in an oval, life scale, dressed in linen, and meditating with a thoughtful smile, head in hand.—G. H. Boughton is favorably seen with the "Duel from *Twelfth Night*" (24 × 20 inches), executed in 1871; it is a picture painted in a high key, set in a good study of the old Illyrian pleasaunce, divided in two by a sun-dial and cluster of sunflowers. The handsome young Viola receives the advice of Fabian, whispered behind his hand, and the washed-out looking Aguecheek, in mortal terror, is egged on by Sir Toby, the gouty old reprobate.

Mr. GEORGE B. COALE has a collection, showing a particular interest in historical portraiture. In another line, however, is the "Vintage in the Champagne Country" (66 × 32 inches) by A. R. Véron (a pupil of Delaroche), painted 1858; it is a lively scene of animated figures in an extensive landscape, under a well-painted sky made of rolling storm-clouds.—Frank B. Meyer, of Annapolis, contributes a picture well-remembered from the Centennial Exhibition, where it conspicuously figured—"The Continentals", a drummer and fifer leading the embattled farmers, in a snow-scene.—A fine old head of Wytenbogaert, the Armenian Remonstrant, chaplain to Prince Moritz' army, bears the legend "Ætatis suæ 88," fixing the date of the painting at 1645. At that date the

only survivor of the four great pupils of Miereveldt (to whose school the work obviously belongs) was Van Nes, and to this delineator of the great reforming protestants of the seventeenth century the canvas may be confidently attributed.—Rigaud's portrait of Vivien is a characteristic work.—Mr. G. B. COALE's treasures of art include a collection of portrait engravings illustrating the rise of the Dutch Republic, including two hundred and ninety likenesses of two hundred and sixteen persons, among which are several originals by Vandyck and Rembrandt.

Mr. D. T. BEEM's collection includes Cabanel's "Angel of the *Ave Maria*" (36 × 26 inches), a sitting spirit with wide white drooping wings, looking over a town which curves, Genoa-like, around a bay, at the hour when all the bells send up into the heavens the voice of a city's devotions.— Bouguereau's "The Oranges" (24 × 30 inches) is one of his elegant compositions, of three figures, comprising a nude baby, with an orange, and an Italian contadina in whose lap he reposes, while a pretty girl of six, with brown hair and blue eyes, hands another orange.—Chierici, the most celebrated Italian genre painter of the older school, contributes "Feeding the Cats" (14 × 18 inches), showing a little girl standing and feeding from the dish which she holds the group of cats at her feet, and laughing at their antics.—Erroli is seen with a "Cabaret," where a judge of good spirits, who has paid for his experience with many a tumble, staggers down the cellar-steps for one more drink.—Schreyer's "The Retreat" (30 × 24 inches) depicts Arabs leaving their camp-fire, galloping off on splendid horses, the chief shading his brow with his hand.—E. Dubufe contributes a "Swiss Girl," a life-size half-length, representing a handsome peasant maid, in her picturesque velvet-trimmed bodice, who drops her knitting and looks out with a meditative expression as she thinks of her lover.—De Coninck's "Violin Girl" exhibits her violin, and a tame bird settling on her hand.—Escosura's "Fencing Lesson" (14 × 12 inches) includes four gallants, in Louis XIII costume, and a full-blown fencing-master.—"The Music Party" by J. Carolus, a Belgian painter, shows a group of three around a painted spinnet.

Mr. GEORGE SMALL's collection includes a dashing and conspicuous work by Carl Becker, "Olivia Unveiling, from *Twelfth Night*," showing the heiress making a delicate frame out of her laces for a bewitching face, with the proverbial speech to Viola,—"We will draw the curtain and show you the picture"—also Bouguereau's "Maternal Admiration," Coomans's "Julia," and Sanford Gifford's first-painted "Golden Horn." This collector owns authentic copies from the hand of Thorwaldsen of the "Night" and "Morning," executed forty years syne.

Mr. JOHN W. McCOY includes at least seventy pictures in his collection, comprising Hovenden's first emphatic success, the "Vendean Soldier" (20 × 26 inches); the same artist's "Breton Image-Seller;" Quartley's "Star Island," with some uncommonly faithful studies of brown rocks, and his "Sinepuxent Bay," Kensett's "On the Thames," from the J. Taylor Johnston sale; and Dr. A. J. Volck's "General Lee in his Study at the Washington-Lee University." Mr. McCoy's collection

Isabella and the Pot of Basil

ARTIST

WILLIAM HOLMAN HUNT

BORN AT LONDON, 1827.   PUPIL OF THE ROYAL ACADEMY

COLLECTION OF

MR. J. W. GARRETT, BALTIMORE, MD.

announces a very intelligent patronage of American art, while it is the adjunct of an enviable library, rich in sumptuous illustrated works. The masterpiece of the late sculptor Rhinehart, a nude figure of "Clytie," has been given by Mr. McCoy to the Peabody Institute, where it may now be seen. This richly-endowed sculptor, by the way, a generous son of Baltimore, set at his death an example to his brother artists not often followed or anticipated in the ranks of his profession;

considerable quantity among his relatives of the Winans and Whistler families, but they are generally included in domestic portrait-galleries having no claim to be collections of art. Mr. THOMAS D. WHISTLER is the proprietor of this artist's celebrated "White Girl," a matchless study of different shades of white, formerly seen at the Paris Universal Exposition of 1867.

Among the pictures owned by Dr. GEORGE REULING is

THE BREAD OF THE POOR.
FAC-SIMILE OF A SKETCH FROM THE ORIGINAL PAINTING BY ALPHONSE MUCATIN.

the bulk of his estate, amounting to some fifty thousand dollars, he left at his death to a company of trustees for the benefit of art in his native city; and the survivors of his family, instead of manifesting the slightest jealousy, did all in their power to further the objects of the testator in this regard.

Baltimore has the good fortune to have given birth to undoubtedly the most famous modern American painter,—to him who has raised the reputation of his country's art the highest in the eyes of experts the world over, and who has introduced an unapproachably strong and even revolutionary influence in the English capital where he at present sojourns. The works of J. Macneil Whistler are owned in Baltimore in

"Autumn," being a work of compound authorship, wherein the shepherdess is painted by Edouard Dubufe, and the sheep by Rosa Bonheur; here the collaboration is similar to that in a well-known likeness of Mlle. Bonheur, where she leans on the neck of a young bull, painted by her own hand, the portrait being by Dubufe. The same owner possesses Victor Navelot's "Cavalry Charge," G. Wolf's "Portia," and other canvases.

At the Historical Society's gallery (where is preserved, by the by, the original Pulaski's Banner, sung by Longfellow, a patient work of chain-stitch upon silk, with the embroidered motto "Unita virtus fortior") may be seen a superb head of Jérome Bonaparte by Gilbert Stuart. This is the only occasion in which a member of the Bonaparte family had the delicious fortune to be painted by an artist of the very first class. Stuart, upon the death of Reynolds, was beyond controversy the foremost portraitist of the world, and this time his embalming magic was luckily extended to perpetuate the worthless brother of Napoleon, then in America on the unfortunate business of his boyish marriage. In powdered hair, and with a poetic expression of fatigue and dissipation, the face gains from the painter's magic a winning air of distinction and grace, probably foreign to the original. It was the irony of fate that the ne'er-do-weel future King of Westphalia should be immortalized by the best talent then extant, while Napoleon himself was condemned to be the stalking-horse for all the infelicities of David, Gros, and such artiblasters of the French school. In the same collection, and likewise the property of Mr. C. J. Bonaparte, is David's portrait of Elise Bonaparte, in pearl necklace and huge pearshaped eardrops; also, Sir Joshua Reynolds' portrait of Charles Carroll, of Carrollton, a bust-portrait, three-quarter size, of some artistic importance and great historic interest.

Reynolds is seen, again, in the portrait of the English officer Lieutenant Tarleton, which may be mentioned here, as preserved in the gallery of the Historical Society of Virginia; a mention which must be excused, however inappropriate in an article on Baltimore, on the plea that it will probably be impossible for this work to return again to the art collections of the South.

A word may be added to specify a picture in a Baltimore gallery which has been previously considered. In the chapter on Mr. WALTERS' collection there has been selected for illustration, since that article was written, "The Synagogue at Amsterdam," by Jacob Emile Edouard Brandon, of Paris. It is a picturesque scene of Hebrew worship, the men crowded together without feminine admixture, and wearing orientally their head-gear and their scarves—one venerable patriarch even sporting knee-breeches in eighteenth-century style. This picture was shown in the Paris Salon of 1867, where it won his first medal for M. Brandon, who is a pupil of Picot. Thus is closed the notice of art collections in the South, by a return to Mr. WALTERS' gallery, the finest Southern collection.

COLLECTIONS IN THE CITY OF BALTIMORE.

MR. D. T. BUZBY'S COLLECTION.

MR. J. CAREY COALE'S COLLECTION.

MR. J. CAREY COALE'S COLLECTION.
Concluded.

MR. J. W. GARRETT'S COLLECTION.

MR. J. W. GARRETT'S COLLECTION.
Concluded.

MR. J. W. McCOY'S COLLECTION.

THE RIGHT PATH

ARTIST
HUGUES MERLE

BORN AT SAINT MARCELLIN, FRANCE   PUPIL OF COGNIET.

COLLECTION OF
MR. THOMAS WIGGLESWORTH, BOSTON

FEEDING THE CAMEL.
FAC-SIMILE OF A LITHOGRAPH BY EULERS LENOIR FROM THE ORIGINAL PAINTING BY MARILHAT

COLLECTIONS IN NEW ENGLAND.

BEGINNING this synopsis of the New England galleries from the starting-point of Boston, we find in the first place a very choice and fastidious collection owned by Mr. MARTIN BRIMMER of that city. This gentleman has several fine specimens of the great French painter Millet, including "The Washerwomen," a scene where one graceful laundress loads upon the shoulders of another the cleansed linen, beside a stream near the ocean, whose far-reaching glories under a sunset sky fill the recesses of the view; also the "Rabbits Leaving their Burrows," a curious morning effect, with lively figures of the little creatures disporting around their dewy haunts, beneath a pearly sunrise sky; the

"Knitting Lesson;" and a "Peasant-Girl Knitting," a study in pastel for the oil-picture deposited at this writing in the Boston Museum. A pair of larger canvases than either of these, and also by Millet, are of great importance as examples of his earlier rustic style,—just emancipating itself from the pseudo-classic subjects, with romantic treatment, by which the artist first tried to capture public attention. The "Ruth and Boaz" belongs to the period of his removal to Barbizon, in the Fontainebleau region, where he sketched the subject in crayon on the wall of his cottage. "They were real peasants," says Sensier—"a harvest-scene, where the master, as in the Scripture, finds a young gleaner and leads her, blushing, to the feast of the country-people." This canvas was exhibited in the Paris Salon of 1853; Millet at that time had an artist's romantic notion that the best judges of rustic subjects must be the rustics, and that the fine practical every-day sense of the public was a better criterion than the judgment of an expert. When the "Ruth and Boaz" canvas was finished, he placed it on an easel in the miserable room which served for a studio, and was one day descanting to a friend on his favorite theory. The door suddenly opened, and a tall, handsome country fellow came in. At a glance he saw the picture— Ruth with the barley-sheaves under her arm, escorted by Boaz. The rustic began to laugh. "What are you laughing about?" asked Millet. "Dame, Monsieur Millet, your picture!" "My picture! What is the matter with it?" inquired the artist. "It is so funny! You have hit it so well!" "What?" "Why, you have so capitally painted this garde-champêtre arresting that girl, because she has been stealing a bunch of garlic!" This sagacious interpretation, made almost inevitable by the

Michel,—a peculiar and sensitive modern artist, whose habit it was to take his donkey daily into the environs of Paris, with his wife and family loaded into the cart, and sketch the exquisite gray French skies and sombre twilights,—is a fine rolling "Landscape, with Tower."—By Diaz is "The Pond."— By Frank Duveneck, a "Head of a Young Man."—Hector

LA CURÉE.
ENGRAVED FROM THE ORIGINAL PAINTING BY G. COURBET.

artist's modern arrangement of his theme, put Millet out of conceit of intelligent country criticism for the rest of his life. —"The Buckwheat Harvest," forming a pendant to the last-named, and here illustrated, is a most brilliant and animated farm-scene, with women binding the crackling stems into sheaves in front, and a background of sturdy peasants in a ring, whose lively flails seem to flutter in the air as you regard the picture; these eminent masterpieces show the rustic painter successful in the treatment of a crowd,—an unusual problem in his career. "The Coming Shower," a pastel, is another noticeable specimen of Millet.—By G.

Leroux is represented characteristically enough, by a "Prayer to Esculapius," where a despairing mother holds up her child in terror to a placid statue of the health-god.—"Love as a Paroquet" is one of Hamon's fantastic inventions; Cupid figures with downy wings, like a strange half-tamed bird, and a maiden has provided a perch with a range of pegs, up which the god can mount according to his moods, and form a living thermometer of the state of his mistress's affections. The damsel who has thus affixed her Love to a graduated scale is represented as playing gayly with her pretty familiar, the resemblance to a common modern scene at a parrot-stand being carefully kept up.—One of William M. Hunt's "Marguerites" is in this collection.—A small Constable depicts

LAUNDRESSES.

"Woods in a Breeze."—By Gilbert Stuart is a likeness of Counsellor Dunn; by Copley his own sister-in-law, Mrs. Startin, and a finer portrait of Mrs. Skinner, with additional likenesses from his hand of Col. Watson and his wife. Some old masters, selected with good judgment, but which it is not the province of this work to certify to, are, Agnolo di Domino's "Nativity," painted on the circular base of a tub, a Zuccarelli 5 feet by 4, and a Pierona della Vaga.

Mr. H. P. Kidder has a varied and representative collection in Boston, showing the chief lights of modern popular art. His unusually fine specimen of Bonnat, "The Elder Sister" (40 × 70 inches), painted in 1873, was eagerly desired by the painter as a loan for the last Universal Exposition at Paris, but not obtained, owing to a wise apprehension of the dangers of the sea. Nobly modeled figures, endowed besides with exquisite vivacity of expression, are the Italian girl of twelve, and the naked laughing baby she carries—a boy sturdy enough to make a Roman Emperor.—By Hébert the collection contains a work of uncommon interest, a color-study for the "Girls of Cervara," of which the large life-size picture is at the Luxembourg Gallery in Paris. The illustration of the descending water-bearer, in these pages, has the charm of being from Hébert's own pencil, and reveals an attitude statuesque enough for Phidias. Seldom have the women of the Roman campagna been painted with such splendor of swarthy beauty.—By the late Hugues Merle is the subject of "The Butterfly," two nude baby-boys, one brown and one blonde, chasing the insects through the woods; this is similar to the larger picture illustrated in the Borie gallery.—J. F. Millet is found with a "Shepherdess," a figure looking away rather wistfully to the distance, with a close-pressed flock of sheep and a spindling fringe of trees behind her.—A fine Fromentin is "Washing the Horses," a scene of Arabs leading four or five horses down to the edge of the sea to bathe them. —A pair of fine large early landscapes by the Roman artist Vertunni, both painted in 1868, are the "Lake Avernus" (5 × 3 feet) and the "Pæstum" (6 × 4 feet).—Of French land-

scape, there are two small examples by T. Rousseau, one "The Stream," showing trees closely shutting over a very narrow, crooked rivulet, the foliage at the left shaded, that at the right bathed in Rousseau's own vigorous light; this specimen is about twelve inches in size; the other, "Open Landscape" (18 × 12 inches), a plain with trees, is from the collection of Count Lavalette.—Jules Dupré contributes "The River" (24 × 18 inches), an unusually luminous effect, with light trees balancing in a brilliant sky, and a river floating down the middle of the scene.—By Schreyer is to be noted the "Kabyle Horsemen" (36 × 18 inches) and by Voltz a large specimen, "Cattle at the Stream" (40 × 14 inches).—"School Dismissed," by Spangenberg of Düsseldorf, and Andreas Achenbach's "Norway Torrent," are examples of German studios in the same city, and Burnier's "Coming Home with the Cows" (14 × 10 inches) is a good Belgian specimen.

Mr. THOMAS WIGGLESWORTH is one of the notable picture-owners of Boston; a very large proportion of his paintings having been generously lent by him at various times for the public enjoyment, the privacy of his gallery (one by no means paralled to the curious inspection of strangers) has been materially lost; this exposure of his possessions has indeed been so liberal that the idea of seclusion intended for them by their owner may be considered as practically annulled, and this by the most liberal, public, far-reaching and generous of revelations. One of his pictures, long exhibited in the Boston Museum, forms the subject of a plate in this work,—"The Reception of an Ambassador,"—by the young Spanish painter residing in Paris, Ignace Leon y Escosura. It is a pompous court-scene, laid in that glittering period of the Renaissance which the painter has studied to the very foundation, by means of an indefatigable accumulation of articles, weapons, furniture and costumes belonging to the era; the accessories may here be relied on, down to the heads of the nails and the stitches in the embroideries.—Another plate from a painting in

THE BUCKWHEAT-HARVEST.
ETCHED BY COURTESY FROM THE ORIGINAL PAINTING BY J. F. MILLET.

the same collection, shows "The Right Road," by the late H. Merle. It depicts the peculiar temptations of a life of art, and the fortitude which repudiates them. Young Giorgione, or Masaccio, grasping the implements of his ennobling profes-

LA CENERELLA.
FAC-SIMILE OF THE SKETCH MADE FOR HIS PAINTING BY E. HÉBERT.

sion, pressing meditatively forward in the road of duty, and deafening his ear to the calls of Pleasure and Folly as they hail him from their portico, is a sufficient allegory of life at large. It is very unfortunate that this pictorial sermon of good advice was not concocted till the nineteenth century, as the artists of the period to which Merle's hero belongs were especially in need of it, and usually went quite counter to the way it inculcates.—Courbet's "Les Demoiselles du Village" (7 by 6 feet), which at the present writing is on view at the rooms of the Art Club, is a typical specimen of the great revolutionist in his mid-career, recalling the style of his "Stone-Breaker" and "Interment at Ornans." Of this debatable picture, a milestone in the history of French art, a curious illustration is given, being a fac-simile of the artist's original sketch. Courbet's drawing has become reversed in the painting. This large canvas has mighty realistic qualities, the depth of the blue sky and the verdure of the rolling hills being given with masterly truth. On its exhibition in France, however, it met the censure which was never spared by the advocates of routine when one of Courbet's disquieting studies of honest Nature came forth. The lively writer, Edmond About, called the Demoiselles "hétéroclite." They represent provincial society-ladies, and were deemed too awkward for Paris, too sophisticated for the country. When the canvas was shown at the Universal Exposition of 1855, About objected: "The 'Demoiselles du Village' is an excellent land-

scape, spoiled by the presence of certain figures that are entirely hétéroclite. The dog is a charming dog, and the cows are in good drawing, but the artist takes pains to redeem merits with vices, the goodness of the design with the faults of the perspective." Perhaps at Paris the orthodox aspect of provincial ladies was not understood; but indeed Courbet might have better established the difference in condition between the country "frumps" who give alms and the beggar-girl who receives them. Over these faults of taste reigns the undisturbed supremacy of technical strength, which knows how to represent air and light and the solidity of objects as these things are only represented by the masters of art.—"Ruth and Naomi" (2 × 3 feet), in this collection, is by Miss E. J. Gardner, a New England lady who has long resided in Paris. The style of her instructor, Bouguereau, is sufficiently obvious, but there is much grace, much classical dignity, and much solemn church-feeling in the way these symbolic figures of grand biblical story are arranged. Ruth, the heathen ancestress of the Redeemer, seems to feel the majesty of her great vocation as she sets her back to the road that Orpah is taking, and lays her fingers in pledge upon Naomi's hand.—Merle contributes "The Return from the Fields" (3 × 5 feet), a picture of 1879, which shows an ideally fair country maiden, with her apron full of clover, leading a little girl who trails a leafy branch.—By the late J. A. A. Pils

RUTH AND NAOMI.
FAC-SIMILE OF A SKETCH FROM THE ORIGINAL PAINTING BY MISS E. J. GARDNER.

(1813–1875), a professor at the Beaux-Arts school and one of the official war-painters of the Crimean period, is seen the

The Reception of an Ambassador

ARTIST
IGNACE DE LÉON Y ESCOSURA

BORN IN ASTURIAS, SPAIN, 1837.

PUPIL OF Gérôme

COLLECTION OF
MR. THOMAS WIGGLESWORTH, BOSTON

"Zouaves Behind a Redoubt" (24 × 12 inches)—five of them kneeling at a barrier of gabions.—By Jacque is a "Landscape

LES DEMOISELLES DU VILLAGE
FAC-SIMILE OF A SKETCH MADE FOR HIS PAINTING BY G. COURBET

with Sheep" (40 × 24 inches), showing a distant plain and a screen of blackish trees, a shepherdess standing in front with her sheep-dog, and a score of her woolly subjects behind.— A flashing bit of sunlight is Daubigny's "Landscape" (22 × 12 inches) with a sky of pure blue and white downy clouds, and feathery trees reflected in the gleam of the river.—Lambinet's "Landscape and Figures" (18 × 30 inches) shows ladies promenading by a rivulet among plumy trees.—The little "Landscape" by Diaz (10 × 7 inches) forms an open theatre of trees around a pool, with an oak at the left. A somewhat larger Diaz, "Binding the Faggot" (18 × 24 inches) shows a countrywoman stooping to tie up her bundle of firewood, in the interior of the forest. By Diaz, also, is a "Blindman's-Buff," a subject he often painted, showing nine or ten Eastern children at a juvenile game.—A "Landscape" by Rousseau opens up the perspective of a stream which recedes from the eye, its banks cushioned with flourishing trees.—Clays shows an admirable "Marine" (3 × 2 feet) with a dark lugger seen side on, and a sky filled with silver-gray clouds.—Ziem contributes "The Sweet-Waters, near Constantinople" (3 × 2 feet).

GRAND PIAZZA AT VENICE
ENGRAVED FROM THE ORIGINAL WATER-COLOR BY W. WYLD.

—Courbet, besides the "Demoiselles" above noted, shows a "Swiss Castle" (3 × 2 feet), a souvenir of his latter exile among

the mountaineers.—César de Cock contributes "Fishing" (18 × 36 inches), with light trees on a stream, and a couple of figures angling.—Corot is exemplified in a "Landscape with Goatherd" (10 × 16 inches), a composition of slender upright trees, and recumbent goatherd with a white goat.—R. Burnier contributes a large and fine "Watering-Place" (40 × 30 inches) painted in 1875, representing a woman who leads her cows to drink, the animals straggling over a hillside.—Meyer von Bremen reveals his dainty hand in "The Wayside Cross" (36 × 30 inches), where a family of five, including a mother with a baby at her breast, kneel at the crucifix by a country road, showing their blonde little heads against the evening sky.—The example of E. Frère is unusually fine, "The Faggot-Bearer" (12 × 18 inches), revealing a peasant-woman toiling through the snow with her fardel of sticks.—Pasini's "The Ford" shows an oriental cavalcade crossing a river, a splendid palanquin being carried among them.—Jourdan's "First Step" discovers a nursery-group, a mother kneeling before her toddling baby girl. The same artist's "Reading Maiden" is a half-length, life-size.—Chialiva contributes "Feeding the Sheep" (36 × 18 inches), a pleasant scene of little girls giving hay to a large flock, whose yearling lambs are crowded

HUNTING DOGS.
FAC-SIMILE OF A SKETCH FROM THE ORIGINAL PAINTING BY C. JACQUE

all over the field.—Desgoffe shows "A Cup of Rock-Crystal" (8 × 12 inches), a large carved vessel of quartz, with a bunch of pansies beside it.—Bouguereau's "Holy Family" brings up with dignity this series of pictures mostly French; it is a life-size group, the Virgin showing her calm Greek face in profile, and the little nude St. John running eagerly up to kiss the holy Babe.—Of American artists in the collection may be mentioned S. Colman, with the "Harbor of Seville" (4 × 2 feet), Copeland, with the "Stone House at Antwerp" (3 × 2 feet), and Walter Shirlaw with the "Ecclesiastical Violinist," a lean young kappelmeister *tout de noir vêtu*, standing as he plays his sounding shell. This enumeration will suffice to give an idea of Mr. WIGGLESWORTH's varied collection, so careful of its privacy, yet so liberal in contributions when an art-institution solicits a loan.

Another recluse is the collection of Mr. QUINCEY A. SHAW, of Jamaica Plain, near Boston. The veil of privacy which

DANTE AND BEATRICE.
ENGRAVED BY DRAWN FROM THE ORIGINAL PAINTING BY ARY SCHEFFER.

would otherwise hang impenetrably over this gallery has been removed by an account issued—alleged as by permission—in a public magazine in September, 1881; and, making use of "Greta's" information, our work may properly convey to the community the facts about one of the most exquisite cabinets of a special kind of art in the world. Mr. SHAW simply has the finest collection extant of works by J. F. Millet. He was one of those appreciative and sympathetic American friends who dawned upon Millet in his gloomiest hour at Barbizon, when poverty was a darkness that could be felt, and French experts had not learned to place even a reasonably paying estimate on his finest works. "An American gentleman and his wife," wrote Millet, in 1872, "came to ask me for a picture a short time ago,—Mr. and Mrs. Shaw, from Boston. I am to paint them one. From among my drawings they chose for a subject the Priory of Vauville." The twenty-one oil paintings and thirty framed drawings and pastels by Millet in this collection embrace every phase of his mind and every attitude

of his genius, and include "The Sower," (the first done of two with that title) and the design of "The Spaders," of which we reproduce the artist's sketch. The original "Sower" (about 2 x 3 feet) was the first of Millet's rustic subjects which excited a veritable sensation among those shrewd young art-students who subsequently make a painter's fame. Executed in 1850, "the young school talked about it," we are told, "copied it, reproduced it in lithography, and it has remained in the memory of artists as Millet's masterpiece." Though painted at Barbizon it is not at all a Barbizon model, but a young fellow proud, independent and free; not one of the bowed-down, crushed farmers of the environs of Paris, but a character showing tameless rusticity and ignorance of cities. In fact, it is a memory of Millet's own youth at Gréville, and breathes the vicinage of the sea. Théophile Gautier was won at once, and published about the "Sower" a pen-picture never surpassed. "He is bony, swarthy, meagre," said the critic, "under this livery of poverty; yet it is life which his broad hand sheds. He who has nothing pours upon the earth, with a superb gesture, the bread of the future." He also fancied that "it seemed to be painted with the very earth that the sower is planting." The "gesture as he throws the sacred wheat into the furrow," said the admiring author, was "so beautiful that Triptolemus, guided by Ceres, on some Greek bas-relief, could not have more majesty." Two important landscapes by Millet, hung in the hall and parlor of the villa, show the epoch when he had ceased to give his early academic predominance to the human figure, and had begun to bask in the full luminous breadth of out-door nature. The first is a large hillside, like a quarry, torn up with ruts and water-gullies, and with a square building at the summit. The other is a view of his native place at Gréville, in Normandy, with a blue burst of the ocean. Other subjects here seen in oil are, a girl carrying a new-born lamb; a mother, with her arms round her standing child, teaching the girl to knit; a woman reeling yarn, as she sits at the large reeling-wheel. A dramatic pastel shows a

THE QUOTE WOMEN.
ENGRAVED FROM THE ORIGINAL PAINTING BY ARY SCHEFFER.

farmer's yard, with a dog aroused, in the moonlit night, listening for a sound which you can almost hear; a simple

A Schism

ARTIST

JEHAN G. VIBERT

BORN AT PARIS, 1840. . . . . PUPIL OF FÉLIX J. BARRIAS.

COLLECTION OF

MR. JOHN DUFF, BOSTON, MASS.

drawing shows a peasant-woman doing up her hair before a poor chip of looking-glass; another, a village street in the snow; two rather large pastels represent, the one cowslips, the other, dandelion-balloons. Paintings of the "Potato Planters" and "An Old Woman and her Cow" have wonderful largeness of style.—It must not be supposed, however, that Millet was absolutely the only predilection of the thoughtful collector. The house is a museum of the best art, ancient and modern. In the hall are two marble bas-reliefs of the Holy Family, in the half-archaic style of Mino da Fiesole and the Della Robbias. Two or three Tintorettos, with pedigrees, obtained at Venice, have every aspect of authenticity; one is a Nativity, (perhaps 7 × 3 feet), showing St. Ann at the right, Joseph in the middle, bending over the Babe, and at the left the Virgin, sitting, her head in profile and finely carried on the shoulders; the second Tintoretto is a standing half-length of a young girl; a third picture, ascribed most reasonably to Veronese, is a large "Mystic Marriage of St. Catharine." By Troyon is an early cattle-piece (perhaps 3 × 2 feet.) The herd are strewn abundantly in the foreground, on a small scale; much of this canvas was painted in the patron's presence, "as easily as writing." Several of Rousseau's landscapes are seen, and are mostly unconventional; a large one in the hall, about 3 × 2 feet, is a simple hillside, red with the sinking sun; another, a valuable study, is a view of the plains of Fontainebleau from his house, (about 24 × 28 inches); it is a mere unaccented level, showing immense distance, above which the flat clouds are edged with the vermilion of sunset. There are several Corots; one, a small upright-shaped picture, exhibits a row of spindling tree-trunks, like a railing; another, with a silvery effect, ranges the white cubes of a row of village houses on a river, and is painted with unusual finish. Three drawings are by Barye, the sculptor of animals, one showing the prowling king of beasts for the "Lion of July," another, a lioness lying down, with her head between her paws. This unique gallery has a sort of subterranean fame, a renown almost legendary, on account of the lack of published particulars, and of the oracle universally whispered among

THE SPADERS.
FAC-SIMILE OF THE SKETCH MADE FOR HIS PASTEL, DRAWING BY J. F. MILLET.

artistic people, "If you would comprehend Millet, get a sight of Mr. QUINCEY SHAW'S series." The cash value of

the Millets alone must amount to three hundred thousand dollars. Many were obtained at the sale of the painter's

FIGURES FROM "LES GRANDES MANŒUVRES."
FAC-SIMILE OF THE SKETCH MADE FOR HIS PAINTING BY E. DETAILLE.

friend, the architect Gavet. Mr. SHAW also owns a Salvator-like "Study of Rocks" (24 × 14 inches) by G. Michel, the late Paris artist whose harmonies of tone have raised him to such preëminence in the judgment of the æsthetic world. Brion's "Coming Out of Church" (4 × 3 feet) is his too, showing a rustic church-portico at the right, with Alsatian girls descending its steps, and a sitting beggar-woman with her little boy in the right foreground.

Mr. C. C. PERKINS, the well-known author of "Italian Sculptors," and President of the Boston Museum, which has in him incomparably the most capable chief of any gallery in this country, possesses a few select works of art, among them a small standing marble statue of Dante, by the eminent artist Vincenzo Vela, author of the "Dying Napoleon" at Washington. He also owns the important "Dante and Beatrice," by Ary Scheffer, who formerly instructed him in art. This painting, a household word throughout the world, and perhaps the most eminent example of spiritual expression achieved by our century, needs no description. The figures are half life-size, and illustrate the passage of the *Purgatory* translated thus by Longfellow:—

> Striving to paint thee as thou didst appear
>   Where the harmonious heaven o'ershadowed thee,
>   When in the open air thou didst unveil.
>
> So steadfast and attentive were mine eyes
> That all my other senses were extinct.
>   And upon this side and on that they had
>   Walls of indifference, so the holy smile
>   Drew them unto itself.

Mr. H. SAYLES retains the remains of a once prodigal collection. Among his noble canvases is one of Courbet's *chefs-d'œuvre*, "La Curée," or game-quarry. The superb painting of the suspended venison is the "last word" of broad realism; the standing figure represents the artist, at the time when his florid comeliness reminded beholders of "an Assyrian man-bull." Mr. SAYLES' "Tobit" (4 × 3 feet) is a

large and important work by J. F. Millet, showing the peculiar manner of representing Scripture scenes in their modern
peasant parallels, which the artist adopted soon after his

HIS PICTURE.   (COLLECTION BY W. SAWIN, TAUNTON, MASS.
FAC-SIMILE OF A SKETCH FROM THE ORIGINAL PAINTING BY C. SAVIGNY.

removal to Barbizon, and of which Mr. Brimmer's "Ruth
and Boaz" is a corresponding example. The "Tobit" was
invented in 1853, but not finished and exhibited until the
Salon of 1861. In the first-mentioned year, on the death of
his pious peasant mother, Millet, a hundred leagues away,
sketched the sorrows of a distant and expectant parent—
those sorrows of absence with which her dying missives had
been filled. He imagined the scene of Tobit and his wife,
who also waited, and he drew a scene in which two old people
look towards the sky, and try to find a human form amid the
glories of the setting sun. Millet, on the exhibition of this
picture was abused, as the saying goes, like a pickpocket.
He was the culprit of a police-court, with critics for accusers.
The canvas on which he had poured the private griefs of his
filial heart was singled out for concentrated attack, the solemn
decree of high authorities supporting the light artillery of the
pitiless jesters and caricaturists. "If I wore dancing-shoes,"
remarked Millet to a friend while thus bemired, "I might find
it made the road rather heavy, but with my wooden shoes I
think I can get out of the mud." Yet the picture is sublime,
and speaks a language that all might have understood, with
its rustic home of Tobit's aged parents, a real home of poor
folks who live in the solitude of the country, and with its expression of their lonely expectancy. The two old people are
drawn with a strong, broad execution, with all the wonderful
knowledge of Millet, while the sun, the wood, the road, are
a painted silence over the canvas.—Of two Corots remaining
to Mr. Sayles one is a "Road," an upright-shaped canvas,

showing two women in an avenue among the birch-trees, and
the other, of low shape, depicts a couple of cows in a stream.

Mr. Peter C. Brooks, Jr., owns one of the grandest life-
size figures ever painted by J. F. Millet, "The Sheep-Shearer."
In reality of modeling, and in harmony of tone, this example
is a full justification of the wonder which seizes the craftsman
over Millet's sublime success. This large "Sheep-Shearer"
was exhibited at the same Salon with the "Tobit," and found
a defender among the Paris critics. "Here is great art,"
wrote Th. Pelloquet, "art that raises the mind. It is full of
character, firmness, grandeur. It reaches the highest style
without apparent effort. One cannot find the least trace of
false tricks of painting, but instead the real strength which
does not try to display itself—a large way of painting,
serious and solid, a style of drawing full of energy and ease
and grace, which we can only accuse of an affectation of
suppressing detail, an excess, in fact, of austerity."

Mr. Thomas G. Appleton has long been an intelligent
patron of art. Among his pictures are an apparently authentic Tintoretto, a first study (18 × 30 inches) for the
"Ascension of the Virgin," at the Jesuit's Church in Venice,
eloquently described in Taine's "Italy;" a Bonington, being
a scene from Gil Blas; the owner's portrait, by Mr. Frank
Vincent; Elihu Vedder's "Lair of the Sea-Serpent;" and
Bridgman's "Market in Nubia;" also Decamps' water-color
sketch of the "Suicide" in the Walters' gallery, Couture's
small "Family Scene," and Palizzi's "Goats." This gentleman
has presented twenty-three Tanagra statuettes to the Museum.

ARAB FALCONER.   (COLLECTION BY S. WELL, PROVIDENCE.
FAC-SIMILE OF A SKETCH FROM THE ORIGINAL PAINTING BY E. FROMENTIN.

Prof. Charles Elliott Norton, of Cambridge, has a
large canvas painted with a woman-figure, held to be an
indubitable Tintoretto; a number of water-color studies by

THE CHILDREN'S FAVORITE

ARTIST

JOHN GEORGE MEYER,

(CALLED MEYER VON BREMEN.)

BORN AT BREMEN, 1810

PUPIL OF SOHRADER AND OF SOHN

COLLECTION OF

MR. JOHN A. BROWN, PROVIDENCE, R. I.

Mr. John Ruskin; and the original sheet of pen-drawings representing Voltaire in different moods, by the Swiss Huber, a series of sketches celebrated in the Voltairian iconography.

Mr. HENRY L. HIGGINSON includes among his pictures the fine specimen of Troyon we illustrate, "Hunting-Dogs in Leash" (5 x 3½ feet).—Mr. FREDERICK L. AMES owns Daubigny's delicious "Evening" (7 x 3 feet) representing a road beneath apple-trees, and corresponding in style with his exquisite May-scene in the Luxembourg; also Bonnat's "The First Step," a justly celebrated picture of Italian models.—Mr. E. HASKIWELL has a small Delacroix, an "Arab Encampment by Torchlight."—The late Miss ALICE HOOPER's estate has Turner's painting of "The Slave Ship," a picture of immense English celebrity, long owned by Mr. Ruskin, and purchased from the famous critic's collection by Mr. J. Taylor Johnston, to be soon afterwards offered at the sale of the latter gentleman's gallery. This picture inspired one of the most glowing pages of the "Modern Painters."—The late Mr. JOHN DUFF was the owner of a brilliant collection of modern art, shared by his surviving family since his decease; a most piquant picture from the DUFF gallery is Vibert's "Schism in the Church," where two holy men, cardinal and archbishop, have reached a pitch of voiceless exasperation over some sacred doctrine; the chairs suddenly wheeled back to back, the crossed leg violently swung up and down, the two faces crumpled into furrows, continue the quarrel in dumb show, or with a kind of rumbling subterranean eloquence. This awful example of the odium theologicum forms the subject of one of our most striking plates. Another conspicuous canvas from the DUFF collection is Adrien Moreau's "Concert of Amateurs in an Artist's Studio," an agreeable and elaborate scene of pretty ladies and handsome Bohemians, being fourteen figures in an elaborate interior; this subject has now passed into the possession of a daughter of the purchaser, Mrs. Dr. BULLETT, of New York.

THE SWING.

FAC-SIMILE OF A SKETCH FROM THE ORIGINAL PAINTING BY J. CAEMANS.

Mr. ALVAN ADAMS, of Watertown, has a pleasant collection of contemporary art, including Erskine Nicol's "Bother the Change!" Meyer von Bremen's "Sleeping Beauty," "Girl

Reading," and "Youth and Age," specimens of Schreyer and Schenck, Tissot's "The Model," and other notabilities to be found in the catalogue.

MORNING DREAMS.

FAC-SIMILE OF A SKETCH FROM THE ORIGINAL PAINTING BY PIERRE TOM MARES.

Among the pictures owned by Gen. WHITTIER, of Boston, is De Neuville's important "French Spy," from the Salon of 1881. It represents a sub-lieutenant disguised as a farmer, seeking to penetrate into Metz, but arrested by the Prussians at St-Marie Aux-Chênes, in September, 1870. He awaits his fate, patient and proud, knowing that a proved spy is instantly shot, and that his death will be futile, for Bazaine, whatever might happen, resolved to reply to no appeal, and to sacrifice his army rather than afford any help to the government of the National Defence.

In the Boston Art Museum are to be found the head of Washington by Gilbert Stuart, painted in 1796 and accepted as the standard portrait, and his head of Mrs. Martha Washington; several works by Allston, including his unfinished "Belshazzar's Feast;" and Benjamin West's "Lear," the companion to his "Ophelia" at Cincinnati. In foreign art, some admirable gifts have been made to the Museum. Corot's "Dante and Virgil" (5 x 10 feet), presented by Q. A. Shaw, shows a landscape, with the two poets, the entrance to Hell, and the three symbolic beasts, the panther signifying Florence and worldly pleasure, the lion France and ambition, and the female wolf Rome and avarice. J. F. Millet's "Sitting Shepherdess" (3½ x 5½ feet), presented by S. D. Warren, is a finely modeled seated figure with distaff in lap, and sheep at the side. The group of two heads by Couture, a study for "The Volunteers of 1792" (24 x 36 inches) is in his better, and the "Bacchante" (14 x 18 inches) in his tamer, manner. —The scholarly arrangement of the antique casts in this Museum, under the learned eye of President C. C. Perkins, makes the series decidedly the best extant, in any country. The Gray gallery of engravings is our finest public collection.

In Boston are some public statues of mixed quality. By the late Dr. Wm. Rimmer, a strange Blake-like genius, is that of Alexander Hamilton, commenced in 1864, erected on Commonwealth Avenue. The group representing Emancipation, by Ball, is on Park Square; his Josiah Quincey, at City Hall. The statue of Winthrop, by R. S. Greenough, is in Scollay Square; Franklin's, at City Hall; Webster's and Mann's, at the State House; in the Public Garden, Washington's, Everett's and Sumner's, with a memorial of the Ether discovery; there are, again, the Army and Navy Monument in the Common, the Dorchester Soldiers' Monument on Meeting-House Hill, the Soldiers' and Sailors' Monument at Charleston, the Soldiers' Monument in a cemetery at Roxbury, the John Glover monument on Commonwealth Avenue, the marble statue of Warren at Bunker Hill, and, at Mount Auburn, Story's fine marble portrait of his father, Chief-Justice Story, and the statue of Bowditch. At Memorial Hall, Cambridge, are over one hundred historic portraits and busts, such as Copley's Cooper, Hubbard, Appleton, Boylston, and Samuel and John Adams, G. Stuart's J. Q. Adams, Story, and Fisher Ames, and Smybert's Benjamin Colman.

Mr. WILLIAM MASON, of Taunton, Massachusetts, has a collection, from which we illustrate "His Portrait" (2 x 2½ feet), a scene of a widow and sister before a painting, and Meyer von Bremen's little "Morning Dreams," a pretty German girl dreaming beside a love-letter, under a luxurious red silk coverlet. There are also Caraud's "Convalescent" (3 x 2 feet) with six figures; Bouguereau's "A Poor Scholar" (2 x 3½ feet) a barefoot girl with finger in mouth; his "Meditation," an oval half-length, of a maiden with prayer-book; Escosura's "Introduction," a white-satin lady with half-a-dozen courtiers; Willems' "The Letter," another white-satin maiden with a standing page; Toulmouche's "Billet-doux," three girls at a table, putting their heads together over a note; Court's "Seraglio Window" (4 x 5½ feet) a fair sultana and her slave-girl; "Innocence" by Dubufe père, a life-size reclining girl with a dove; Merle's "Maternal Affection" (18 x 24 inches) a mother and two children in close embrace; Boutibonne's "The Broken Heart" (30 x 18 inches) a weeping girl on a sofa, her head in her mother's lap and a sister playing consoling melodies on the organ; C. L. Müller's "Pride of the Desert," a life-size Zuleika at the well, with jar poised on hand; and a pair by Zimmermann (3 x 2 feet) "Love's Messenger," an urchin bursting with a bouquet into a dinner scene, and

ARREST OF A FRENCH SPY BEARING DESPATCHES
FAC-SIMILE OF A SKETCH MADE FOR HIS PAINTING BY A DE NEUVILLE

then the consequence, "A Betrothal," a diplomatic procession of youth and parents invading the girl's family.

In the rich city of Providence there are several pleasant collections, hospitably accessible to visitors. That of Mr. B. WALL is a remarkable one to find everywhere,—a gallery for artists to pasture in. Where else, in America, do we group specimens of Chardin, the great tone-master, of Marilhat and Belly, those earlier Orientalists, of Léopold Robert and Decamps, of Daumier the caricaturist, of Bonington and Ary Scheffer and Horace Vernet, of Courbet and Couture, of modern impressional painters like Monticelli and Michel? The reader must go to the catalogue for the particulars of this fascinating collection, where the brightest artists of the century seem to have emptied their portfolios. There is only space to mention the remarkable "Falconer" (24 x 26 inches) by Fromentin, a masterpiece of energy and strength; the rare Marilhat which forms the head-piece to this article, "Feeding the Camel," an exquisite dream of an oriental evening, conceived in days before the East was cheapened as now; the curious Ary Scheffer, a color-study for his celebrated "Suliote Women" in the Luxembourg, that desperate challenge thrown down by the painter to Delacroix, that unprecedented awakening of an intellectual artist to sensuous impressions; and the admirable Chardin, "Kitchen Utensils"—a copper kettle, some crockery jars, and a large ladle on a table; and the nectareous colors of the Monticelli, "Nymphs and Cupids;" and the three Bondins, coast scenes, with their valuable gray tones.

Mr. J. A. BROWN, of Providence, has at least fifty well-selected pictures, including an elaborate Meyer von Bremen, "The Tame Bird," with four children feeding a canary, and "L'Escarpolette" or swing, a group of six figures at a Pompeian portico, by Coomans; "Reverie," by Jourdan, a life-size maiden figure in muslin morning-gown, holding a book; Julien Dupré's fine Breton-like "Haymaker," with her pitchfork; Boks's "The Miller, his Son, and the Ass," conceived as a picnic scene; Matteson's pair of "Pilgrim Father" subjects; and Bouguereau's unusually spirited "Italian Beggar-Girl."

Mr. R. C. TAFT, of Providence, includes among his pictures "Autumn Manœuvres," by Detaille, with soldiers occupying a field as a parade ground,—a row of haystacks, on one of which a row of rustic spectators are perched; Van Marcke's important picture of "The Village Herd after the Storm," with a rainbow and a score of cattle; Millet's pastel of the "Knitting Shepherdess and Flock;" Jules Breton's important "The Lookout" (3½ x 2 feet) of 1876, a peasant-girl lying on her breast and looking at the sea; Escosura's spirited "Hardwick Castle," with a girl hiding her cavalier behind a portrait from a squad of ironsides; and "Venice," a water-color by William Wylde, an English painter who associated with the best French artists of a dozen years ago.

Mr. WALTER RICHMOND, of Providence, owns among other pictures Le Roux's "Suppliant to Hygeia," and the splendid "Greek Christian Girls Captured by Bashi-Bazouks," by Cermak, whose biography was published in Vol. 1, page 135.

The brothers SAYLES, of Pawtucket, near Providence, have their palace-like houses filled with art treasures. For one brother, Mr. F. C. SAYLES, we must refer the reader to the catalogue; as Mr. W. F. SAYLES', we may mention the

WAR BOOTY

ARTIST

JAROSLAV CZERMAK

BORN AT PRAGUE, BOHEMIA, 1831.   DIED, 1878.   PUPIL OF CHRISTIAN RUBEN

COLLECTION OF

MR. WALTER RICHMOND, PROVIDENCE, R. I.

"Girl and Dragonfly" (2 × 4 feet), by Bouguereau. O. Achenbach's "St. Peter's," Mr. Perry's "Huldy," and Barzaghi's graceful statue of "Moses and Miriam," (cut page 92) a subject seen also in replica at the Pennsylvania Academy.

Mr. MARSHALL WOODS, of Providence, has a delightful collection of pictures and statuary, including Lombardi's marble "Ruth," Blavier's bronzes of "Dante" and "Virgil," Gott's "Bacchus," Powers's busts of "Faith," "Hope" and "Charity," Macdonough's portrait-bust of a little girl, and Powers's and Fantacchioti's joint portrait-statue of a babe.

without a pedigree. The canvas and its certificate are the complete thing, not the canvas and its merit. Many of these pictures are clothed in a full armor of stamped paper, and the modest connoisseur is at liberty to fall in love with them with full authentication of character. Thus the colossal Angel by Tintoretto in the hall is one of a group of four, of which Judge BRADLEY possesses two, from an Annunciation, described in Boschini's compendium; and this, as well as the Madonna of the same artist, on the adjacent stairway, the Bacchus, by Giordano, and the large fragment of a Resur-

THE VILLAGE HERD AFTER THE STORM.

ENGRAVED ON PALLADIUM FROM THE ORIGINAL PAINTING BY E. VAN MARCKE.

In oil-paintings, may be remarked Troyon's "Cowherd" and Oudry's "Puppies and their Mother."

Judge C. S. BRADLEY, of Providence, has a truly fine collection of ancient paintings, of seemingly unimpeachable authenticity. It is here especially regretable that the scope of this work quite excludes any judgment upon the genuineness of presumed old masters. One canvas is, however, guaranteed. It is the Terburg, "A Trumpeter taking orders from his General," a repetition of the picture at the Hague, engraved in the Hague Catalogue and in the *Musée Napoléon*. Only a flying inspection can be permitted now, while awaiting the infallible Dr. Waagen who shall give these claimants their conclusive rank. Not to slight too much a collection which has the best claims on the lovers of great days and great artists, I will mention a few, giving the preference to those most amply reinforced by guarantees. In America, unlucky refuge of cracked pretensions, an old master is nothing

rection, in an upper chamber, as well as the "Manna in the Wilderness" (8 × 6 feet) and "Moses Striking the Rock" (14 × 9 feet), both by the son of Tintoretto, and appropriately placed in the dining-room,—all this group have a perfectly straight history; they were taken from churches and religious establishments by the French about 1795, remained in Austrian governmental custody until the surrender of Venice by the house of Hapsburg, and were sold by auction, carefully catalogued, when Venice was restored to Italy. Another fine Tintoretto, "Saint Mark, Writing," in the hall, is mentioned in the lives of the artist, and was procured in Venice through a trusted correspondent of Charles E. Norton, the art-professor at Harvard. A pair of Morettos, the "Annunciation" and "Supper at the House of Simon" (placed back to back on a large easel) and the same artist's "St. Agnes," are probably authentic, the "Supper" being a smaller replica of a well-known original described by Crowe and Cavalcaselle. The small Vandyck, "Cardinal Bentivoglio," is "signed all over," as artists say. Del Sarto's "Holy Family" (30 x 40 inches), Schidone's "Madonna and Child" (24 x 36 inches), and Sasso-ferrato's "Head of the Virgin," are all supported by written certificates of the professors at the Academies of Rome. A "Venice," by Canaletto, was represented by Mr. and Mrs. S. C. Hall, the well-known art-writers, as a missing one from a set belonging to Queen Victoria; and a "View of the Salute Church," also by Canaletto, was procured, again, by the con-fidential correspondent of Professor Norton. In a notice so necessarily restricted, these vouchers are perhaps better than critical estimates. A "Portrait of a Lady in a Ruff" by Scipione da Gaeta, prized by the owner as his best picture technically, was procured by Mr. Perry when consul at Venice, and its color said to be beyond the reach of modern art by the American painter Page. Some old Venetian portraits are seen in the dining-room—one of that queen of romance, Caterina Cornaro by Francesco Vecellio, Carlo Contarini by Sebastiano Bombelli, Francesco Contarini by Jacopo Palma, Francesco Donati by Horatio Vecellio, and Leo Donati by Andrea Vincentino. In the same room is the younger

Hoesmans' portrait of his wife, with a group of fruit, melon, and musical instruments. A landscape by Wynants is a prize in the Dutch school, and Franz Hals's study of figures for one of his chief pictures is full of interest. The collection does not absolutely exclude modern art, an "Old Woman" by Campobianchi, of Rome, being exceptionally fine, and some flower and figure-pieces by Diaz presenting his secure magic of color. Altogether, the BRADLEY collection is one to set a man dreaming, and waft him off these new shores of ours by the enchantment of Art and History.

In the city of New Haven are some interesting works of art, of which there is only space here to mention the public gallery, with its Smybert's "Bishop Berkley and Family," Allston's "Jeremiah," Trumbull's studies for his Capitol pic-tures, and the collection of old masters certified by Mr. J. Jackson Jarves.

The celebrated cartoon of the "Reformation," by Kaul-bach, was purchased by Mr. DURFEE, of Fall River, Mass. and has reverted to that gentleman's mother on his death.

Scheffer's "Larmoyeur," in the Boston Museum, was described in replica with the Corcoran Gallery.

MOSES TAKEN FROM THE WATER.
FROM THE STATUE IN MARBLE BY F. BARZAGHI.

Watching the Manœuvres

ARTIST

J. B. EDOUARD DETAILLE

BORN AT PARIS, 1848.   PUPIL OF MEISSONIER

COLLECTION OF

MR. R. C. TAFT, PROVIDENCE

COLLECTIONS IN NEW ENGLAND.

COLLECTION OF MR. M. BRIMMER,
BOSTON, MASS.

CONSTABLE, J.—*Weeds in a Ravine.*
COPLEY, J. S.—*Portrait of Col. Watson.*
    "   "   *Mrs. Col. Watson.*
    "   "   *Mrs. Skinner.*
    "   "   *Mrs. Startin.*
DIAZ, N.—*Pond.*
DOMINGO, AGNOLO DI.—*The Nativity.*
DUVENECK, F.—*Head of a Young Man.*
HAMON, J. L.—*Love as a Paroquet.*
HUNT, W. M.—*Marguerite.*
LEROUX, H.—*The Prayer to Esculapius.*
MICHEL, G.—*Twilight.*
MILLET, J. F.—*Ruth and Boaz.*
    "   "   *The Buckwheat Harvest.*
    "   "   *The Coming Storm.*
    "   "   *The Rabbits.*
    "   "   *The Washerwomen.*
    "   "   *The Knitting Shepherdess.*
STUART, GILBERT.—*Portrait of Counsellor Dunn.*
ZUCCARELLI, F.—*Cattle.*

COLLECTION OF MR. H. P. KIDDER,
BOSTON, MASS.

ACHENBACH, A.—*Norwegian Torrent.*
BÖKER, GEO.—*The Image-Seller of Pompeii.*
BENSON—*The Flight from Pompeii.* Marble.
BONNAT, L.—*The Elder Sister.*
BOUGUEREAU, W. A.—*The Tambourine-Girl.*
CANTALAMESSA.—*The Storm.*
DAUBIGNY, C.—*Landscape.*
DE HAAS, M. F. H.—*Sunset at Pigeon Cove.*
DIAZ, N.—*Fontainebleau.*
DUPRÉ, JULES.—*Landscape.*
FREEMAN, J. E.—*Girl and Parrot.*
FRÈRE, E.—*Going to School.*
FROMENTIN, E.—*Arab Horses Going to Water.*
HERBERT, A. A. E.—*Les Cervantiles.* Study.
INNESS, GEO.—*Pontine Marshes.*
MEISSONIER, J. L. E.—*Cavalier.*
MERLE, H.—*Chasing the Butterfly.*
MEYER VON BREMEN, J. G.—*Blindman's-Buff.*
ROBBE, W.—*Landscape and Sheep.*
ROUSSEAU, TH.—*Landscape.*
ROYBET, F.—*Flowers.*
SCHREYER, A.—*Arab Horses.*
SERGENT, A.—*Looking Out.*
SPANGENBERG, L.—*Leaving School.*
TROYON, C.—*Cattle.*
VAN OSTADE, A.—*Dutch Boors Regaling.* [*Sheep.*
VERBOECKHOVEN, E. AND KLOMBECK.—*Landscape and Sheep & Dogs.*
VERTUNNI, A.—*Pæstum.*
    "   "   *The Campagna.*
VOLTZ, F. J.—*Landscape and Cattle.*
    "   "   *Cattle at a Stream.*
WATTEAU, A.—*Children Playing Soldier.*
ZAMACOIS, E.—*Faust and Marguerite.*

COLLECTION OF
MR. T. WIGGLESWORTH,
BOSTON, MASS.

BOUGUEREAU, W. A.—*The Holy Family.*
BURNIER, R.—*Leading Cattle to Drink.*
CHIALIVA, L.—*Interior of a Barn.*
CLAYS, P. T.—*Marine.*
COLMAN, SAMUEL.—*Harbor of Seville.*
COPELAND, A. B.—*The Stone House, Antwerp.*
COROT, J. B. C.—*Landscape with Goat.*
COURBET, G.—*Les Demoiselles du Village.*
    "   "   *Swiss Landscape.*
DAUBIGNY, C.—*Landscape.*
DE COCK, C.—*Landscape.*
DIDIOTTE, B.—*Crystal Cup and Pansies.*
DIAZ, N.—*Forest with Faggot Gatherer.*
    "   "   *Blindman's-Buff.*
    "   "   *Landscape.*
FRÈRE, ED.—*Winter Scene.*
GARDNER, ELIZABETH J.—*Ruth and Naomi.*
JACQUE, CH.—*Landscape with Sheep.*
JOURDAN, A.—*Reading Girl.*
    "   "   *The First Step.*
LAMBINET, EMILE.—*Landscape with Figures.*
LEON Y ESCOSURA, I.—*Reception of the Ambassador.*
MERLE, H.—*The Right Path.*
    "   "   *Return from the Fields.*
MEYER VON BREMEN, J. G.—*The Wayside Cross.*
PASINI, A.—*The Palempain.*
PILS, J. A. A.—*Zouaves Behind a Redoubt.*
RESER, J.—*Roses and Flowers.*
ROUSSEAU, THEO.—*Landscape.*
SCHISLAW, WALTER.—*Ecclesiastical Violinist.*
ZIEM, F.—*Sweet Waters near Constantinople.*

COLLECTION OF MR. A. ADAMS,
WATERTOWN, MASS.

BARALOWICZ, I.—*In the Library.*
BEWER, C.—*Lorelei on the Rhine.*
BIERSTADT, A.—*The Nevada Mountains.*
    "   "   *Lake Lucerne.*
BOUTIBONNE, E.—*The Readers.*
    "   "   *"Be Quiet, Sir!"*
BRENNER, G.—*In the Wine-Cellar.*
CALDEN, M.—*Bedtime.*
CAMPHAUSEN, W.—*Riderless.*
DELL'AQUA, C.—*The Mirror.*
DETTI, C.—*L'Amour.*
DIEFFENBACH, A.—*The Attack.*
DILLENS, A.—*Return from a Masked Ball.*
HERZOG, H.—*Landscape.*
HILL, THOS.—*The Yosemite Valley.*
JALABERT, E.—*Diana and the Nymphs.*
JACOBSEN, S.—*Fox in the Snow.*
JAMIN, D. T.—*The Passing Regiment.*
MEYER VON BREMEN, J. G.—*Youth and Age.*
    "   "   *The Sleeping Beauty.*
    "   "   *Girl Reading.*
MONDLAGER.—*The Cut Finger.*
NICOL, ERSKINE.—*"Rather the Change?"*
PIOT, A.—*Spanish Dancing-Girl.*
PORTAELS, J. V.—*Thought.*
ROBIE, J.—*Flowers.*

ROMAKO, A.—*The Last Hours of Beatrice Cenci.*
RUMP, P. A.—*The Natural Mirror.*
SCHENCK, A. F. A.—*Sheep.*
SCHREYER, A.—*Horses.*
TISSOT, J.—*The Model.*
VERBOECKHOVEN, E.—*Cattle.*
VIBERT, J. G.—*A Good Fit.*
WEBB, D.—*Dutch Canal.*

COLLECTION OF MR. W. MASON,
TAUNTON, MASS.

BAUGNIET, C.—*His Picture.*
BOUGUEREAU, W. A.—*Meditation.*
    "   "   *A Bad Scholar.*
BOUTIBONNE, C. E.—*The Broken Heart.*
BRADFORD, W.—*Deserted Among the Icebergs.*
BRAITH, ANTON.—*Cattle.*
CALISCH, M.—*Which is the Taller?*
CARAUD, J.—*The Convalescent.*
COURT, J. D.—*The Seraglio Window.*
DUBUFE, CLAUDE.—*Innocence.*
LEON Y ESCOSURA, I.—*The Introduction.*
LE POITTEVIN, E.—*Dutch Market on the Ice.*
MERLE, H.—*Maternal Affection.*
MEYER VON BREMEN, J. G.—*Morning Dreams.*
MILLNER, CARL.—*The Zuckspitz, Bavarian Alps.*
MULLER, C. J.—*The Pride of the Desert.*
RAFFAEN, F.—*Lake Lucerne.*
ROTTMANN, T. A. AND M. HOW.—*Skating Scene.*
SADEE, PH.—*Interior.*
SINKEL, J.—*St. Cecilia.*
TOULMOUCHE, A.—*The Love-Letter.*
VERBOECKHOVEN, E.—*Shepherd Dogs.*
WILLEMS, F.—*The Letter.*
ZIMMERMANN, R. S.—*Love's Messenger.*
    "   "   *The Betrothal.*

COLLECTION OF MR. B. WALL,
PROVIDENCE, R. I.

ANTIGNA, J. P. A.—*Fisherwoman.*
    "   "   *The Thunderstorm.*
    "   "   *A Waif of the Streets.*
    "   "   *Peasant-Girl.*
BELLY, LEON A.—*Moorish Nuns in Algiers.*
BERNE-BELLECOUR, E.—*Trumpet Practice.*
BONINGTON, R. P.—*The Letter.*
BOYTON, I.—*Stranded Ships.*
    "   "   *Harbor of Bordeaux.*
    "   "   *Beach Scene.*
BRASSAUT, J. B.—*Study of a Horse.*
BROWN, J. LEWIS.—*Out to Pasture.*
CHARLET, LEONCE.—*The Old Guard.*
CHAPLIN, C.—*Copy from Boucher.*
CHARLES, J. B. S.—*Still Life—Kitchen Utensils.*
CHENU, F.—*Winter Landscape.*
COROT, J. B. C.—*Lake in a Morass.*
    "   "   *A Sand-Bank.*
    "   "   *Landscape with Washerwomen.*
    "   "   *Dunegat.*
    "   "   *Landscape.*
    "   "   *Study in Brown.*
    "   "   *Scène Britannique.*

COLLECTION OF MR. B. WALL,

PROVIDENCE, R. I.

Concluded.

CABOT, J. B. C.—A Bird's-Eye View.
" " View of Rouen.
" " Meadows.
CORBET, G.—Twilight.
" " Study of Two Boys.
" " The Glen.
COUTURE, T.—Study of a Head.
DAUBIGNY, C.—Spring.
" " Lake.
" " Shady Pool.
" " Before the Storm.
" " Coast of Normandy.
" " Sunset.
DECAMPS, O.—Study of a Head.
DECAMPS, A. G.—The Good Samaritan.
" " Richmond's Mate.
DE DREUX, A.—Fox Hunting—The Start.
DELACROIX, E.—The Somnabula.
DIOGENES, B.—The Crown of Louis XIV.
DOLL, N.—The Bathers.
" " Study of Flowers.
" " Fortune Telling.
DORE, G.—Gipsy Girl.
DUPRE, J.—We Americans.
DURSTER, A.—Lost.
EYES, A.—The Lovers.
FAVEN-PERRIN, F. N. A.—Fisher-Girl.
FROMENTIN, EUG.—Arab Falconer.
GERICAULT, J. L.—Cavalry Charge.
" " Still Life.
GIACOMETTI, F. B.—The Poems.
GIRARDY, K.—Monte.
" " Peasant Women.
GUIN, J. A. T.—Sunrise on the Beach.
HERBERT, JULES—Harvest of Hay.
" " Going to Market.
" " Landscape and Sheep.
HUTCHINS, T.—Study—Head.
JACQUE, C.—Landscape and Sheep.
JOHANESS, J. B.—Herd of Hayfields.
LANDSEER, CHAS.—Pool and Fireplace.
LATOUCHE, L.—Coast View.
" " Harbor View.
LEYS, BARON HENRI—The Interview.
LAMINAIS, F. V.—Gaulish Warriors Crossing a Stream.
MEYERS, RENE—Landscape.
MONTCALM, E.—Sunset.
" " Feeding the Camel.
MEYER VON BREMEN, J. G.—The First in the Fold.
MICHEL, G.—Landscape—The Pine.
" " The Marsh.
MONTEVELLI—Landscape with Nymphs and Cupids.
PILS, J. A. A.—Artillery Man.
RIGOLOT, G.—The Autumn Leaved.
ROUSSEAU, E.—Radish.
ROBERT, L.—Roman Ruins.
ROUSSEAU, TH.—Autumn.
SCHREYER, ART—Massacre of the Sultan's Women.
TABAERT, N. F. O.—After the Ball.
TOURMINEX, C. F. V. DE.—Landscape.
TROYON, C.—Landscape and Sheep.
" " Study of Sheep.
VERNET, H.—Battle Scene.
VIBERT, J. G.—The Forager.
VILLEGAS, JOSE.—The Poultry-Tender.

COLLECTION OF MR. J. A. BROWN,

PROVIDENCE, R. I.

BOKS, M.—Fable of the Miller, his Son, and the Ass.
BOUGUER, MME. JULIETTE PEYROL.—Sheep.
BONNAT, L.—A Little Contadina.
BOUGHTON, G. H.—Girl's Head.
BOUGUEREAU, W. A.—The Beggar-Girl.
BROWN, G. L.—Palermo.
CHAVET, V.—The Widow.
CLAYS, J. B. A.—Dutch Boats.
CORTE-CALZA, F. G.—Going to Market.
CORMON, J.—The Swing.
COROT, J. B. C.—Landscape.
CALVERY, J. F.—Sunset in Autumn.
DAUGINEY, R.—American Countrymen.
DIAZ, R.—The Favorite Sultana.
" " Landscape-Study.
DUPRE, JULES—Landscape.
HOMER, JOHNS.—Hay-Making.
GREUZE, W.—The Last Meal.
HUNT, WM. M.—Portrait of a Young Lady.
" " Girl's Head in Shadow.
IRVING, J. B.—The Cavalier.
INNESS, S.—Snow Scene.
JACQUE, CHAS.—Farmyard with Poultry.
" " The Shepherd.
JOVERALA, A.—Reverie.
KEYSER, E.—A Flemish Family Gathering Grapes.
KNAUS, L.—Female Head.
KORROMAN, B.—Jo the Winds.
LAPORTE, J. G.—The First Machines.
MATTESON, T. H.—On the Deck of the Mayflower.
" " The Pilgrim Fathers First Saw
both on Shore.
MOREL, H.—The Byzantine Madonna.
MEYER VON BREMEN, J. G.—The Little Housekeeper.
" " The Time Told.
MALETON, —St. Cecilia.
NARBRY, E.—The Rendezvous.
PORCEL, T.—French Flower Girl.
PORTAILS, —The Moorish Beauty.
ROUSSEAU, TH.—Sunset.
SELL, CHRISTIAN,—The Filten.
TROYON, C.—Sheep.
VAN MARCKE, E.—Cattle.
VERBOECKHOVEN, E.—White Horse.
WAYLEN, L. V.—Cattle.
ZIEM, V.—Venice.

COLLECTION OF MR. F. C. SALES,

PAWTUCKET, R. I.

ACHENBACH, O.—Naples at Midnight.
CROMMER, G.—The Saturday Fair.
DE BOCKSDEVILLE, A.—Garden Scene in France.
DOCKING, —The Discouraged Hare.
ESCOSURA, G.—In his Dotage.
HART, JAS. M.—"The Cattle Seek the Cooling Shade."
KREYER, V.—Winter in Russia.
KULLA, J.—Swedish Sextad Party.
LEWIS, H.—Luxembourg. [In Munich]
LICHTENSTEIN, M.—Searching a Castle for Treasure.
MAES, W.—The Picket.
PERAY, P. W.—Thanksgiving Time.
POPE, A.—Contentment.
PRATT, BELA—Young Again.
PRESTON, J. W.—Frost.

RAFFEL, CARL—Evening on the Sea.
ROBERTS, A.—Hidden Lane.—Marble.
SCHREIDER, V.—Mother's Jewels.
WORTH, R.—Happiness.
XYLANDER, W.—Moonrise on the North Sea.
ZANTROSE, DOG.—Labor and Study—Marble.

COLLECTION OF MR. W. RICHMOND,

PROVIDENCE, R. I.

BICKER, C.—A Cup of Tea.
BIERSTADT, A.—Western Kansas [Sunset].
CARMER, J.—Cheguian Girls Captured by Backs.
CLAYS, P. J.—Sunshine.
COROT, J. B. C.—Landscape.
DIAZ, N.—Landscape.
" " Turkish Women.
" " Marguerite and Mantha.
" " Flowers.
EAY, K.—The Sleepy Kitten.
JACQUET, G.—Cinderella.
LAMBER, H.—Supplement to Nigeria.
MAS, G.—Donation.
MESLE, H.—Autumn.
NEGRY, E.—Spring.
PAST, A.—Flowers.
SCHREYER, A.—The Scout.
TROYON, C.—Les Lavandières.
VERBOECKHOVEN, E.—Cattle.
VIRY, P.—The Falconer.
WAHLBERG, A.—Sunset on the Coast of Norway.
ZIEM, V.—Venice.

COLLECTION OF MR. R. C. TAFT,

PROVIDENCE, R. I.

BOUGHTON, G. H.—Indian Summer.
BRETON, JULES—The Lookout.
BRION, G.—The Banquet.
CORE, T.—Autumn Landscape.
CORBET, G.—The Still Pond.
DEVALLE, E.—Autumn Landscape.
DETTI, C.—The Guess Room.
DIAZ, N.—Land of Enchantment.
" " The Gipsies.
" " The Dead Bird.
DURAND, A. B.—Sunday Morning.
DIVEN, EUG.—The Sisters.
GIFFORD, SANFORD R.—Salute Church, Venice.
JOHNSON, EASTMAN—The Imprisoned Girl.
KENSETT, J. F.—Cliff at Newport.
KNAUS, L.—A Child.
LEON I FRANCIA, J.—Mordaunt Castle.
MERLE, H.—The New Novel.
MILLET, J. F.—The Knitting Shepherdess.
MUNKAS, M.—The Marriage Allotment.
RICHARDS, W. T.—Narragansett Pier.
ROUSSEAU, TH.—Plain of Rochester.
SCHREYER, A.—The Russian White Cart.
SOYER, P.—Little Monkey.
STRICKEN, T.—The Scout—Water-color.
VAN MARCKE, E.—The Village Herd after the Storm.
WEISSER, R.—Two Shadows—Water-color.
WHITTREDGE, W.—Landscape.
WYLIE, R.—The Brittany Fisher-Woman.
ZAMACOIS, E.—Waiting for an Audience.

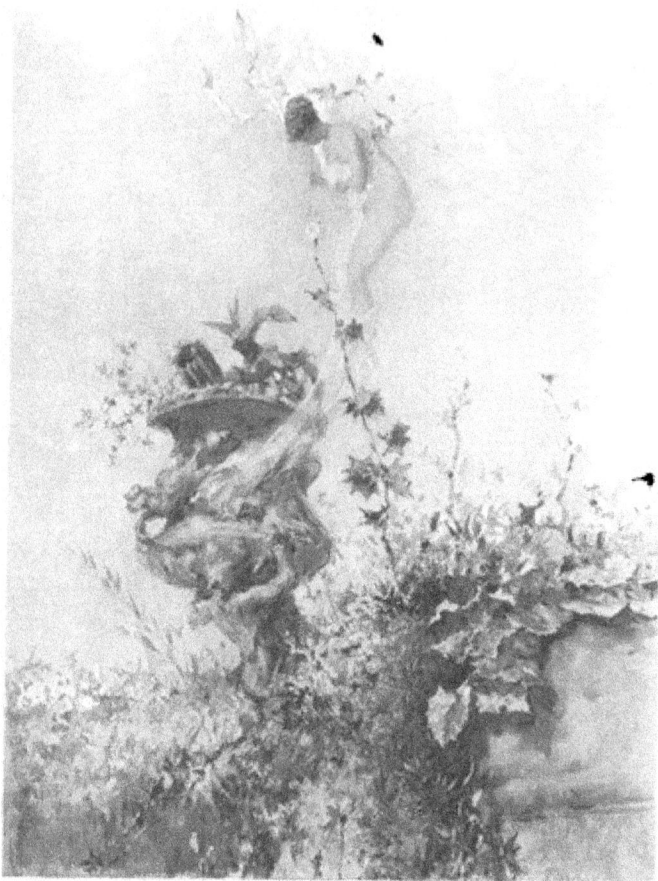

PSYCHE

ARTIST

MARIANO–JOSE–MARIA FORTUNY

Born at Reus, Spain, 1838; Died, 1874.   .   .   Pupil of the Academy, Madrid.

GOING DOWN TO THE RIVER

ENGRAVED BY J. LOUVON FROM THE ORIGINAL PAINTING, BY L. ALMA-TADEMA

THE COLLECTION OF MR. WILLIAM H. VANDERBILT.

THE house of this munificent collector being itself a work of art, whose details have been supplied by the most eminent painters of the old world and the new, it becomes a matter of sacrifice and renunciation to abstract ourselves from the consideration of architecture, of upholstery, or of embellishment for the purpose of doing justice above all to the collection of pictures. Many of the decorations, including the stained windows and the ceilings, have been designed by artists whose easel-works would be the pride of the gallery. The collection, however, is naturally the first object of comment in a book like this, and must be considered as the central jewel for our present regard, though even this rich gem has been far less costly than the casket.

The gallery of Mr. VANDERBILT, in a publication like the present, forms but one of a series of private galleries, and its individual character and importance are necessarily merged to some extent in the impartial justice due to other collections far less considerable in themselves. A limited description, in a series of many descriptions, is all that this publication will accommodate, though the gallery will be completely indexed and its principal treasures noted as minutely as in other cases. For a full understanding, however, of the collector's aims, with those of the architect and the decorators, recourse must be had to the CATALOGUE RAISONNÉ now preparing on a scale quite unprecedented with any such illustrated catalogue, and

to be immediately issued from the press of the present publisher, written by the same well-intentioned critic who indites these pages.

Two fine and memorable works by Alma-Tadema, the eminent Dutch artist established in London, give distinction to the gallery. The "Going Down to the River" (5 × 2½ feet) shows a perfectly characteristic scene of antique life by Tiber-side. The ferrymen are clamoring for custom. One swarthy fellow, with a truly Roman nose, and an outstretched braceleted arm, whose modeling and color and relief are the perfection of minute art, solicits a fare at the foot of the balustrade from a descending lady attended by her slave-girl and little daughter. The heads of these figures form great foreground projections in front of a distance most wonderfully broadened with giddy coiling water, or with the crispness of basking light on the stately white bridge, beneath whose centre arch a decorated galley shoots into view. A light *biga* passes over the bridge, whose driver flourishes his whip under a large umbrella-like canopy. One wishes for the power to soar up to the unusual altitude at which this composition is placed, to take one's fill of the mysterious art with which the textures are represented,—an art equally prodigious in counterfeiting the flesh, the marble, and the deep-looking water. This picture dates from 1879. The other example of the great archæological painter is the "Entrance to a Roman Theatre" (38 × 27 inches). The principal figures are sketched for these columns, as the engraving of the artist's other example distinguishes this page. The great sponge-like frontlet of hair seen on the busts of Roman empresses adorns the foreheads of both the ladies who meet each other in this rencontre. The widow, who has for escort her smartly-dressed little son, bestows the melancholy and stately smile of an Agrippina upon the proud Roman knight, in his weeds of peace, on whose shoulder an extravagantly dressed wife leans with such easy confidence. The honor in which the women are held defines this as a study of Roman, not of Greek, manners, and some such woman's-rights argument was doubtless in the mind of the painter when he composed his scene. A lady descending from the little gig-like chariot at the right, again, is most respectfully handed to the ground by a venerable man with silver locks. Inside, the audience

This is one of the artist's admirable studies of varied draperies, wonderfully antique in appearance, yet almost modern from their figured character. Previous painters of Roman scenes would have adopted for the child merely the white gown bordered with purple, and the manly toga of pure white for the knight, giving an inevitable sculpture-gallery air to the scene; but the present artist has ample justification for every unexpected item in his pictures, and draws upon a depth of archæological lore in which few professed antiquarians can rival him.

There are two of Gérôme's most elaborate compositions in this gallery,—"The Grand Condé," and "The Sword-Dance

HUNGARIAN VOLUNTEERS.
ETCHED BY L. CABLE FROM THE ORIGINAL PAINTING BY A. PETTENKOFEN.

are seen ascending the stairs of the theatre, and the broad daylight drifts into the corridors, for all the representations of Terence or Plautus to which these urbane Romans thronged were matinée performances. On the wall are the *sgraffiti*, scratched inscriptions taking the form of modern placards. Horace, in one of his satires, represents his slave Davus as lingering over these advertisements, and speculating on the merits of different gladiators, all the while justifying his interest by the absorption of his master in the latest works of art at the picture-shops. We have seen the attitude of Horace's lazy knave in Hector Le Roux's picture, in Mr. PIERPONT MORGAN's collection; in M. Alma's composition the inscriptions are not circus but theatrical bills, and the more aristocratic company throng by them without deigning a glance. Just inside the archway sits the ticket-taker at his table, collecting from the audience those ivory *tesseræ*, of which abundant specimens remain in the Naples Museum.

at the Pasha's"—as well as his exquisite gem of a "Bashi-Bazouk Drinking." Both the larger themes form subjects of plates in this work. The "Condé" is a conception based upon one of the few and highly-prized epigrams uttered by Louis XIV. When this model of deportment threw his cane 'out of window lest he should be tempted to use it on one of his officers, or invited an actor to supper out of bravado, or excused the slow gait of a warrior with a compliment, the court burst into ecstasy, the historians sharpened their pens and caught the incident in its freshness for posterity, and the priceless phrase sometimes lasted, as now, so as to spice a painter's art. "Do not hurry, my cousin. It is hard to walk quickly when a man is overloaded with laurel, like you!" The blessed phrase not only cured Condé's gout incontinently, but has taught urbanity to every princelet in Europe since it was uttered, in 1674. Gérôme makes a sort of illumination of it. The stair of honor at Versailles beams with light,

THE SWORD-DANCE AT A PACHA'S

ARTIST
JEAN LÉON GÉRÔME

BORN AT VESOUL, FRANCE, 1824.

PUPIL OF P. DELAROCHE

COLLECTION OF
MR. WILLIAM H. VANDERBILT, NEW YORK

and dazzling cherubim of the court are seen ascending and descending. This stairway was demolished by the grandson

FIGURES FROM "DEFENCE OF LE BOURGET."
FACSIMILE OF A SKETCH BY A. DE NEUVILLE FOR HIS PAINTING.

of the Sun-King, but Gérôme has restored it successfully from an old engraving. The stairs, in fact, support not only Louis XIV, but his little son, the Grand Dauphin, and when Louis the well-beloved had pulled down the steps on which his father and grandfather are now sustained, he soon pulled down the dynasty besides. "After me the deluge," he used to say, with cheerful self-gratulation. Far different thoughts from those of ruin are in the minds of this gorgeous court. The Grand Monarch's victories are still in respectable preponderance; Heidelberg is a cinder, and the Palatinate a waste. The Grand Condé returns from his conquests, and as the gouty prince enters for his first reception, he finds,—unusual favor!—that the king meets him on the landing of the celestial Jacob's ladder. "Sire," says the rheumatic old prince, at the bottom, "I beg your majesty's pardon for making you wait;" and then Louis, with happy repartee, and without any coaching from Bossuet at his side, delivers his epigram, quite neat and prompt and inedited. How these crowded balustrades ring at the godlike speech, and how Vauban's old ironsides wave their oriflammes and golden lilies! Gérôme reconstructs the scene, as usual, with an incisive and plausible accuracy that makes you believe it could not have been otherwise in the minutest particular. With a touch of appropriate poetry, of which the secret never fails him, he makes the proverbial laurels of the speech come forward in person as the living *rôles* of the occasion. He strews the steps with them, and the seneschal tangles his sword with their green freshness, as he draws it in salute.

This seneschal, one of the pair who guard the lower step, and who are the sole spectators wearing their hats like the king, is represented in Gérôme's preparatory sketch on page 100, a drawing which has the artist's usual profound significance of strenuous and sensitive lines. Each seneschal is backed by a couple of pretty boy-pages, the blooming contemporaries of that lean and rickety Dauphin on the landing, who will just succeed in fathering the next king, and will die without reigning. Bossuet, whose genius for polish was employed in giving a gloss to this royal scion, stands behind him, tall, elegant, and thatched with his white hair instead of a perruke. A half-dozen court ladies are grouped at the monarch's left elbow, and others lean out from the lobby of the upper floor. Ladies and courtiers alike stand well, crowded but graceful, subservient yet human, with that perfection of decorous posture never better understood than among the red-heels of Versailles. Through these parted walls of faces, in the solitude of his glory, the Prince of Condé creeps upward alone, in an attitude compounded by the painter's clairvoyance out of gout and reverence. This picture was finished in 1878, and from its multiplicity of detail cost the artist unusual trouble. "I hope I have succeeded," he wrote, "for my toil towards the desired end has been unintermitting. I hope, too, that your own satisfaction will have been attained, for that is a result which I have done my best to reach." The picture of "The Grand Condé" measures 54 by 37 inches.

Like the above picture, the "Sword-Dance at the Pasha's" (38 × 24 inches), abstraction made of its color, is a composition of great merit. The truncated appearance of the squatting Arnauts as they seemingly sink into the floor under favor of a general flourish of white kilts, and the

THE EMIR'S FAVORITE.
ETCHED BY DUMONT FROM THE ORIGINAL PAINTING BY E. ZAMACOIS.

monumental dignity with which they hold themselves upright in this trying posture, contrasts well with the swaying variety of the musicians, also cross-legged. The Pasha attends to his business of amorous stimulus with a dignity which makes

ENTRANCE TO A ROMAN THEATRE.
PRINCIPAL FIGURES FROM THE PAINTING BY L. ALMA-TADEMA.

it seem the noblest moment of his life. Between the two admirably balanced groups of officials at home and intruding nomads, rises the palm-like figure of the Almeh, one curly sabre balanced on her head and another brandished in her hand. She rocks backward and forward on toe and heel of an exquisite foot, and her multiplied collars of coin fly around her body like lariats as she moves. The two-stringed viol and the pipes are played with extreme seriousness by her estimable relatives squatted on the floor, her honest husband, with a fatuous grin, rubs the kettle-drum under his arm with a horny middle finger, and the almehs who are next to dance, beat time, sitting, with their hands or tambourines. Gérôme here exults in his chance to represent a noble house of Cairo, and the eye of the collector of Eastern curiosities is amply refreshed with potteries, rings of glass lamps half full of perfumed oil, the tracery embroidered over the tiles, or woven in perspective into the enormous carpets. In front sits a cynocephalus baboon, with the gravity of an Egyptian god, regarding the performance with a judicial air of extreme good-breeding. The artist repeats the principal figure with

MORNING.
FAC-SIMILE OF A SKETCH FROM THE ORIGINAL PAINTING BY T. ROUSSEAU.

different supporting groups in his "Sword-Dance in a Café" in Mr. C. CROCKER's collection in San Francisco.—In contrast

with these two elaborate compositions, which impress by their studied elegance, and must depend on time to give them tone and unity, is seen the little "Bashi-Bazouk Drinking" (12 × 16 inches), due to the same pencil at its best period, and a masterpiece of delicacy and knowledge.

Fortuny is more than once represented. In a little water-color reproduced by the plate he shows us "Maidenhood as a Butterfly," sipping with a straw the nectar from a gadding gourd, whose blossoms eagerly ascend to meet her breath. A strange rococo garden-vase, upheld by cupids and filled with awkward cactus-leaves, entangles the gauzes which stream around her form and dissolve with the vapors of morning. The vase and the gourd-plant, the cactus and the maiden's petal-like Psyche-wings, are faintly printed and blotted against a swimming sky that spreads behind the crest of the terrace where the dreaming painter evokes this vision of a garden-spirit. The caprice is altogether novel, and not derived from any preceding form of allegorical painting. Fortuny brings in a new breath of art, quite hot and tropical, inspired by the hashish of floating Persian isles, or purloined from the

THE TWO FAMILIES.
FROM THE ORIGINAL PAINTING BY M. MUNKACSY.

imagery of oriental poets who never saw a picture. As the mystical maiden of his fancy closes her broad moth-wings to settle on a flower, the dry song of the cicada, the pulsating light of the fire-fly, and the whisper of the bulbul frightened by morning, seem to throb through the painter's strange vignette. The caprices of artists so entirely unconventional have a wonderful value, in their property of evoking new poetic flavors. This is the picture of which we have already noticed a repetition in the Philadelphia gallery of Mr. WARNER —a great prize, if equally genuine with the little Vanderbilt specimen of 1868—and our plate forms an illustration of either painting.

Another Fortuny, of which we show M. Bocourt's fine drawing on page 102, is of earlier style, and is entitled "The Fantasia" (24 × 20 inches). "Making the powder talk" is a barbaric ceremony which Fortuny repeatedly observed when he went down into Morocco to paint the battle of Tetuan, and he has fastened upon the canvas the full energy and enthusiasm of the scene. The mad Arabs in front, who leap around in a circle, jumping perpendicularly into space and discharging their slim guns among each other's legs while suspended in the air, are represented with an impromptu of movement which was never excelled by Delacroix, and whose abandon is corrected by a very sufficient accuracy of drawing. These fiendish and half-naked leapers, whose horny camels' feet beat the dust, whose girdles are stuck with swords and weighted with powder-flasks, career about in a Tophet of their own gunpowder-smoke, while beyond them the comrades of their celebration are seen like saints in their niches, statuesque in white haiks and spiral turbans. This picture, obtained from the collection of M. Foli, at Rome, is identical with the Fantasia of the W. H. Stewart gallery in Paris, except that in Mr. Stewart's example a tame lion is held in leash, instead of the enormous and ox-like goat here seen retained for sacrifice.—A little oil-color sketch of Fortuny's obtained at the sale of his effects, in 1875, is a sitting figure of a "Court-Jester, Time of Charles V" (5 × 8 inches).

An important picture by Edouard Detaille was painted to the order of the owner, in 1878, and perpetuates with French willfulness the dreary business of the Franco-Prussian war; it represents "The Arrest of an Ambulance Corps in the Eastern part of France, in January, 1871" (46 × 32 inches). A Prussian general has ridden into a captured town to occupy it, and causes the provisional arrest of a party of French civil Ambulanciers. The peaceful and scientific-looking surgeons and nurses, with Geneva crosses tied around the sleeves of their overcoats, stand patiently in the snow, until the Prussians shall have examined their papers and certified them to be in good order: after this they will be distributed through the German hospitals and permitted to collect the wounded of both nations. The snowy street of a Franche-Comté village, with slushy ruts admirably made out in Detaille's photographic style, forms the stage-set of the drama. At the left

CABARET IN THE TIME OF LOUIS XIII.
FAC-SIMILE OF A SKETCH FROM THE ORIGINAL PAINTING BY E. MEISSONIER

are five horsemen—a grave flat-capped General like Moltke, an officer of the cuirassiers in front in his steel corslet (Bran-

denburgisches Cuirassier, Regiment No. 6, Kaiser Nicholas I von Russland), an officer of the Dragoons in blue tunic and

L'ORDONNANCE
ENGRAVED BY STEPHEN FROM THE ORIGINAL PAINTING BY J. L. E. MEISSONIER

yellow collar, a full-bearded officer of the staff, with amaranth-colored lappels and cap, and an abundantly frogged officer of hussars (Liebhusaren, Regiment No. 2). The little group of doctors is guarded by three foot-soldiers of the Prussian Chasseurs (Rheinisches, jäger, Batallion No. 8), and their officer. A dead Bavarian foot-soldier lies at their feet with his face in the snow, which is strewn with his cigarettes and pocket-matches, and a Bavarian contingent swarms in the public place before the little church. The picture is of high value, as portraying with the accuracy of an eye-witness the actualities of a war which raised the conquerors so high in the scale of European powers.—A small oil-picture by the same artist represents "Skirmishing," and shows the incident of fortifying a common wall against an unexpected attack of Prussian troops during the invasion of French territory.—A water-color picture, also by Detaille, shows a "Parade," and was painted in 1880. It is of considerable size, and was sketched during one of the painter's trips across the British Channel. The scene takes place at London Tower, and is crowded with military and spectators, the artist doing special justice to the beautiful Scotch uniform—the most gallant and picturesque in Western Europe.

Emile Van Marcke yields a fine subject for our plate, in his rich but tranquil composition entitled "The Forest" (34 × 24 inches). The contrast of the silvery white standing cow against the dark relief of the trees makes a precious bit of repoussé indeed, when trees and cow are so well painted as they are here. She turns her glossy neck, hung with the droning bell, as if some footstep of the milkmaid were approaching through the velvet grass. The pool she stands in reflects four white limbs, and collects the superfluous drops from her streaming muzzle, while the composition is balanced by a meditative dark cow standing at her right and four others

tangle of beauties and brilliancies. Here the willfully crooked trunks and boughs form a perfect lattice-work across the composition, in which, as in a net, the forms of the cattle are caught in almost every attitude and point of view. A full-uddered cow, rubbing her neck against the most conveniently crooked stem, forms the central object; behind is the brown thatch of a country tool-house, enlaced all round by the

THE CONCERT.
FAC-SIMILE OF A DRAWING OR ETCHING FROM THE ORIGINAL PAINTING BY E. ISABEY.

at her left, whose figures half sink in the minor and trifling hollows of the plain. It is scarcely a demerit that the contrasts of tone and value are a little forced, that there is a kind of rhetorical emphasis about the very sombre trees and very brilliant animal, interfering with the picture's unity as a composition, and suggesting something hard, positive, inlaid like a white enamel on black. Beautiful as are the gray vapory cattle-pieces of masters who more dearly love the country, the massive violence with which Van Marcke models his vigorous alto-reliefs has a tangible impressiveness of its own.—The "Pasture at Soreng," in the Department of the Lower Seine (5 × 4 feet), a picture from the Salon of 1879, is the largest Van Marcke in the collection, and is a wonderful

zigzag limbs of the orchard, which pour upon its roof the shadows from their armloads of rich green leaves. In contrast to the solidity and breadth of the last-named picture, the present one is a glittering distribution of sunny points. Both are rich in all graces save those of simplicity and unconsciousness on the painter's part. Van Marcke is a rhetorician among animal-painters, always in antithesis and paradox.

Kaemmerer's "Ladies of the Directory" (18 × 24 inches) is a picture painted in 1870. Two *merveilleuses*, in short dresses tied under the bosom with a drawing-string, are attended by an *incroyable*, with straggling Brutus locks, half-moon *claque*, two watches in his fobs, and the cock-a-doodle

RECEPTION OF THE GREAT CONDÉ BY LOUIS XIV

ARTIST

JEAN LÉON GÉRÔME

BORN AT VESOUL, FRANCE, 1824.   PUPIL OF P. DELAROCHE.

———

COLLECTION OF

MR. WILLIAM H. VANDERBILT, NEW YORK.

strut of Carle Vernet's caricatures. The ladies are pretty, while the exquisite has fatigued and vapid lineaments, the sure earmarks of an intellect that has passed through a great revolution and learned nothing. The Tuileries, with its hunchback mansards and the tubbed orange-trees of its garden, forms a background for these precious figures, designed with the conscious and posturing grace of the period.

"The King's Favorite," a small picture painted in 1867 by Zamacois, was immediately famous, as much from the political satire involved as from the technical excellence of the execution. It was the grim delight of the Spanish genius to live among the French and to lash them,—to point out the flimsy foundations of their power and their willing subserviency to a comedy government. The twenty years of the third Napoleon's unmolested play-acting gave the artist incessant opportunities for the exercise of a caustic pencil, an instrument of torture which never dropped its point while his hand lived to wield it. The native artists were not always so uncompromising. While Gérôme, for instance, faithfully kept up the sham, designing a portrait of Cæsar for the Emperor's book which looked, and was meant to look, like Napoleon, and demonstrating the fancied resemblance of the court to that of Louis XIV by a series of plausible compliments to the Grand Monarch's urbanity and the Grand Monarch's

STUDY FOR SENESCHAL FROM "THE GRAND CONDÉ."
FACSIMILE OF A DRAWING BY J. L. GÉRÔME.

Imperial and all his supposed ancestors in whitest marble, Zamacois painted him rolling oranges for grave statesmen to pick up. While Yvon painted the Arabs in spontaneous homage before Eugénie, Zamacois painted the palace courtiers doing obeisance to "The King's Favorite." Here, under a symbol borrowed from the court of Francis I and from Triboulet, he satirizes the back-stairs intrigues under Napoleon III, and the infamous court paid by capable men to the Mlle. Bellanger of the day, or to the last impudent American beauty who earned the imperial "remark" at the promiscuous crush of a Tuileries ball. The sarcasm is none the less obvious for being transferred to the sixteenth century. Zamacois shows us a broad palace stair, laid with tapestry, down which the court hunchback advances in company with a dog larger than himself. The entering crowd of place-seekers, who are about to throng into the ante-chamber, and whose stomachs are all hungry for preferment, stop humbly and salute the pocket potentate—the all-important familiar who has the ear of the king. The warrior lays his helmet on the balustrade and bows his bald forehead to the jester; Barkilphedro, in front, advances and droops his velvet cloak in a hypocritical salute; every spine is bent, except that of a fresh, candid young captain introduced for contrast, a figure as perfect in its healthful comeliness as the dwarf in his deformity. This careless youth, in a fine new suit, with "unions" of freshest lustre gleaming in his ears, simply stands and stares, in wonder dashed with pity. Meantime the King's Favorite, with his bauble carried like a sceptre, exposes his

KNITTING SHEPHERDESS OF BARBIZON.
DRAWN BY EMILE VERNIER FROM THE ORIGINAL PAINTING BY J. F. MILLET.

literary taste, the Spanish satirist's persecution never flagged. While the French Guillaume was sculpturing the Prince

fangs in a down-curving smile, the sign of a deformed mind in a deformed body. This satire was displayed to the Paris public in the year of the great Exposition of 1867, and planted its sting in the bosom of the various court favorites while Louis Napoleon was entertaining a company of visiting monarchs.

The two specimens of August Pettenkoffen were obtained from one of the sales of the dealer Sedelmeyer, at the Hôtel Drouot in Paris, in 1877. The biography of this fine artist was given in the article on Mr. J. H. Stebbins's collection,

which follow closely. In the cart are confusedly packed the band of Hungarian volunteers. Standing in the wagon, amongst the would-be warriors, rises a lively young fellow, doubtless the recruiting-sergeant, who howls the national hymn of Hungary, accompanying himself with a rataplan on the drum. The contents of the cart form two distinct groups; in front is the light-headed and light-hearted volunteer, who sits beside the driver and gayly turns his back upon his village, and dashes cheerfully into unknown adventures; behind, the regretful recruits, whose eyes dwell fondly on the

AN ARAB FANTASIA.
FAC-SIMILE OF A SKETCH BY F. BRIDGMAN FROM THE ORIGINAL PAINTING BY H. FORTUNY.

Vol. I. page 103. The paintings, drawings and water-colors of Pettenkoffen have always been highly prized and priced at picture-sales. Born at Vienna in 1823, this artist came in 1851 to Paris; the latter date is that of the picture of the "Volunteers," painted to order for the picture-merchant Van Cuyck, who bought it back from his client M. Roné, and declared that nothing but death should take it out of his possession. He kept his word, and it was only upon the decease of the expert that his heirs placed the treasure upon the market. The drama represented in the "Hungarian Volunteers" (12 × 10 inches) is a cheery one. A country cart, drawn by three galloping horses, races across the steppes of Hungary on a fine autumn morning. Clouds of dust are seething from beneath the wheels, and collect into a long plume of smoky whiteness, whose confused wreaths half hide in their powdery thickness the forms of other vehicles

little corner of earth where they were born, and which they may never behold again. Behind the sergeant is a brooding visage which even sees distinctly the fatal drama of the other picture hung near by, the "Ambulance-Wagon Carrying off the Wounded;" it is the natural sequel, and the volunteer need only pierce a short way into the mists of the future to find his natural destiny. Such are the details of this little masterpiece. They could not have been arranged with a more perfect tact of narrative and expression. And the rigorous observation of detail, the love of truth, equal the dramatic power. The French critic, De Lostalot, remarks: "Everything here is finished with utmost refinement of care, yet the pencil never lingers over improper analysis; we only see distinctly as much as would be reasonably visible in so rapid and precipitate an action. In the painting-method we notice a corresponding good sense; the colors are chosen

LA FORÊT

with so fine a tact as to give the right key without any disturbing brilliancy; they melt into the harmonies of an

THE COMMITTEE ON MORAL BOOKS.
FAC-SIMILE OF A SKETCH FROM THE ORIGINAL PAINTING BY J. G. VIBERT.

atmosphere of golden gray, where the light warmed by early morning is yet threaded with the wisps of dust. We find very few pictures where success reaches such perfection; and it may be this completeness which induces us to look for terms of comparison back of the times in which we live. We must go away to the finest period of Dutch art to find the parallel works from which the artist might have drawn his inspiration." On the revelation of this fine effort at Vienna, in 1873, the Austrian Emperor decided to honor the author especially by making him chevalier, and awarding him the order of the oaken crown. The other Pettenkoffen in the gallery, the "Ambulance Bearing the Wounded," was executed before the subject of which it forms the natural sequel. Both, however, were painted in the same year of 1851, although the greatest possible development of style is visible in the more elaborate picture. His "Ambulance" shows more of the rapid narrative talent of the experienced illustrator, such as we see it exhibited in the pictorial journal; it reveals an intelligent designer, very clever in grouping his figures and making them tell the story, but caring less for technic. Pettenkoffen, living when it was painted on funds allowed him by the Art-Academy of Vienna, did it in routine style, putting into it more execution than what he had learned, and neglecting as yet to inspire himself with the severe nature-study practised by his new neighbors, Troyon, Rousseau, Alfred Stevens and Meissonier. We see in it the facile picturesqueness of the Vienna school of 1850, without any promise of a higher art than that of Vernet or Bellangé. The color is scrambled on in flat scene-painter's masses, with hardly enough gradation to satisfy the necessities of modeling; a broad deposit of paint, hastily fenced in with an outline, makes a figure, and the costumes are executed with sketchy facility, without realism or close study. But the picture is notwithstanding a very interesting one, impregnated with the national observations which the artist had collected during his career as captain in Francis-Joseph's

army. Though the execution is superficial the statement of facts is spirited and true, and the impetuous Vienna style of the smaller painting proves to be a good foundation on which to work up the more refined observation of the recruiting subject. The interest of the "Ambulance" picture results from the maker's deep knowledge of the occurrences depicted, and the ensuing reality of the impression. A wagon heavily dragged by oxen is painfully progressing over a road made deep by rains: two soldiers push it behind. This provisional equipage is taking to the real ambulance near by a load of wounded men picked up on the battle-field. The postures of these stricken men are given with a sober truthfulness which proves that they have been studied on the spot. There is in Art a well-known dying soldier—theatrical and emphatic, all ready for his monument—which the painter takes care not to show. These men have been wounded in reality, and they feel their misery. They are the hapless victims whom the painter has seen in his army career, not boastful of their cause, but suffering humbly and retiringly, for the glory of their commanders. Over the whole scene there is a covering of silence and dejection. Amidst the bloody straw, where lie these prostrate and unlucky victims, confused with the sudden stroke which has menaced their life, we should hear at most a sigh or a grunt, when the wheel jolts over some obstacle. One has fainted quite away, and the surgeon, standing in the forepart of the wagon, is trying to bring him to. In the foreground of the picture one recognizes a figure well-known in military art, the trudging soldier who lifts up his shoulders and back patiently against the rain, followed by the faithful dog who shares his thoughts; one recognizes with some little surprise this hero of Horace Vernet, presented in Hungary with all of his old doggedness by an Austrian painter.

Alphonse de Neuville's "Defence of Le Bourget" (about 8 × 5 feet) is probably its author's masterpiece. It was displayed during the Paris Exposition of 1878, but not at the Champs de Mars, for fear of exciting German susceptibilities. It is said, however, that its resting-place at Goupil's was

THE PORTRAIT.
FAC-SIMILE OF A SKETCH FROM THE ORIGINAL PAINTING BY LOUIS LELOIR.

visited by every German then in Paris, and that one of them, no less a judge than Knaus the painter, declared that he did not see its equal at the Exposition. During the second action which had this little town for its theatre, a handful of romantic defenders—eight officers and twenty men—barricaded themselves in the village church, swearing an oath to die rather than surrender. "It was necessary," wrote General Duroc of this romantic defense, "to shoot them through the windows and bring up cannon, to force a capitulation from the courageous band." The German newspapers have answered this report, to which the celebrity of the picture has given a sort of immortality, with some facts which rather diminish the heroism of the resistance. For the painter, however, all

The display of works by J. F. Millet is very fine in this collection. The "Knitting Shepherdess of Barbizon" (11×16 inches) is one of his tender, evenly-colored masterpieces, where a veil of soft gray atmosphere covers the flock, the woods, and the peasant-girl who stands leaning upon her shepherd's crook, like the central gnomon upon a dial, around which the sheep revolve from morning till night with the stillness of a shadow. The gentle click of the needles, as natural in the fields as a cricket's song, is kept up by the girl, who has a stationary air as she leans a little forward on her crook, to ease her standing position, thus forming a sort

PASTURE AT NORENG (LOWER SEINE).
ENGRAVED BY LANGEVAL FROM THE ORIGINAL PAINTING BY E. VAN MARCKE

is grandeur on the part of the French, all brutality on that of the Prussians. The dying Lieutenant Grison, of the Grenadiers de la Garde, who afterwards expired of his wounds, is seen carried out of the church by a couple of his faithful mobiles, while his officers are ranked in his path under the custody of animal-looking Germans. "You will oblige me much by not declaring," wrote the artist to a critic, "that I have made the Prussian conquerors polite and respectful;—that would make my flesh creep, and would be contrary to the truth." At the foot of the church steps, forming a melancholy guard of honor to receive him, are two of his fellow-officers in the custody of German soldiers; Commandant Brasseur, of the Voltigeurs of the Guard, waits between a couple of obtuse-looking privates, and his friend, Captain O. de Verne, of the Twelfth Mobiles of the Seine, stands next at his right.

of tripod upon the earth. The flock, her daily care, seems to enfold her, and give her a reason of existence; the wood seems to enfold the flock, and the sky the woods; it is all a system of lives which depend on each other, a phase of the simple dignity of country existence,—to maintain which system in proper balance the watchful dog stands a little apart, needful to the business yet not quite of it, like a mechanic's fly-wheel or governor. Millet has found the true poet's secret of composing a cyclic action, in which all the parts seem to depend on each other as truly as the worlds in their orbits.—In the "Woman Going to Draw Water"—a figure of a rather proud well-formed farmer's daughter bearing pails —the artist meant to express a great deal, and he has written a rather long letter on her account, to show that she was not a water-vendor, nor a servant, but a responsible housewife, "going to get water for the household, for her husband and children's soup." The weight of her buckets causes a slight contraction of the features, but through it all "one should see a kind of homely goodness." He has made a well in a curious niche, a very old-fashioned form; and this too has a meaning, and is intended to suggest that many before her had come thither to draw water. What is to the purpose is that in this canvas of 1860 Millet has not quite got rid of his Delaroche manner—a manner which can be best explained by reference to those thoroughly tough figures of Delaroche which seem like some very superior kind of art-leatherwork. Other pictures by Millet, "At the Well," "The Knitting Lesson," and "Hunting in Winter," all small canvases, give the various sides of his intense and concentrated genius.

A number of pictures of high interest must be considered briefly. "The Two Families" (58×41 inches), by Munkácsy,—cut page 98—represents his later manner, having been seen only in 1880 at the Royal Academy; accordingly we find the blonde tone, seemingly caught up from Alfred Stevens, retained for the figures, while portions of the background keep his old vigorous addiction to inkiness, and look like blacksmith's work. The incident is the meeting of a family of dogs with a human family of the same number. A young wife—one of those vigorous and hardly beautiful Czech types beloved by the Hungarian—has given her three children their breakfast, and sits at the table watching the same number of fat pug puppies and their mother. The infants, including baby in its nurse's arms, delightedly watch the little cylindrical pups over their dish of milk.—F. Roybet, a vigorous Paris painter, who is one of the few who can aptly set their French vigor beside Munkácsy's vigor, is seen with "A Musical Party" (46×58 inches). In this rich composition (cut on page 100) a fair lady, alone among a crowd of gentlemen, sings from a sheet of music, while the gallants accompany her on flute, mandolin, or bass-viol. Though the costumes are Louis Treize, there is nothing here to remind us of the faded æsthetes of the Hôtel Rambouillet. Roybet is an artist who would paint even Mlle. de Scudéry as an

A MARRIAGE OF CONVENIENCE.
FAC-SIMILE OF A SKETCH FROM THE ORIGINAL PAINTING BY A. LONTAURAS.

amazon.—L. Ruiperez illustrates the same epoch—see cut on page 99—in his "Cabaret in the time of Louis XIII"

(11×9 inches). The painter was one of the little band of Spanish students who have made of late years a university

THE REALM.
FAC-SIMILE OF THE ORIGINAL SKETCH FOR HIS PAINTING BY T. COUTURE.

city of Paris, so far as the arts are concerned; he painted this picture in 1866, and has since died, at an untimely age. A plump waitress, pouring drink for a table-full of Richelieu's swashbucklers, after the sirge of Rochelle, is not a very new theme, but the Spanish youth has made it salient with his accuracy and impressive with his chiaroscuro.

Vibert, whose pictures come in like the "good things" narrated by a professional diner-out—one who earns his meal by his jolly stories,—is found in the collection with two examples, both illustrated in these pages. "The Peeping Roofers" (see cut at the beginning of the present chapter) is a water-color, painted to order in 1880, in double form, the upper register showing the curious slaters and the lower one what they see. What they detect is a family bath, with ladies in beautiful bathing-dresses splashing about, or taking refreshments, in a luxuriously decorated *hammums* fit for the Arabian Nights. The oil-color specimen, the "Committee on Moral Books," by the same wit, (26×19 inches), is a picture which facetiously supposes that the clergy who prepare the annual *Index Expurgatorius* secretly enjoy the light literature they condemn. The composition shows (cut page 103) two members of the committee of cardinals, which is called the Congregation of the Index. Their weapons are a blazing fire and a pair of tongs. The pincers hover threateningly over the light leaves of Dumas or Balzac, while the holy inquisitor dips into the doomed pages with rare enjoyment.

Louis Leloir, in a daintily-painted canvas called "The Portrait" (38 x 26 inches), painted to the owner's order in 1879, shows a wealthy Holland home in the early part of the seventeenth century (cut page 103). Some pupil of Miereveldt has brought up his palette and paint-pots to the porch of the mansion, a quaint brick house with *mascarons*

novel by Daudet, whose hero Numa repeatedly notices how French officials and bureau-clerks always sit with their legs stretched out, lest the bagging at their knees should reveal that they are desk-men and not riding-men. The husband adjusts his eyeglass and turns the leaves of his paper with a breakfast-knife, profoundly oblivious of his young wife who

THE DANCE OF "LA PAVONE."
FAC-SIMILE OF THE ORIGINAL SKETCH FOR HIS PAINTING BY F. WILLEMS.

and arabesques on its stone facings. The heiress of the house sits on the steps to be painted, on a fine bit of tapestry, while her governess or "reader" thrums the mandolin to amuse her, and a gallant is particularly detailed to keep her smiling with his wit, as the buffoons were employed by Leonardo to create the smile of the "Joconde."—Loustauneau, a young pupil of Vibert's, shows "The Marriage of Convenience" (31 x 21 inches) an incident of post-nuptial antipathy (cut page 105). The posture of the cold-looking cavalry officer would seem to indicate that the artist had read a late

bites her lip across the table; a cavalry soldier employed as servant, with an apron tied over his army trousers, looks with youthful and intelligent sympathy at the neglected bride.— Grison, who paints "A Good Omen" (26 x 25 inches), is a Strasburg artist, like Brion and Doré. He shows (cut on the next page) an elderly bride and matter-of-fact groom stepping through the mud into a church to be married, but interrupted by a smiling nurse, who carries out a baby from its baptism. —Willems, the Belgian painter, shows the old stately dance of "La Pavone" (30 x 42 inches) which, as the name indicates,

ARREST OF AN AMBULANCE CORPS

ARTIST

J. B. EDOUARD DETAILLE

BORN AT PARIS, 1848.

PUPIL OF MEISSONIER.

COLLECTION OF

MR. W. H. VANDERBILT, NEW YORK

was imitated from the tail-spreading of a peacock, with much gorgeous expansion of petticoats and trains. His own portrait is introduced among the musicians, as also that of Gérôme, with his recently-acquired crown of gray hair. This picture (cut page 106) is from the Exposition of 1878.

"The Realist" (15 x 18 inches) was painted by Couture to ridicule Courbet and the brutal naturalistic painters. The misguided disciple (cut page 105) uses the head of a hog for his model, and the classic head of Ariadne for a seat. A color-study of "Les Enrôlements Volontaires" shows one of the dreams of Couture's career, which he never lived to realize; his intentions are fully developed in the curious memoirs he has left.

As a specimen of the landscapes, Rousseau's "Morning" (21 x 12 inches), from the Laurent-Richard collection, is illustrated on page 98. It is one of six Rousseaus present—a scene of sluggish water and scrubby trees, made rich with the artist's opulence of color and infinite with his knowledge of atmospheric perspective. A fine snow-scene by Munthe, and good specimens of Dupré, Daubigny, Corot, Troyon and the English Linnell, give proof that landscape art is a paramount object of the collector's attention.

The VANDERBILT gallery is a perfect treasure-house of Meissoniers. The specimen illustrated is "L'Ordonnance" (15 x 18 inches), seen at the Paris Exposition of 1867; in this group (cut page 99) a general, comfortably installed in his cabinet with an aide, receives a written instruction from his commander-in-chief at the hands of a grisly-looking orderly in the powdered and plaited locks of Daugereau's hussars.— "General Desaix" (16 x 12 inches) from the same Exposition, recalls the retreat through Bavaria with Moreau. Learning from a captured Bavarian the position of the two Austrian forces, he arranges that masterly march of the Army of the Rhine which had all the success of a victory. The intellectual and astute face of the young nobleman shows the integrity which afterwards caused him to be called the Just Sultan, in Egypt, and the intelligence which enabled him to change to a triumph the defeat of Marengo, just before dying on its field. Essays might be written on these varied and representative Meissoniers, not forgetting the portrait of Mr. VANDERBILT, so like a Gerard Dow, and that of Meissonier with his wife, a successful challenge to the famous Rembrandt with the fair Saskia on his knee.

A GOOD OMEN.
PRINCIPAL FIGURES FROM THE PAINTING BY P. A. COSSON.

CATALOGUE OF MR. W. H. VANDERBILT'S COLLECTION.

BEFORE THE ALCALDE

ARTIST

JULES WORMS

BORN AT PARIS, 1832.   PUPIL OF LAFOSSE.

COLLECTION OF
MR. D. W. POWERS, ROCHESTER, N. Y.

PRESENTATION OF THE INFANT LOUIS XIV TO THE COURT.

FAC-SIMILE OF THE SKETCH MADE FOR HIS PICTURE BY J. E. LEMAN.

LIST OF PERSONAGES, COMMENCING ON THE LEFT.

1 Lady of Honor the Court's   2 Madame de Lisieux   3 Princesse de Carimine   4 Prince de Condé Setimé   5 Comtesse St. Salvator   6 Duchesse de la Trémouille   7 Duchesse de Montpensier (young girl)   8 Duchess de Bourbon.   9 Maréchal de Bassompierre.   10 Duke de Chevreuse.   11 Duke des Longueville.   12 Duke de la Trémouille.   13 Duke de Luxicourt.   14 Duke de Chevigny.   15 Bishop of Beauvais. (King's Confessor.)

THE COLLECTION OF MR. D. W. POWERS.

ARTIST, FROM A SKETCH BY E. ZAMACOIS.

LIKE a pleasant chapter of Washington Irving, the picture of "El Pelele," by A. Garcia-Mencia, in the large art gallery of Mr. D. W. Powers, at Rochester, N. Y., takes us straight to Grenada and the Alhambra. On the right of the scene is introduced the entrance to the grand Cathedral at Grenada,—in the sacristy of which, by-the-by, Fortuny has placed the famous "Marriage in the Vicaria." Over the tiled roofs in the distance, a little out of place for the actuality of the view, but brought in arbitrarily to add to the interest of the locality, is one of the turrets of the Alhambra—that "tower of the two sisters," from whose window a romantic leap was made, as Irving has narrated. In the foreground is taking place a sacred frolic eminently characteristic of Spain; it is the religious comedy of "El Pelele," wherein, on the night before Easter, the effigy of Judas Iscariot is tossed by girls in a blanket for his crime. The boneless traitor, in a white wool wig, flies high in the air on the impulse given by these little zealous brown hands, and the arched Spanish insteps are gayly treading a measure as the handsome *majas* circle round the open plaza with their blanket. The painter neatly contrives a modern street-scene

in which there is not a single spectator in modish and commonplace dress. Instead of modern dandies and cits, we have a street-crowd entirely made up of romantic characters—the guitar-player in his *marsillé* jacket, the bare-limbed fruit-seller sitting on his striped blanket, the shoeless begging monk making off with his presents of poultry, wherewith to break his long lenten fast, and casting a satisfied glance at the torture of Judas, the girls with their high combs and mantillas and silken ankles, and a barber-shop fit for Figaro in the middle distance. "El Pelele" was exhibited in the Paris Salon of 1876; the painter, Antonio Garcia-Mencia, was born at Madrid; his first instructor was the director of the Academy in that city, Federico, father of Ramon de Madrazo; he also took lessons from Señor C. Rivera; arriving in Paris to share the good fortune of so many immigrants from over the Pyrenees, he established himself in the studio No. 20, rue des Martyrs.

Jacques Edmond Leman, who was born at Laigle in the department of Orne, and who studied under Picot without ever obtaining a medal, executed in 1873 the careful rule-and-line picture, "The Presentation of the Infant Louis XIV to the Court." It is a gala scene of pompous Louis XIII costumes—the same dress that we see in English pictures of Cavalier and Puritan subjects. The ladies all wear extinguisher collars that quite cover their shoulders, and the men are suffocating in Venice point and long curls like the supernumeraries of an opera. The king shows a ray of joy on his saturnine and hypochondriac face as he stands beside the nurse who wraps ermine around the infant and holds it up on a cushion before the multitude. Anne of Austria, daughter of Philip III, of the Austrian dynasty of Spain, reposes among her pillows and smiles upon the courtiers out of a cloud of lace. The hangings of the bed are embroidered with the symbolic dolphin, beside the shields of France and Austria. The court physician stands watchfully behind the noble patient, whose best health will soon be needed for long years of regency. In front of the scene, at the right, appears the great Richelieu, the brain of the government, attended by his confidential counsellor Friar Joseph, whose practical rank

Richelieu, the *deus ex machina* of Leman's scene, is the guiding spirit of Adrien Moreau's canvas, "A Reading of Richelieu's Comedy of 'Mirame.'" The interest here turns on one of the Cardinal's favorite and most creditable projects, his patronage of literature. Finding that more social success than he liked was attained by the Hôtel Rambouillet, with its senate of blue stockings, and its patronage of writers like Mlle. de Scudéry and Voiture, he set up a rival *salon* in his own palace, where his nieces acted the part of learned ladies to their best ability. They are here found sitting in resigned and patient attitudes, among a company of standing courtiers of both sexes, while the Cardinal's young secretary, or

"EL PELELE." TOSSING THE EFFIGY OF JUDAS AT GRENADA.
THE WHOLE OF A DESIGN FROM THE ORIGINAL PAINTING BY J. GARLIO-MENELL.

was indicated by the envious of his day in the mock-heroic nickname of the Gray Cardinal. Louis XIII, who plants himself in the middle as if he were of some importance, occupies no share in anybody's thoughts. He will only last five years longer, and will never be anything more than Richelieu's stalking-horse. The inexorable Cardinal will soon induce him to exile his intriguing mother, Marie de Médicis; and when he is dead, and the lady now in the straw becomes Regent, Richelieu will apply himself to combating her Austrian ideas. Among the ladies will be noticed the princess de Condé, sitting at the head of the bed, and the youthful duchess de Montpensier, standing as a little girl just behind the king. The latter of these, assuming a place close to Louis XIII as his niece, is that famous "Mademoiselle," who left such interesting memoirs, who conducted campaigns and fired upon the royal troops, and who failed in so many noble matches, to fall in love with Lauzun when she grew old. In this year, 1638, she is a girl of twelve, with her future yet before her.

possibly Vincent Voiture (whom he tried to draw away from Rambouillet), declaims the choice passages from the half-forgotten production of his youth. The company are rather decorous than enthusiastic, but the pleased author, stretching his legs luxuriously before him, takes the full pleasure of authorship among an audience that cannot escape. Already there is finished and locked up in Corneille's worm-eaten desk the first masterpiece of French drama, the 'Cid.' Out of readings like this is to spring Richelieu's admirable idea of the Académie Française, which this proud, jealous and vain old man will found, to his undying glory.

"Before the Alcalde" is one of the numerous scenes of Spanish manners devised by the Paris painter Jules Worms. Like an eastern king of old, the good magistrate administers justice at the gate. Before the door of his house, beneath its spreading vines and wooden portico, the good old man sits examining a bundle of love-letters and photographs tied up with a ribbon. The culprit is the indiscriminate lover

of the village, who courts all the girls impartially, and who
now defends himself from the two inamoratas, one elderly,
severe and implacable, and the other young and passionate.
Meantime the magistrate and the priest at his shoulder are
absorbed in his love-letters, which give them the most
intense delectation. The rustic Don Juan is likely to pay
dear for his epistolary talent.

"The Education of Azor" is one of the pleasant childish
subjects of Léon Perrault. A lap-dog, just learning to sit
alone, rears himself on a fine table and balances loaf-sugar
on his nose, while the girl in the carved chair warns him
severely, delighted to play the part of a schoolmistress against
whose authority there is no appeal, and her younger brother
and sister look on absorbed. This canvas was originally
contributed to the Paris Salon of 1872.

E. Eroli, an artist of Rome, is the author of the slight
but spirited painting of "La Fille du Régiment." A gipsy
girl pours drink for a dissipated-looking young soldier of the
period of Masaniello and Salvator Rosa. Her royal hostelry,
decorated with the king's ensign, is a thatched hut on the
outskirts of the camp, and she pours the drink with a mock
modesty that savors of the stage still more than of the
regiment.

LA FILLE DU RÉGIMENT.
FACSIMILE OF A SKETCH FROM THE ORIGINAL PAINTING BY E. EROLI.

F. Roybet has taken the splendid likeness of the Infanta
Marguerite by Velasquez, which is a jewel of the Louvre,
and by the process of reconstructing history has imagined

the great portraitist achieving it. Here stands the courtly
Spanish artist, an enormous palette on his thumb, his curly
head set in a saucer of lace, his shoes of raw Cordova

THE EDUCATION OF AZOR.
ENGRAVED BY ROBERT FROM THE ORIGINAL PAINTING BY L. PERRAULT.

leather tied over his long gartered hose, and on his back a
smart velvet jacket fit to wear in the presence of the king.

Ludwig Knaus uses his favorite juvenile model of latter
years for the lively picture of "The Butcher-Boy," painted in
1879. The urchin, looking from under a wonderful thatch
of light curling hair, sharpens his knife on the steel tied to
his side. The hit of the picture is the sympathetic motion
of the lad's jaws as he crosses the blade from side to side
of the sharpener.

Bruck-Lajos, the sentimentally-humorous painter, contributes to this gallery a scene of nine figures, entitled
"The Unwilling Scholar." In the midst stands a hesitating
urchin of five, a model of Shakespeare's famous second stage
of life. The family of a comfortable French cottage are seen
around him, the grandmother cutting a loaf for the oldest
girl's luncheon, two more little women in the doorway with
primers in their hands, and the adults grouped around the
table with looks directed towards the young rebel.

Anton Seitz, on a canvas of 1874, paints "The King of
the Shooters," a hale old man who has won the prize at many
a schützenfest, and who now enters a crowded tavern.

One of the best pictures here is the "Children Interceding
with the Hussites before Naumberg, 1431," by Nechutrey, a
Vienna painter.

CATALOGUE OF MR. D. W. POWERS' COLLECTION.

A READING OF RICHELIEU'S COMEDY OF "MIRAME."
FAC-SIMILE OF A SKETCH FROM THE ORIGINAL PAINTING BY A. MOREAU.

The Grafter

ARTIST

J. F. MILLET

Born at Gréville, France, 1814.   Died, 1875.   Pupil of Delaroche

COLLECTION OF

MR. WM. ROCKEFELLER, NEW YORK

THE FLORENTINE POET.
FAC-SIMILE OF A SKETCH FROM THE ORIGINAL PAINTING BY A. CABANEL.

ADDITIONAL COLLECTIONS IN THE CITY AND STATE OF NEW YORK.

INITIAL FROM A DESIGN BY F. BOISBAUDRAN.

EAL is not wanting, but merely space, for the pursuit of our interesting subject to its utmost development. Our theme does not pall, but notices of even the most fascinating pictures must now be curtailed, in order to preserve the impartiality of the work without exceeding its allotted length. The interest of these examinations rather augments than wanes, but they are made uneasy and hasty by the prospect of a closing door—the inevitable word Finis which gapes at every author when he puts pen to his last chapter.

The collection of Mrs. Paran Stevens, in New York city, is distinguished by several names of comparative rarity. Here, for instance, is the large and serious figure of a "Woman Carding Wool" (2×3 feet) by J. F. Millet, which was contributed to the Paris Salon of 1863. That year the exhibit of the peasant painter provoked an unprecedented storm among the critics,—one of the three pictures he sent,

the "Peasant Leaning on his Hoe," having been remarkably daring in its unconventionality. Théophile Gautier, the arbiter of opinion, changed from an advocate to an enemy in this year's discussions, and became ferocious. The Salon of 1863 was a theatrical performance in which Millet unwillingly played the part of principal actor. The "Wool-Carder," however, has nothing in it to arouse the dismay of Philistia; the figure is a grave, simple study, true to its peasant character, and with an appropriate look of enduring strength, broken only by the tired and discouraged droop of the back. The quality of painting, in which every designated surface is exquisitely true to nature, culminates in the art by which the laps of wool are realized—thrice-driven sheets of down, which the spectator holds his breath not to disturb. Millet's drawing for this subject is reproduced on page 115.—" Mirabeau in the Convention," sketched on page 114, is a color-study of limited size by Ary Scheffer. This historical subject, so different from the ideal and religious themes on which the painter's fancy chiefly dwelt, will recall Mirabeau's famous words to the mind of many a spectator—those stinging and ringing words uttered to the King's master of ceremonies as Mirabeau pointed to the empty throne in the Convention, at the beginning of the revolutionary troubles, in 1789,—"Go back to your master, and tell him that we hold our seats by the will of the people!" In reading the history of Mirabeau, and the eloquence in panegyric form which he has inspired in Carlyle and others, we are tempted to think that there never was a man who effected so little, who left on the minds of his contemporaries such an impression of power.—Makart's "Falstaff in the Buck-Basket" (4 × 3 feet) makes one rub one's eyes, it is so rich and imposing, and at the same time so un-English and so un-Shakespearian. The two merry wives, the laced table-cloths, and the fat knight, altogether make up a gorgeous confused pyramid of glossy stuffs, of which the laughing faces of the women and the purposeless one of Falstaff are hardly noticeable incidents. In the distance a grinning page announces the return of the master, and gives the pretext for the concealment.—"The Sisters," by Couture, is a little empty in style, yet noticeable from its size, and from a certain theory of grace and beauty which

soldier; but the emotion of the scene is dry and hard, owing to the merely galvanic and mechanical kind of energy which Vernet commanded.—"The Betrothal Ring," by the Belgian artist Willems, is one of his most pleasing compositions, and was selected by the artist for a contribution to the Universal Exposition of 1878. A lady stands under a portico, draped in the refined-looking satins of Terburg's time, and musingly extends her finger for the lover to imprison in its environs of gold.—Merle is represented by a "Good Sister Teaching the A. B. C.," and by the "Lisette of Béranger" (3 × 2 feet). The latter depicts the faithful companion of the poet telling his virtues after his death to a company of blooming grisettes.

MIRABEAU IN THE CONVENTION.
FACSIMILE OF A SKETCH FROM THE ORIGINAL PAINTING BY ARY SCHEFFER.

belonged to Couture alone, and which our better-read Cabanels and Lefebvres do not attain; in Couture we seem to see the man of the people, trying to force on the attention of the refined world those charms which he has perceived in the wives and sisters of the artisans; Couture's pretty women seem to have read no books, while Cabanel's look as if they could stand a rigorous examination in sentimental literature. "The Sisters" are gleaners, one leaning on the shoulder of the other; they have animal grace, and that culture which comes of passion, without letters, as if they studied in Cupid's college, "and kept his rosy terms in idle languishment."—The hard and newspaperish style of Horace Vernet is seen in "The Idol Overthrown." A bust of Napoleon has been overturned from its pedestal in the galleries of Versailles, during the refurbishing carried on for the restoration of Louis XVIII. Two of his Vieille Garde pass, and grieve over the insult. A truly poetical painter could have made much of the incident, and Vernet doubtlessly felt his theme like a

None who has seen it can forget what an exquisite impression Déjazet used to make with a song of this title. Attired in the old classic cap and costume of the artisanne of 1810, and surrounded by a stage company of pretty actresses dressed like working-girls of fifty years later, the inimitable artiste would sing of her lost poet, of his misfortunes and imprisonment, and of his love for her:

> Children, could you but know
> How I was pretty and bright,
> Laughing, I and the girls—
> That was long, long ago!
> Laughing, showing my pearls;
> Eyes with a dancing light,
> Peaches buried in curls—
> I was admired so,
> Little grisette of fifteen!

The painter has imagined the scene with unusual grace and tenderness. A repetition of this picture is in another New

FALSTAFF

THE FLOWER MARKET, PARIS

ARTIST
FIRMIN GIRARD

BORN AT PARIS, FRANCE.   PUPIL OF GLEYRE

COLLECTION OF
MR. THERON R. BUTLER, NEW YORK

York collection, that of Mrs. W. H. Aspinwall.—One of the softly-romantic ballad subjects of Compte-Calix, "Happiness

CARDING WOOL.   COLLECTION MRS PARIS STEBBINS N.Y.
FAC-SIMILE OF THE SKETCH MADE FOR HIS PAINTING BY J. F. MILLET.

Better than Riches," shows a chevalier and his wife taking rest after the hunt with a peasant family, and contrasting their childless lot with the baby-nursing felicity of the rustic mother.—By Meissonier, in this collection, is a seated "Gallant, Sleeping;" by Alfred Stevens, a beautiful "Lady in a Blue Sacque," sitting with a letter; by his brother, Joseph Stevens, a capital "Butcher's Dog," watching a round of beef; by Vibert, "The Standard-Bearer," a castle-guard in a waiting-room, grasping the folds of his banner; by Rosa Bonheur, "Sheep," on a Scotch hillside; by Lagye, "The Fair Historiographer," a mediæval girl sitting at a Gothic desk with her unclasped folio, acting as secretary to a standing sage at her side; by Isabey, "Heliodorus," painted in 1858; and characteristic works of Troyon, Comte, Diaz, Gérôme and Plassan. A few specimens of sculpture decorate the saloons, two of which illustrate respectively the romantic and the austere treatment; Benzoni's "Flight from Pompeii" is an agitated, tormented and dramatic bit of rhetoric in marble; "Cleopatra," by the American Story (cut on page 116), is calm, undemonstrative and restrained to the point of vapidity.

The costly modern collection of Mr. Theron R. Butler, in New York city, catalogues more than fifty pictures; none among them is so great a favorite as "The Paris Flower-Market," of which this connoisseur possesses both the finished painting and a small color-sketch. The scene takes place in

the heats of August, or when the first chrysanthemums of autumn are blooming. The customers are middle-class people who do not go to Trouville or the Spas, and to whom a Sunday inspection of the Grandes-Eaux is all that is known of the country. The bouquets, in those exaggerated extinguishers of white paper which the French florists love, are shaded by the umbrella's humble dome. The dog, puzzled by so many useless scents, turns round upon himself and upon his chain; the child laughs, gratified with a pot of mignonette; the Seine is banked with flowers, which send their perfume into the old prison-windows of Marie Antoinette, under the funnel-shaped towers of the Conciergerie. Over the water, on the more aristocratic right bank of the river, is seen the long stretch of the picture-galleries of the Louvre, basking in heat and light that make their outlines faint in the perspective. The foreground is filled with an army of pleasant children, girls, and young wives, who occupy the cartway in defiance of the advancing soldiers, secure in the rights of youth, happiness and leisure. A florist, harnessed to his cart by a yoke of leather, draws along the load of plants, in their rustic bark-baskets; another unloads his barrow, his sleeves rolled to the shoulder; and the coco-merchant carries about his pagoda with shining bells, dispensing to the children his warm mawkish drink of licorice-root. It is a flower festival worthy to be sung by Moore, of which the priestesses are large market-women with faces distinguished by tufted warts and gray moustaches, while the worshipers are the city clerk and the neat grisette. This picture, while it aims at no exalted technical quality, is so neat and vivacious in its transcript of modern manners that it is calculated to amuse a throng of spectators for hours like a well-played drama.—"Selling Rosaries in front of a Spanish Church," by Ramon de Madrazo (cut on this page), in the same collection, shows beggars ranged outside the sacred portal, possessing their souls in a fund of unfathomable patience; their vis-à-vis are humble merchants, occupying a corresponding row on the hither side of the church-door, stringing beads and offering amulets for the

SELLING ROSARIES IN FRONT OF A SPANISH CHURCH.
FAC-SIMILE OF A SKETCH FROM THE ORIGINAL PAINTING BY RAMON MADRAZO.

purchase of the faithful. The child of one of them plays on the pavement, with a child's complete want of sympathy for the consecrated business going on around—a shrewd dramatic touch. The graceful lady at the left, emerging from the

ST. AGLAIA AND ST. BONIFACE.
FAC-SIMILE OF A SKETCH FROM THE ORIGINAL PAINTING BY A. CABANEL.

confessional with her conscience purified, dresses in black and masks her face with a deep mantilla, a perfect model of the *morgue espagnole*. Inside is perceived the impressive peculiarity of the Spanish church, a giant bleeding Christ in a sepulchral light—Mr. BUTLER's gallery shows various other "works of choice"—a Knaus, "Priest and Poacher;" four Viberts, "The Preparatory Sermon," "On the Rampart," "A Dealer in Pottery," and "The New Clerk"—a comedy-scene, where a smartly-dressed youth, in a span-new Directoire suit, stands in the agonies of bashfulness in an opulent village kitchen, before the town doctor, who reads his recommendation, and his buxom daughter, who quizzes; a well-colored Zamacois, "The Costume Shop;" and the usual Plassan, Merle, Rosa Bonheur, and Gérôme. A particularly crisp work by the last named is "The Master of the Hounds," with its fawning dogs and smiling Arab.

The peculiarity about the collection of Mr. ISRAEL COREE, in New York city, is that one meets so many celebrities in diminished form, that is to say, in smaller repliche from the hands of the artists. Cabanel's "Aglaia" and "Florentine Poet," Hamon's "Aurora" and "Sister is not at Home," and Aubert's "Jeunesse," are works so pleasantly familiar in the print-shops that to see their originals in full color seems like surprising the very "origin of species" (whatever that is) in the act of preparing its first types. We seem to see the art of the nineteenth century through the diminishing end of an opera-glass. The masterpiece of Cabanel's life is the "Florentine Poet;" we see Sordello sitting on a garden bench, rapturously listened to by languid lovers and a wet-eyed Francesca; the sentiment is so just and true, the culture so pronounced, the taste of the thing so perfect, that we wonder how Cabanel could have sunk into his present plati-

tude; this replica loses none of its chaste finish by being only some two-and-a-half feet across. Another replica of the picture is in the possession of Mr. J. H. WARREN, of Troy, and is attributed to him in the caption to the head-piece of this article.—His "Aglaia and Boniface," also a diminished study of 2½ by 2 feet, or some two-thirds the original's size, is another composition of refined grace, though it cannot be denied that the sentiment is rather Virgilian than Christian. The married saints, newly converted to the doctrine of the Redeemer, sit on their terrace at the close of the day; the culture and luxury in which their pagan years were passed reveals itself in the cast of their faces, and in Aglaia's lyre, whose strings have been taught a Christian hymn, and yet tremble with their novel burden.—Hamon's "Aurora," in this collection, is a little replica painted at Capri in 1866 from the charming picture executed for the Empress; most readers know the fancy—Aurora treated as a pretty gourmande, tiptoeing upon a burdock-leaf to empty the dew out of a morning-glory; the bright drop on her lip emulates the liquid diamonds in her hair. By the same artist, "My Sister is not at Home," a replica from the first conception of 1853, shows a little lover coming with an oleander-plant and a cage of birds to give to his child-mistress, who skulks

CLEOPATRA.
FROM THE STATUE IN MARBLE BY W. W. STORY.

behind the babies of the family, delighted to conceal her with all the bravado of infancy. The classical playhouse in this

THE PURITAN GIRL

ARTIST
DOUGLAS VOLK

BORN AT PITTSFIELD, MASS., 1856.   PUPIL OF GÉRÔME

COLLECTION OF
MR. THOMAS B. CLARKE, NEW YORK

MAGDALEN

ARTIST
J. J. HENNER

Born at Bernweiller, Alsace, 1840   Pupil of Drolling and of Picot

-----

COLLECTION OF
MISS HITCHCOCK, **NEW YORK**

picture, stuck over with captured butterflies and crowned with a Tanagra statuette or its like, is a pseudo-classical item worth noting for its applicability.—Aubert's "Jeunesse," a Greek maid defending her bosom—*boutonière* from her lover's pretence of smelling at it, has been praised by Hamerton for its fine sense of manners. It is an idyllic little picture-poem. —Jalabert shows, with more tenderness than dignity, the miracle of "Jesus Walking on the Waters." A column of distant light encloses the Christ, while the long row-boat labors in the foreground with its wild-gestured passengers. A very wet, saline character has been introduced in the quality of the light forming the celestial aureole, than which no halo round a rainy moon can be more damp and dewy.—Jalabert's "Peeping at the Nymph," a sort of "Chaste-Susannah" subject, and his "Galatea" and "Widow," form, with the Christian theme, a pretty broad showing of his refined but not mascu-line art.—Gérôme's "Prayer in the Desert," a whole liturgy in miniature form, is distinguished by a depth and purity of feeling he seldom attains. Very solemn and very near to God is this Arab, who has washed his feet in sand and stands on his cloak alone in the immeasurable desert, his camel browsing behind him, his spear stuck in the ground.—Plassan is seen in one of his daintily-dressed illustrations of Molière, the "Bourgeois Gentilhomme," Act 4, Scene 2, and in "The Bouquet" and the "Lady at her Bedside."—The line of

as Landelle's "Angels' Whisper," Merle's "Primavera" and "Contadina" (3×4 feet), Dykman's (of Antwerp) "Magdalen

WOODLAND VOWS.
ENGRAVED BY KRUSELL FROM THE ORIGINAL PAINTING BY A. SEYDELMAN

at the Cross," Toulmouche's "Dead Bird" (18×24 inches), Brion's "Decorating the Village Cross," and Riefstahl's "Pro-cession in the Tyrol."—A picture in the group that might with reason be thought to outweigh all the rest is a small color-sketch by Delaroche, "The Temptation."

A gallery of lively anecdotic pictures is to be found at the house of Mr. R. G. Dun, in New York city. Here is "The Indiscreet Friar" (20×14 inches), by A. Casanova, from the Paris Salon of 1879; it is a character-piece, seemingly sketched in the antechamber of Godoy; as the irresistible Spanish beauty awaits her audience with arms akimbo, a lean-faced monk advances to spy upon her charms, lowering his capuchin; another friar, fat and owlish, hooded and hid-den, has placed himself as her guardian at a prudent distance, and repels the intrusion. Of this expressive scene the artist's very snappy sketch is reproduced on page 120.—"A Pretext for a Conversation," by Vibert, shows a nobly-built woman of the people advancing with her marketing under the dis-charging gutter-spouts of a Spanish by-street, and an oily monk offering his red umbrella as an excuse for pious flirtations.—By Louis Alvarez is "The Inopportune Visitor;" a priest enters to a very tender tête-à-tête feast, and the lover is obliged to consult with his lacquey as to the best mode of getting rid of the superfluous caller.—By Martinetti, there is a painting of 1875, of seven figures, entitled "A Practical Joke." A musician is asleep, and some gay girls are teasing him, while a violinist enters at the right.—By

A PRETEXT FOR A CONVERSATION.
FAC-SIMILE OF A SKETCH FROM THE ORIGINAL PAINTING BY J. G. VIBERT.

sentiment in this whole collection is rather pensive than aggressive, and is harmoniously carried out by such examples

F. Leyendecker is "Une Présentation chez M. Tallien;" the frivolous society over which that magnate presided is shown

FIGURE FROM " HIS FIRST TOOTH."
FAC-SIMILE OF A SKETCH OF PRINCIPAL FIGURE MADE FOR HIS PAINTING BY P. PERCHALT.

in all its dissolute gaiety.—Firmin Girard contributes "A Wedding in the Eighteenth Century," showing a fiddler and piper leading a merry nuptial throng down the side of a hill that is crowned with a distant church.—G. Detti is shown by "The Sad Lover"—two figures across a card-table—and G. di Chierico by "The Sheriff's Arrest"—the taking into custody of a little snow-baller who has bombarded an officer, in a staircase street of Italy.—By P. A. Cot, in this collection, is a picture well known from engravings—"Don't Peep!" a life-size head of a young girl, finger on lip, looking mischievously out from the curtains of a bath; it was painted in 1869.

Mr. WILLIAM ROCKEFELLER, of New York, has secured some admirable pictures for his gallery. From the Frédéric Hartmann collection, sold at Paris in 1881, he has selected "Grafting," by J. F. Millet, and "The Parish Oven," by T. Rousseau. The "Grafting" picture is almost as faithfully illustrated by the careful etching of Gaujean (page 119) as by the photogravure plate. Of this painting, shown to the public in the Universal Exposition of 1855, Théophile Gautier at once recognized the typical, monumental, representative character. "The man seems to accomplish some mystic ceremony, and to be the dark priest of a divinity of the fields. The woman certainly is not pretty; the beauty of peasant-women goes quickly, in the weariness of country life; but there is a

pensive and touching expression in her face, a tranquil greatness in her posture, and the caught-up end of her apron makes a drapery whose flexible and well-arranged fold might be carved in marble." The "Parish Oven in the Landes," by T. Rousseau, was hailed as "a chef-d'œuvre" by the critic Mantz when Hartmann lent it for the Alsace-Lorraine charity. M. de Lostalot has more recently called it "one of those well-sunned pictures such as Rousseau knew how to paint at the fortunate time when his palette only admitted tones of gold. One would attribute it to a Hollander of highest mark; the finish of the workmanship makes us think of Ruysdael, as well as the charm and freshness of the color and the elegance of line." A large "Landscape with Pond" is another Rousseau, and "At the Fountain" and a "Sitting Shepherdess" are other Millets. For a better idea of the subjects included in this collection the catalogue must be consulted; there may be mentioned, however, Delacroix's "Marguerite and Mephistopheles," a small picture of 1846; Rosa Bonheur's "Sheep," Gérôme's "Arabs in the Desert," Meyer von Bremen's "Making Garlands for the Festival" (five figures, with a blazon inscribed Vivat,) Meissonier's "Historiographer," dated 1872, Bonnat's life-size "Italian Girl, Smiling," Merle's life-size "Infant Moses," Vibert's "The Bouquet" and "Spanish Girl and Duenna," and Troyon's "Cattle." The Dupré, "Sunset Landscape with Water," is one of the finest in existence.

Miss HITCHCOCK, of New York, has a small collection containing some rare specimens. Especially fine is the "Magdalen," by Jean-Jacques Henner, an Alsatian painter born at Bernwiller in 1839; at Paris he studied in the ateliers

ARAB FALCONER.
FAC-SIMILE OF FIRST SKETCH MADE FOR HIS PAINTING BY E. SCHMARTEL.

of Drolling and Picot; from the studio of the last-named he passed to Italy as a recipient of the Prize of Rome, and

DESDEMONA

ARTIST
ALEXANDER CABANEL

BORN AT MONTPELLIER, FRANCE, 1823.   ARTIST OF PROOF

COLLECTION OF
MR. J. HOBART WARREN, HOOSAC FALLS, N. Y.

astonished Schnetz, of the French Academy there, by admiring the pictures of Caravaggio. His Magdalen, seen in a cave-light, and a pretty close replica of the example secured for the museum of Toulouse, is a wonderful piece of flesh-painting and of chiaroscuro—so grand in these purely technical qualities that it hardly gets its deserved credit for feeling and expression.—Beyschlag's "Woodland Vows," (cut page 117) prettily shows the mediæval maiden watching the decoration of the forest with her initials, like those which Rosalind saw in the forest of Arden. The mediæval lover's knowledge of writing can carry him so far; it would not

tuny, but who in this example chooses a quiet family theme worthy of Greuze. The whole scene is conceived with a pleasant and graceful simplicity, the most vivacious figure being that of the hopeful father, sketched by the artist on page 118. His vis-à-vis is a proud and smiling nurse, who sits on the steps of an old-fashioned porch; as if to do honor to the newly arrived cargo of ivory, Margot has put on her best things, her quilted petticoat and lace collarette.—In another vein is the sumptuous life-size figure called "Zaida the Favorite," by Don Jose Casado del Alisal, a nobleman of Old Castile, who received lessons in painting from Madrazo,

GRAFTING.

ETCHED BY GAUJEAN FROM THE ORIGINAL PAINTING BY J. F. MILLET.

carry him much farther.—Miss HITCHCOCK is fortunate in possessing G. H. Boughton's "Passing into the Shade," his first piece of pure and true sentiment, never excelled. It was the picture with which he made his mark in England, after his removal from America, and excited the liveliest admiration from the critics. It was sent to the British Institution about 1863, before the author had exhibited in the Royal Academy. It was an acute, touching thought to make the sylvan shadow show a prophetic and figurative character, like that which Dante entered, in the mid-road of his life.—There are two paintings by Bouguereau in the collection, one a female subject, the other an "Italian Peasant-Boy with Mandolin," similar to but not identical with Mr. W. H. VANDERBILT's.

Colonel R. C. HAWKINS's collection, in New York, includes some rather unconventional pictures and some quieter ones. Among the last is "The First Tooth," by Pinchart, an artist who has usually followed in the luminous footsteps of For-

the father, in the Academy at Madrid. The flesh-painting of this recumbent figure, whose supple torso emerges from a tumult of rich draperies, is distinguished by a Rubens-like opulence of florid color.—Kaemmerer's "Promenade in the time of the Directory" is one of several similar scenes he has painted—the terrace of the Tuileries garden, a lightly-robed Merveilleuse on the upper step, a dozen other figures in the background, and the proper complement of vases, balustrades, and marble stairs; Musset, who wrote a poem on these steps of pink marble at Versailles, could have written a ballad on this picture.—P. Bouvier, of Milan, is the painter of "Salvator Rosa Improvising," a composition of four figures; this canvas obtained in 1876 the Umberto Prize, a premium instituted by King Humbert of the interest of a hundred thousand lire.—By Achille Guerra, of Naples, is the picture of "Cardinal Bembo visiting Raphael while painting Julius II."—The Italo-Spanish character of the collection is carried out by such pictures as P. Blanchi's "Hunter Winding his Horn," Mose Bianchi's "Rococo Girl," Dilliani's "Malignant

THE PARISH OVEN.

FAC-SIMILE OF A SKETCH MADE FROM THE ORIGINAL PAINTING BY P. WOUWERS

Gossips," Luis Alvarez' "Ancient Coquette" and "Modern Coquette," and Barbaglia's "A Morning with Pasini."

From the collection of Mr. J. SLOANE, of New York, the picture by E. Munier, "Doing Penance," is a canvas of 1879, representing a little rebel of singular but stormy beauty, who has been turned round at table for a punishment. The artist has also sold a replica of his picture to America, the repetition being in the gallery of Mr. Cox, in Brooklyn.—Boughton's "Our Village" (4 × 3 feet), in this collection, shows the flirtations of quaint dandies and old maids of 1820 in a town-street.—Gérôme's "Old Prayer-Reader," (2 × 3 feet); Jazet's "The Orderly;" Leyendecker's "The Guard-Room," a canvas of 1873; Willems' "The Flower's Perfume," a maiden in white satin smelling a blossom from a corbeille which she holds; De Neuville's "Waiting for Orders" (1880), a mounted orderly at his post, with a background of artillery and horses; L. Glaize's "Connoisseurs in Faience" (1874), with two ladies before a cabinet, and his "Japanese Robe;" C. Baader's "Soubrette at the Well;" Jacovacci's "Visit to the New-Born Heir" (2 × 3 feet), with numerous figures in Henri II costume; Pasini's "At the Fountain" (16 × 24 inches), a picture of 1880, with Arabs and steeds; Bouguereau's "Luncheon" (3 × 4½ feet), of 1879, a ten-year old girl slicing bread as she walks; Knight's "At the Fountain" (2 × 3½ feet), with two figures in flirtation; Jules Rose's "Swiss View" (4 × 3 feet), painted at Munich in 1872; with Carodi's "Island of Philœ" (2 × 3½ feet) and "Pincian Hill," are pictures which illustrate the tasteful character of this gallery.

Mr. ROBERT GORDON has a collection of art, American in origin, except an imposing marble bust of Queen Victoria. Here is "The Road to Concarneau," by H. L. Picknell, illustrated on this page; it is a diminished replica by the artist—the original, which made an unusual sensation in the Paris Salon of 1880, having been added to the Philadelphia collection of Prof. FAIRMAN ROGERS since his pictures were described in this work. "The Old Clock on the Stairs," by E. L. Henry, and "Twilight in Long Island," by C. H. Miller, may also be mentioned as meritorious pictures in this collection.—Mr. H.

B. FAHNESTOCK possesses a few choice pictures, among them "Paul Carrying Virginia" (12 × 24 inches), a graceful tribute to the lovers of Mauritius, executed in 1866; Compte-Calix's "Departure of the Swallows" (18 × 24 inches), well known from the engraving; C. Becker's "Return from the Masquerade" (3 × 4 feet), a masked gallant giving flowers to two ladies; Boughton's "Peasant-Girl Blowing Bubbles" (24 × 32 inches), Houghton's "Peasant-Boy and Girl with Kitten," and Lejeune's "Red-Riding-Hood."—Mr. T. B. MUSGRAVE owns a few conspicuous pictures, such as Gérôme's "Crucifixion" (5 × 3 feet), a very original if a rather parenthetical and allusive treatment, with the shadows of the three crosses upon Calvary, instead of the originals; Van Lerius' "Death before Dishonor" (3 × 4 feet), with a woman leaping out of window from a couple of landsknechts; Bouguereau's "Tambourine-Girl," of 1873, and Lessel's "Mediæval Flower-Woman."—Mr. H. R. BISHOP, whose interesting "Spalatro's Vision," by Allston, was burned in a fire at his country-place on the Hudson, has the remains of a good modern collection, including Lagye's "The Historiographer," Merle's "Nursing Baby," W. V. Morris' "Pointer, Retriever, Grouse, and Hare" (5 × 3 feet), the late A. H. Bakkerkorff's "Old Lady Knitting," Detaille's "Shaving in Camp" and "Sapeur," Vibert's "Valet," Lambinet's "Noon" (4 × 2½ feet), Bouguereau's "The Pet Bird" (2½ × 3 feet) and Émile Breton's "Stream between the Hills" (3 × 2 feet).—Mr. W. E. DODGE's collection includes Huntington's "Christiana and her Children Fleeing from the Burning City," Merle's "Maternal Tenderness," V. Huguet's "Arab Market," A. Borckmann's "The Lesson," C. Hübner's "Reading the Book," F. E. Church's "River of Light," W. Meyerheim's "On the Scheldt" and "Winter," and a quantity of water-colors.

Two interesting canvases were publicly sold in New York, March 1, 1882, in the collection of the Hon. L. P. MORTON, U. S. Minister to France. One was "The Burial of Manon Lescaut" (39 × 27 inches), by P. A. J. Dagnan-Bouveret. At the auction, this painting was bought to go back to France. It is illustrated on page 122, as a picture long associated with the interesting MORTON collection. This touching canvas, the highest attainment of an artist of excellent technique, shows the devotion unto death of Chevalier Des Grieux, who follows

THE ROAD TO CONCARNEAU.

FAC-SIMILE OF A SKETCH MADE FOR HIS PAINTING BY H. L. PICKNELL.

his inamorata when she is transported to the French penal settlements in the American colonies; a breath of pure feeling

PAUL AND VIRGINIA

ARTIST

EMILE LÉVY

Born at Paris, 1826.

Pupil of Abel de Pujol, and of P.

COLLECTION OF
MR. H. C. FAHNESTOCK, NEW YORK

blows through the Abbé Prévost's story and has saved it from oblivion, when most of the romances of the pre-Rousseau period have sunk to rest among the hoop-skirts and hair-powder of their century. "It was not hard to open the earth in the place where I found her," says the poor lovesick boy. "It was a country covered with sand. I broke my sword to assist me in making the grave, but I received less aid than by

leading the horses which spoke. Xanthus, the chestnut-colored steed, and Balius, the black, are properly depicted, not with the "hog-necked" trimming of the mane which we see with the Parthenon cavalry, but with "the whole mane, which, drooping from the ring near the yoke, streamed to the ground." The painter has had a perfect inspiration in show-ing the horses that talked, the horses that predicted the

THE MARTYR JULIA.

my hands." The chevalier's figure plainly shows breeding and race; that of hapless Manon, the piquant charm and ineradicable neatness of the French demoiselle.—Regnault's noble "Automedon," the other picture alluded to, was sold for $5900 to Mr. S. A. Coale, of St. Louis, for his collection already described, and must henceforth be regarded as a part of that gentleman's private gallery. Our photogravure plate gives in oval form the important part of this canvas, which is really a rectangle of 129×124 inches. The picture was painted by Henri Regnault in Rome, in 1867, while Hébert, painter of the "Cervarolles," was Director of the French Academy there, and was sent back to Paris by the young alumnus as a prize-essay. It represents Automedon, the charioteer of Achilles,

leader's death in the action to which they are being led; the power with which this is done is so imposing, so young and imperial, that attention is almost drawn away from the excellent academic study of Legraine the model.

Gabriel Max's painting of "The Martyr Julia" is illus-trated on this page. The large canvas devoted to this conception by the artist, sent to the Paris Exposition of 1867, was about the first of his contributions to attract the attention of French critics, and give him a place in their hierarchy of great names, owing to the novelty of a female crucifixion, and the sad interest of a pagan admirer decora-ting the cross with wreaths. The smaller American replica belongs to Mr. H. M. Johnston, of New York city.

The gallery of Mr. W. H. VANDERBILT having been already considered, it remains to be said of a family which of late years has become prominent in art-patronage, that a large ceiling-decoration has been made for Mr. W. K. VANDERBILT by Baudry, being the first noteworthy example of that artist brought to this country; also the great "Cloth of Gold" window by Oudinot. Mr. CORNELIUS VANDERBILT owns among other pictures, Corot's "Dance of the Nymphs," J. Lefebvre's "Sposa da Torrente," E. Nicol's "Looking for Investment," Villegas' "The Rare Vase," Díaz' "Clairière de la Reine Blanche," A. Moreau's "Wedding Party," Vautier's "Post

of the Pacha;" Winslow Homer's finest work, "Confederate Prisoners to the Front;" and a "Landscape" by Kensett.

Mr. M. GRAHAM has a small cabinet of brilliant modern pictures, signed with the sparkling names of Alvarez, Agrasot, Jimenez, Palmaroli and Zamacois. A glance at the catalogue will afford an estimate of this collection. The specimen of Palmaroli is a good type of the mass of pictures, representing the "Petit-Lever" (or levee in demi-toilet), of a belle in the last century. The attentive cardinal is on hand, of course, sipping his chocolate, and ogling with a moist eye the reclining heiress in morning-gown; a picturesque youth in

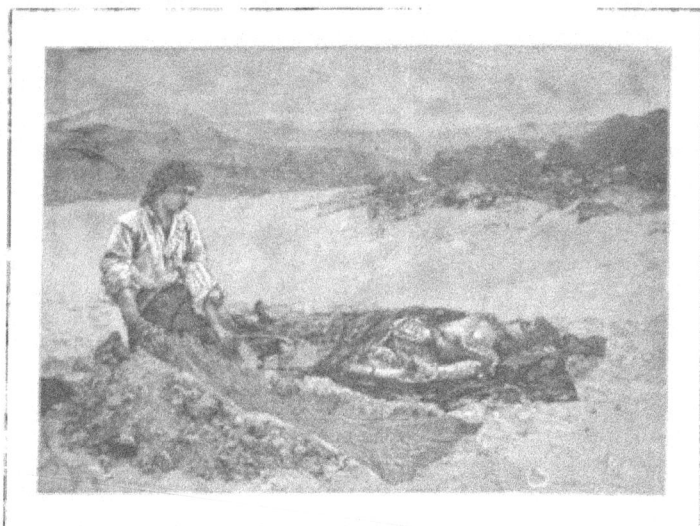

BURIAL OF MARÓN LESCAUT.
ENGRAVED BY SAUVE FROM THE ORIGINAL PAINTING BY S. A. J. PAUTAIN-BRUNEAU

Station," Madou's "Flemish Cabaret," M. von Bremen's "What has Mother Brought?" and a "Cattle-Piece" by Van Marcke.

Mr. R. L. KENNEDY, who presented Munkácsy's "Milton" to the Lenox Library, includes among his collection the masterpiece of Zamacois, "The Education of a Prince." This scene, with its gouty statesmen stooping to pick up the oranges rolled by a royal baby, is not only diverting, but is superbly painted. It contains, however, a prominent error natural in a young artist. The foreshortened infant is small-headed, having been sketched from a model too close to the painter. A composition of this kind always supposes a wall of the room to have been removed, and the scene drawn from a remote position; and the figures should be consistent with this theory, instead of precipitating their perspective just beneath the eye. There are also included in this collection Gérôme's fine "Bonaparte in Egypt," showing the consul and his staff on camel-back; his "Call to Prayer;" Pasini's "Escort

jacket and turban plays the guitar, and the beauty's love-letters are read to her by a most indulgent duenna.

Mr. J. M. FISKE owns one of the finest Boldinis in existence, a subject with a horse in it, and a direct challenge to Meissonier. It represents "Delivering the Dispatch," and shows an orderly riding his horse up to a porte-cochère over a streaming just-washed footwalk. His Zamacois, the "Demand in Marriage," with contrasted fathers, bashful Tony Lumpkin, and peeping girl, is a joke "put" with richness, and a painting executed with felicity.—Mr. J. G. BENNETT is fortunate in having secured Bridgman's "Burial of a Mummy," containing perhaps the best landscape background ever done by one of the Gérôme school, and Palmaroli's "Souvenir of Grenada," with the ideal Moorish princess, tame educated swan, and Alhambra architecture.—Mr. JAY GOULD luckily keeps the sweetest of the pictures by Kaemmerer, "A Wedding under the Directoire."

AUTOMEDON AND THE HORSES OF ACHILLES

ARTIST

A. G. HENRI REGNAULT

BORN AT PARIS, 1843; DIED, 1871.

PUPIL OF LAMOTHE AND OF CABANEL.

COLLECTION OF

MR. LEVI P. MORTON, NEW YORK

To particularize these ownerships is not a task admitting much eloquence, but it is the first duty of a work like this, and is not without interest among the readers most especially addressed.—Thus Mr. O. D. MUNN owns so well known a canvas as L. Leloir's "Grandfather's Birthday," with its fifteen Henri-Quatre figures; he has also Vibert's "Roman Censor," Kaemmerer's "Love-Making," Villegas' "Morocco Guard," and Madrazo's "The Swallows."—Mr. JORDAN L. MOTT owns a well-known Vibert, "The Painter's Rest," with the burgomaster asleep, and his portraitist kissing the daughter; and L. E. Adam's "Dancing Lesson."—Mr. S. S. FISHER possesses three Hasenclevers from the famous "Jobsiade" series, the student's "Departure," "Examination," and "Return;" the last of the set, "Jobs as a Watchman," was sold in New York not long since with the FALES gallery.

Mr. ALBERT SPENCER, who has already parted with a fashionable collection, is now accumulating works of higher style, such as J. Breton's exquisite "Evening" (with harvest-women stretching themselves or reposing), Gérôme's "Snake-

THE HONEYREST FRAR.
FAC-SIMILE OF A SKETCH MADE FOR HIS PAINTING, BY A. CASANOVA.

Charmer," Diaz's "Edge of the Forest" and Corot's "River Landscape."

Mr. ERWIN DAVIS owns that superb work of expression and inspiration, the "Joan of Arc" by Bastien-Lepage; also "The Children of Ribot," by that Ribot whose "St. Sebastian" is one of the glories of the Luxembourg, but whom we have not before encountered in America; and Courbet's "Blacksmith Shop," Billet's "Noonday Rest," Couture's "Portrait of Himself," Decamps' "Calais Fisherman," Henner's "Nymph at the Fountain," Millet's "After the Bath," Munkácsy's "Hay-Field," and other works collected in the true artist spirit.—Mr. D. H. McALPINE has Piloty's "Death of Cæsar," a small color-study, whose stilted style it is interesting to compare with the controlled intensity of Gérôme's; also, R. Wylie's "Breton Neighbors Reading Hugo's '93,'" Josef Brandt's "Tartars in Flight," Horace Vernet's "The Hurried Consultation," Isabey's "Smugglers' Retreat," Riefstahl's "Chapel in the Tyrol," and E. M. Ward's "Young Breton Housekeepers"—about sixty pictures altogether.—Mr. H. G. MARQUAND possesses "The Fisher-Girl," by Boughton, "The Reading-Girl," by E. Frère, Willems's "Lady at the Cradle," R. Madrazo's "Waiting," a "Landscape" by T. Rousseau, and

Trumbull's portrait of Alexander Hamilton.—Mr. ROBERT HOE, senior, owns many exquisite works of modern art; among them are Couture's "Belated Lawyer" (28 x 23 inches), one of his elegant satires in the Aristophanes vein, showing the barrister imitated by a turkey-cock and his clients by unfledged chickens; Alfred Stevens' thoughtful picture of "Amours Eternels" (19 x 24 inches)—a maiden decorating her mother's portrait with rue on all-saints' day—painted before Paris had made a mere chronicler of him; Joseph Stevens' "Hackman and Horse" (14 x 18 inches); J. Breton's "La Fontaine" (24 x 18 inches), two girls at the spring in pure statuesque poses; Boughton as a comedian, with "Ichabod Crane and the Village Maidens" (46 x 30 inches; 1870) Boughton as a tragedian, with "The Pilgrim Scouts from the Mayflower" (40 x 30 inches; 1869) Boughton as a troubadour, with "The Minstrel" (60 x 40 inches; 1875) a composition of seven figures, with the patrician's boy regarding the bard's boy; Boughton as an anecdotist, with "A Bit of Advice;" Lagye's "Early Flemish Interior" (26 x 20 inches) with mother, nurse and cradled baby in Holbein dresses; and Vollon's "Snow-Scene" (13 x 10 inches).—Mr. ROBERT HOE, junior, a noted book-collector, owns among other works of the painter's art, Alma-Tadema's "Gallo-Roman Women," two life-size antique dames leaning over a garden wall.

Mr. CHRISTIAN HERTER has contrived to obtain a study of Couture's for the celebrated "Décadence Romaine," and one of Vibert's for his ambitious "Thiers in Death."—Mrs. A. F. KIDD is the possessor of Cabanel's smaller replica of his Luxembourg picture, "The Death of Francesca di Rimini."—Mr. N. B. SARONY owns Mr. Eastman Johnson's best work, "Corn-Husking," compared by good judges with a Decamps, and two oil-pictures by Chifflart.—Mr. H. F. SPAULDING has "The Breton Conscript's Departure" and "The Return," both by E. Dubufe.—Mr. DEMAS BARNES has "The Anatomist," a terrible subject by Gabriel Max, with a dissector and dead maiden, unmercifully made the size of nature.—Mr. LUTHER KOUNTZE owns an unusually fine Watteau, called, of course, "The Fête Champêtre."—The estate of the late Mr. LOUIS DURR includes an imposing series of old masters, without guarantees, however; among them, a "Mathematician," by Ribera, is especially fine.

The gallery of the late W. T. BLODGETT, which was almost a complete synopsis of modern French painting, (not to speak of Spanish art like Goya's, of English art like Bonington's and of that of several old masters), has been mostly dispersed since his decease; some relics of it are still held by his widow, however, and a fine series of his water-color pictures by his son.—Mrs. W. H. ASPINWALL has a large collection of old masters, many of them apparently authentic and certainly fine; among them, a superb "Reclining Boy," by Murillo, Velasquez' "Knight of Malta," Vandyck's "Marquis Laganes;" Reynolds' "Miss Bingham and three other portraits, representing the Four Ages;" together with various modern works, including Ary Scheffer's "Lafayette," two Gilbert Stuarts, one of them a "Head of Washington," Stuart Newton's "Sir Walter Scott," Piloty's "Death of Wallenstein," Baron Leys' "Street at Night," and

Merle's "The Lisette of Béranger," resembling that described among Mrs. Stevens' pictures in this article.—A large and fine "Landing of the Pilgrims," with life-size figures, by Baron Wappers, was long owned and kept in New York by Señor Miguel de Aldama, a Cuban gentleman, but he now writes the author that it is "sent to Havana as a present to the City, and to be seen in the Hall where the Common Council meet."

Mr. G. B. Fearing is the possessor of Laurens' "Execution of d'Enghein," whose darksome sadness may be compared with the painter's "Honorius," in Mr. D. O. Mills' collection.—Commodore Garrison owns "Sur le Terrain," by Berne-Bellecour.—Mr. Frank Work has Kaemmerer's spirited "Dispute," a scene in a Directoire tea-garden.—Mr. S. L. M. Barlow has rich bric-à-brac, tapestries and pictures—including repliche, approved by artists, of Vandyck's "Children of Charles I," and of Titian's Venus of the Florence Tribune. —Mr. Sewell's collection of engravings, comprising the rarest masters in the most inaccessible states, is a feast.

Mr. Thomas B. Clarke has a most refined collection, intended especially to demonstrate the present attainment of American art in its best representation. His catalogue is given at the close of this article. Bridgman's "The Caïd's Escort at Rest" is an interesting example of a most talented painter; but nothing in Mr. Clarke's treasury exceeds in beauty and feeling the "Puritan Girl," by Mr. Douglas Volk, as she stands, deserted, by the trysting tree, where her initials are already covered from sight by the oblivious snow.

The Historical Society owns about six hundred paintings, largely made up from the gift of the late T. J. Bryan, and including the fine "Infanta Margarita" by Velasquez and a glorious "Portrait" by Rembrandt.—The Lenox Library possesses the original and famous "Milton Dictating," by Munkácsy, three pictures by Reynolds, including the "Mrs. Billington," and two Turners, the "Staffa" and "Stranded Frigate;" also "The Spanish Café," by Jiminez, a smart and crisply-painted scene of manners in the Goya period.—In the City Hall, the "Governor's Room" contains some fine old portraits.—The Union League owns, among other pictures, "Ready for the Ride," by W. M. Chase.

Central Park shelters Ward's big-headed "Shakespeare," his "Indian Hunter," and "Seventh Regiment Soldier;" Cain's "Tigress;" Sir John Steell's "Scott" and "Burns;" portrait statues of Webster, Hamilton, Morse, and F. G. Halleck; busts of Humboldt, Schiller and Mazzini; and statues of "A Falconer," "Commerce," and "The Angel of Bethesda."—Union Square has Bartholdi's "Lafayette," with H. K. Brown's "Lincoln," and his equestrian "Washington;" also a statue of Seward.—In Madison Square is St. Gaudens' admirable "Farragut." A model of Ward's has been approved for the "Washington" to be placed on the Sub-Treasury in Wall street. Bartholdi's colossal Liberty is preparing for an island in the Bay. The above are all in bronze.

The permanent collection of the Metropolitan Museum

has an interesting series of old masters secured by the late Mr. Blodgett, including Franz Hals' "Hille Bobbe," Van der Helst's "Burgomaster," and Vandyck's "St. Martha." It contains General Di Cesnola's curiosities from Cyprus, including the treasure of jewelry from the site of Curium, and statuary attributed to the lost temple of Golgoi. It would yield volumes of description—not quite, however, within the scope of this work.—Winterhalter's famous "Florinda" has for years had a peripatetic existence, being seen sometimes at the Historical Society's rooms and sometimes in those of the Metropolitan Museum.

In Mr. W. W. Kenyon's collection, in Brooklyn, is G. R. Boulanger's huge group of "Hercules and Omphale." We seem to see the Farnese Hercules broken up on the ground, with its joints snapped, and with the power accompanying the statue's connected posture wholly dissipated and irretrievably lost.—Mr. G. I. Seney, of Brooklyn, a philanthropist and a liberal art-patron, includes in his very select gallery "A Helping Hand," by E. Renouf, from the Salon of 1881, and Bouguereau's "Madonna and Angels," from the same Salon. —Mr. Henry F. Cox, of Brooklyn, has a cabinet of over forty paintings, including Cabanel's "Trysting-place of Souls," illustrating that passage in the *Midsummer Dream* where "ghosts, wandering here and there, troop home to church-yards;" also Munier's "Doing Penance," a replica; Boughton's "Widow's Acre," Gérome's "Bashi-Bazouk," Steinheil's "In the Studio," Schreyer's "Russian Traveler and Wolves," Glaize's "Pompeian Interior," M. von Beckmann's "Reading Girl" and "Little Cook," and Jacque's "Cattle at the Stream."

Mr. J. H. Banker, of Irvington, owns Makart's "Diana Hunting," a large work executed in 1880.

Mr. J. Hobart Warren, of Troy, has a small and choice collection, including Cabanel's masterpiece, "The Florentine Poet," illustrated at the head of this article; a word about this picture has recently been said, apropos of its repetition in Mr. Corse's collection. "Desdemona," also by Cabanel, is a tender treatment of a gentle listener, who gives her tears and her soul to a story of hair-breadth escapes. Fromentin's "Arab Falconer," in this collection, is one of his finest works, resembling, but not exactly matching, that in the possession of Mr. Wall, of Providence; the artist's first sketch, on page 118, has the merit of being an autograph; but the head of the Falconer, and some minor matters, were changed slightly in committing the subject to canvas. The catalogue at the close of this chapter specifies Mr. Warren's Roybet, Diaz, Detaille, and Isabey, his Boughtons, and Jacques, and Duprés.

The Capitol, at Albany, contains the large decorative demi-lunes by the late W. M. Hunt, representing "The Discoverer" and "Anahita, or the Flight of Night."

These summary notes, which certainly do not sin from loquacity, complete a survey of the galleries in New York, when taken with the earlier chapters on individual New York collectors.

LE PETIT LEVER

ARTIST
V. PALMAROLI

BORN AT MADRID, SPAIN, 1837.   PUPIL OF A

COLLECTION OF
MR. MALCOLM GRAHAM, NEW YORK

COLLECTIONS IN THE CITY AND STATE OF NEW YORK.

COLLECTION OF MRS. P. STEVENS.

ACCARD, E.—Visit to the Convalescent.
BAKALOWICZ, L.—Petition to the King.—Lady and Bouquet.—The Ladies and the Mandolin.
BAUGNIET, C.—A Lady's Night-Toilet.
BARON, H.—The Fair Naturalist.
BENJON, G. M.—The Flight from Pompeii. Marble.
BERNARDONI.—The Erring Wife. Sculpture.
BONHEUR, ROSA.—Scotch Sheep.
COL, D.—A Family Reading.
COMTE, P. C.—Two Ladies.
COMPTE-CALIX, F.—Happiness better than Riches.
CORTAZZO, O.—The Amateurs of Bric-à-Brac.
COUTURE, T.—The Two Sisters.
CRETIUS, C.—Mazeppa.
CULVERHOUSE.—Interior, Woman seated with Baby.—Playing Bowls.—Gallants Playing Cards.—Dutch Landscape.—An Old Inn.
DE LOOSE, A.—A Village School.
DIAZ, N.—Oriental Mother and Child.
EBERLE, A.—Parting with the Cow.
FREUVELET, J.—Lady with Fan.
FICHEL, E.—The Cabaret.
GÉRÔME, J. L.—Arab Seated.
ISABEY, C.—Heliodorus.
LACTE, V.—The Fair Amazaronic.
LOWENTHAL, E.—Romeo and Juliet.
MAKART, HANS.—Falstaff in the Buck Basket.
MEISSONIER, J. L. E.—Gallant Seated, Sleeping.
MERLE, H.—The Lizette of Strangers.—The Good Sister.
MEYER VON BREMEN, J. G.—Watching the Baby.—Mother and Baby.
MEYER, O.—The Poacher.
MULLER, J. V.—Carding Wool.
PECRUS, C.—Concert.—Lace Knitter.—A Visit.
PLASSAN, A.—The Maiden's Night-Toilet.
RAVEL, JULES.—Prison Scene.
ROTA, JOS.—Mother and Boy at Prayer.
SCHEFFER, ARY.—Mirabeau in the Convention.
STEVENS, ALF.—Lady Seated and Holding a Letter.
STEVENS, JOS.—Butcher's Dog Watching.
STORY, W. W.—Cleopatra. Marble.
TOULMOUCHE, A.—Girl with Kitten.—The Sleeping Letter-Writer.
TROYON, C.—Cattle.
VAN SCHENDEL, P.—Torchlight Party.
VERBOECKHOVEN, E.—Storm.—Sheep in Stable.
VERNET, H.—The Courtroom Idol.
VIBERT, J. G.—The Standard-Bearer.
WILLEMS, F.—The Betrothal Ring.

COLLECTION OF MR. T. R. BUTLER.

ANTIGNA, J. P. A.—Industry and Reverie.
BAUGNIET, C.—A Difficult Answer.—The Dead Canary.—Drawing the Bride.
BONHEUR, R.—Landscape with Sheep.
BOUGUEREAU, W. A.—Maternal Solicitude.
BOUTIBONNE, E.—The Inquisitive Maid.
BULLOUIN, F.—A Cavalier.
COL, D.—The Wine-Tasters.
DESGOFFE, B.—Objects of Art.

GÉRÔME, J. L.—The Bull-Fighter.—Guard Louis XIV.
GIRARD, F.—The Paris Flower-Market.—A Study for the "Paris Flower-Market."
HAMMAN, E.—The Pearl Necklace.
KNAUS, L.—Priest and Poacher.
LEON Y ESCOSURA, I.—The Convalescent Prince.
MEISSONIER, J. L. E.—The Vedette.
MEYER VON BREMEN, J. G.—The Little Coquette.—Leaving Home.—Meditation.—Prayer.
PALMAROLI, V.—The Listener.—The Connoisseur.
PLASSAN, E.—Table Supplies.
ROYBET, F.—The Halberdier.
SCHREYER, A.—A Russian Inn.
VIBERT, J. G.—The Preparatory Sermon.—Dealer in Pottery.—The New Clerk.—On the Ramparts.—The Smoker.
ZAMACOIS, E.—The Costume Shop.

COLLECTION OF MR. ISRAEL CORSE.

AUBERT, J.—Jeunesse.—Idyl.
BIERSTADT, A.—Residence of Sir Morton Peto.
BRION, G.—Decorating the Village Cross.
CABANEL, A. E.—The Florentine Poet—St. Agléa and St. Boniface.
CHAVET, J. V.—Music.—The Artist.
DELAROCHE, P.—The Temptation of Christ.
DUVERGER, T. E.—Threading the Needle.
DUCKMANS, J. L.—Magdalen.
ERDMANN, O.—Blindman's-Buff.
FRÈRE, E.—Putting on the Stocking.
GRAEBER, J. L.—Prayer in the Desert.
HAMON, J. L.—"My Sister is not at Home."—Aurora.
JALABERT, C.—Christ Walking on the Water.—Widow and Fatherless.—Peeping at the Nymph.
JORDAN, R.—Fisherman's Wife.
KOEKKOEK, B. C.—Landscape—Old Castle.
KRAUS, F.—Going into Church.
LANDELLE, C.—The Angel's Watch.
MERLE, H.—Courtship—Maiden in the Forest.—Italian.
PLASSAN, A.—Lady at the Bedside.—At the Mantel.—Scene from "Le Bourgeois Gentilhomme."
RIEFSTAHL, W. L. F.—Procession in the Tyrol.
RONETTI, A.—The Hindoo Slave. Sculpture.
TOULMOUCHE, A.—Dead Bird.—The Family.
TRAYER, J. B. L.—Consolation.
WILLEMS, F.—Plucking the Rose.
ZIEM, F.—The Camel.

COLLECTION OF MR. R. G. DUN.

ABBEY, E. A.—The Stage-Coach Office.
ACCARD, E.—Dressed for the Ball.
ADAM, E.—A Stud of Horses.
ALVAREZ, L.—The Inopportune Visitor.
ARNOUX, M.—The Little Lace-Maker.
BONHEUR, AUG.—Sheep and Shepherdess.
BORCHERVILLE, A. DE.—The Visit.
BOUGHTON, G. H.—Gipsy Children.
BRIDGMAN, F. A.—The Almeh.
CASANOVA, A.—The Indiscreet Friar.
CHIERICI, G. OL.—The Sheriff's Arrest.
COL, D.—Sports in the Old Barn.

COGHRAM, J.—My Sister is not Here.
COT, P. A.—Don't Peep!
COUDER, A.—Gathering Wild-Flowers.
DAMMART, L.—The Inn Door.
DETTI, G.—The Sad Lover.
GIRARD, FIRMIN.—A Wedding in the Last Century.
HIRTS, H.—The Greedy Grape-Gatherer.
KUWASSEG, C., FILS.—Venice from the Giudecca.
LEYENDECKER, F.—Introduction at Tellini's Salon.
LITSCHAUER, K. J.—Young Monk Reading.
MARTINETTI, A.—A Practical Joke.
MEISEL, E.—Courtship of an "Incroyable."
MEYER VON BREMEN, J. G.—The Letter.
PALMAROLI, V.—Reading Girl.
PLASSAN, A. E.—Lady Disrobing.
RICCI, PIO.—The New Dress.
RODIES, J.—Samuel.
VAUTIER, L.—Greek Dancing-Girl.
VERBOECKHOVEN, E.—Cattle.
VERNON, PAUL.—Girl and Bird's-Nest.
VIBERT, J. G.—A Protest for a Conversation.
VOLTZ, F.—Cattle.
WAGNER, ELOI.—Old Man and Soubrette.
WORMS, J.—Guitar-Player. Water Color.

COLLECTION OF MR. W. ROCKEFELLER.

BONHEUR, ROSA.—Sheep, Scotch Landscape.—Pyrenees, Landscape and Sheep.
BONNAT, L. J.—Roman Girl.
BOUGUEREAU, W. A.—The Prayer.
BRETON, JULES.—The Harvest.
COL, D.—The Wine-Tasters.—Storm-Bound.
CORDY, J. B. C.—The Confidence.
DELACROIX, E.—Marguerite and Mephistopheles.
DE NEUVILLE, A.—Cavalryman and Two Horses.
DESGOFFE, B.—Objects of Art.—Two Subjects.
DETAILLE, E.—Vedette.
DIAZ, N.—Ladies of Seraglio.—Venus and Cupid.
DUPRÉ, J.—Landscape with Water.—Sunset effect.
GÉRÔME, J. L.—Arabs in the Desert.
KAEMMERER, F. H.—The Cold Shoulder.
KNAUS, L.—Girl's Head.—The Little Scholar.—Gretchen.
MEISSONIER, J. L. E.—The Historiographer.
MERLE, H.—Mari in the Rubrucker.
MEYER VON BREMEN, J. G.—Preparing for Papa's Birthday.—Little Girl.—Study, Head.
MILLET, J. F.—Grafting.—The Water-Drawer.—The Shepherdess.
MUNKÁCSY, M.—Interior, Lady at Table.
PALMAROLI, V.—The New Volume.
RODIES, J.—Ruses.
ROUSSEAU, T.—The Parish Oven.—Landscape and Pond.—Landscape and Forest.
SCHREYER, A.—Wallachian Team in Snow.
SEITZ, E.—The Birthday.
TOULMOUCHE, A.—The New Novel.
TROYON, C.—Landscape and Cows.
VERBOECKHOVEN, E.—Sheep.—Bull.
VIBERT, J. G.—The Bouquet.—"Why Comes He Not?"
ZAMACOIS, E.—The Disputed Game.
ZIEM, F.—Shipping at Venice.
ZO, ACHILLE.—The Siesta.

COLLECTION OF MR. M. GRAHAM.

ACKERT, J. — Mand and Children.
SAVILLE, I. — Her Forefather' Devotion.
AUBERT, J. Y. — Cupid at the Fountain.
BEARD, W. H. — Rejoicing at the Grave of Nimrod.
BOUGUEREAU, W. A. — The Little Rogue.
CHOCARNE, L. — Fishing in the Pool.
CHASE, F. J. — Marine.
CHRON, J. B. C. — Landscape with Female Courtcard.
DIAMOND, C. — Landscape.
DETAILLE, E. — Sentry.
DIAZ DE LA PENA, N. — Summeration Landscape.
HEILBUTH, I. — In the Field.
JIMENEZ Y ARANDA, J. — Change from the Bourbon Régime.
KAEMMERER, F. H. — The Honeymoon.
KNAUS, L. — The City Belle.
LEFEBVRE, J. — Flowering Branch Girl.
LEROLLE, L. — Gallants Playing Cards.
MEYER VON BREMEN, J. G. — Girl in a Fountain.
MORALS, C. — At the Well. [Continued]
PALMAROLI, V. — Petit Lever; or, La Bouchée du Matinée.
PLASSANS, L. — Reference to the Law-Book.
MARTIN, H. — Reading the Recommendation.
SCHREYER, A. — Launch in the Snow.
SEIGNAC, V. — The Card Castle.
VAN MARCKE, E. — Cattle at the Fountain.
VERY, L. — Courtiers at Louis XIII.
VOLLKMANN, H. — Old Woman Reading.
KNAUS, V. — The Message.
ZIEM, F. — The Laguna, Venice.

COLLECTION OF MR. ROBERT HOE.

ACHENBACH, A. — Steamers Meeting on the Lower Rhine — Stormy Scene.
BRIDGEPORT, CHA. — Horses.
BONHEUR, ROSA & H. — Pilgrims — Souvenir d'Italie — cross and old Buildings — A Pot of Olives — The Moment.
BOUGUEREAU, W. A. — Far from Home.
BRETON, J. — Solitary Postman.
BODIN, E. — Italian Peasants.
COUTURE, THOS. — The Reclined Toilet.
DUPRÉ, J. — Meadows, with Sheep.
FORTUNY, M. — Plaza near Madrid — Departure à la Fête — Arab at Arms.
GÉRÔME, FIRMIN — Sport in St. Roman, Paris.
KLEIN, Plantation Negroes.
LAGYE, V. — Flemish Interior.
LANDELLE, CHAS. — Roman Girl — Circassian Girl — Circassian Girl.
MERLE, H. — Mother and Child.
MEYER VON BREMEN, J. G. — The Awaking — Morning Prayer.
PLASSAN, E. — The Lesson.
SCHREYER, AD. — The New-Born.
STEVENS, ALFRED — Les Amours Faréolles.
STEVENS, J. — By the Hour.

COLLECTION OF MR. TH. B. CLARKE.

BIERSTADT, A. — View on Kern River, Cal.
BLACKMAN, WALTER — Elsie.
BOUGHTON, G. H. — The Widow's Garden.
BRIDGMAN, F. A. — The Gael's Escort at Rest. — After the Bath.
BROWN, J. G. — A Merry Air and a Sad Heart. — "That's Good!"
CHASE, W. M. — The Coquette.
CHURCH, F. E. — Landscape. — Sunset in the Wilderness.
COLMAN, SAMUEL — Corpus Christi Day, Seville.
DEWING, T. W. — A Shoe.
DIELMAN, Frederick — My Own Fire-side.
FREER, F. W. — Showing a Study.
GIFFORD, R. S. — Landscape.
GIFFORD, S. R. — Palisades, Lago Maggiore.
GAY, S. J. — The Bedtime Story.
HENRY, E. L. — Waiting for the Steamer.
HOMER, W. — A Happy Family.
HOVENDEN, T. — Chloe and Sam — "So Happy!"
HUNTINGTON, W. — M. Taxine.
INNESS, G. — Landscape, Noon.
JOHNSON, E. — New England Fireside — Blackbird Pie.
JONES, H. BOLTON — Landscape.
KENSETT, J. F. — Summer Mountains and Lake N. H.
LATHROP, J. — Apple Orchard in Spring.
MAGRATH, W. — An Old Gardener.
MCENTEE, J. — November Day.
MORAN, E. — Foggy Morning, English Channel.
MORAN, P. — Good Friends.
MORAN, T. — Asleep the Wire.
MURPHY, W. S. — In Arcadia Grand.
PAXTON, ARTHUR — Landscape.
PEARCE, H. S. — Casual over the Bar.
POORE, H. R. — A Church Holiday.
QUARTLEY, ARTHUR — Low Water, Long Island Shore.
RICHARDS, W. T. — Coast near Atlantic City.
SNYDER, J. W. — The Swine.
SMITH, J. H. — Still Drawing.
THOMPSON, W. — The Old Stone Church, Stony Hollow, N. Y.
YORK, D. — The Persian Girl.
WEEKS, E. W. — Merry Man in Own Doors.
WYANT, A. H. — Morning, Esopus Creek, N. Y. — An Old Lady.

COLLECTION OF MR. G. I. SENEY.

BROOKLYN, N. Y.

BOUGUEREAU, J. — Rembrandt near Café Au fait.
BAILLY, E. — The Gleaner.
BONNAT, L. — An Italian Girl.

BOUGUEREAU, W. A. — Virgin and Angels.
BOULANGER, G. R. C. — The Home of Horace.
BARTON, T. — Going to Mass.
CHARNAY, A. — Pic Nic Party.
COROT, J. B. C. — Landscape near Ville D'Avray.
DE BEAUMONT, E. — The Old Beau.
DELORT, C. — Richileu and Père Joseph.
ISABELLE, E. — A Council of the Don.
DIAZ, N. — Autumn Landscape.
DURRIEUX, J. — In a Spanish Café.
DUPRÉ, J. — Band of the Oak at Fontaine.
FORTUNY, M. — Santa Lucia, Naples.
GIRARD, V. — Fishing.
GOUBIE, J. A. — Wedding Journeys.
HILDEBRANDT, F. V. — Girl Casting a Letter.
JACQUE, C. — Pastoral in France.
JACQUET, J. — Gossiped.
JIMENEZ Y ARANDA, J. — A Spanish Pharmacy.
KAEMMERER, F. H. — The Sleigh Ride.
KNAUS, L. — The Hard Step.
LELOIR, L. — Dressing the Dog.
LEYS, H. — Luther.
LOBRICHON, E. V. — The Call of the Arms.
MARCHETTI, L. — A Festival Day.
MAX, GABRIEL — Watching the Butterfly.
MUNIER, E. — The Pet Lamb.
RIBERA, EMILIO — A Helping Hand.
ROYA, D. MARTIN — Lamb to Road, Alice to Body.
ROUSSEAU, THEO. — Early Morning — Fontainebleau — Clump of Trees.
ROYBET, F. — The Rover of Dispatches.
SCHREYER, ADOLPH — Sandstorm — Arabs.
TROYON, C. — Return to the Farm, Twilight.
VAN MARCKE, E. — Normandy Cattle — Landscape and Cattle.
VIBERT, J. G. — The Grasshopper and the Ant.

COLLECTION OF MR. J. H. WARREN.

TROY, N. Y.

BOUGHTON, G. H. — Pride and Humility. — French Brook, Brook? — Pleasant Interior, Bethany.
CAZIN, A. — The Flowerless Past — Deckhouses.
DUPRÉ, I. — The Festival. — Water Colour.
DE BLAEMONT, E. — The Englishman in Paris.
DETAILLE, E. — French Infantry Manoeuvring.
DIAZ DE LA PENA, N. — The Coquette.
INNESS, J. — Glow on the Pool — Scene near Pennsylvania.
FRANCKFORT, E. — Arid Volume.
GODDARD, TH. — Seeding the Calf.
GUILLAUMIN, A. — Grandmother's Birthday.
JOSEPH, F. — Betrothal of Henry II.
JACQUET, C. — Return to the Sheepfold.
LARCH, C. — Breton Girl Going to Church.
MINER, H. — The Poor Mother. — A Young Mother.
MORLAS, A. — The Lesson. Richaud.
PEYROL BONHEUR, JULIETTE — Sheep and Heather.
ROYBET, F. — The Music Pension.
ZIEM, F. — Across the Grand Canal, Venice.

The Education of a Prince

ARTIST
EDWARD ZAMACOIS

BORN AT BILBAO, SPAIN, 1840.

PUPIL OF MEISSONIER

COLLECTION OF
MR. ROBERT LENOX KENNEDY, NEW YORK

TABLE OF PHOTOGRAVURES.

VOLUME III.

END OF THE TABLE OF PHOTOGRAVURES IN VOLUME III.

INDEX OF COLLECTIONS MENTIONED IN THIS WORK.

INDEX.

INDEX.

INDEX.

www.ingramcontent.com/pod-product-compliance
Lightning Source LLC
Chambersburg PA
CBHW030403270326
41926CB00009B/1243